Urban Life and Urban Landscape Series

DESIGNING MODERN AMERICA
THE REGIONAL PLANNING ASSOCIATION OF AMERICA AND ITS MEMBERS

EDWARD K. SPANN

Ohio State University Press
Columbus

711.3
S73d

Copyright © 1996 by the Ohio State University Press.
All rights reserved.

Library of Congress Cataloging-in-Publication Data

Spann, Edward K., 1931–
    Designing modern America : the Regional Planning Association of
America and its members / Edward K. Spann.
        p.   cm. — (Urban life and urban landscape series)
    Includes bibliographical references and index.
    ISBN 0-8142-0722-7 (alk. paper)
    1. Regional Planning Association of America—History. 2. Regional
planning—United States—History.   I. Title.   II. Series.
HT392.S64   1996
711'.3'06073—dc20   96-9514
                                                                    CIP

Type set in Garamond 3 by Huron Valley Graphics, Inc., Ann Arbor, Michigan.
Printed by Thomson-Shore, Inc., Dexter, Michigan.

The paper in this publication meets the minimum requirements of American National
Standard for Information Sciences—Permanence of Paper for Printed Library Materials.
ANSI 239.48-1992.

9   8   7   6   5   4   3   2   1

To
Jason, Laura, and Suzan
with Love

University Libraries
Carnegie Mellon University
Pittsburgh, PA 15213-3890

CONTENTS

Acknowledgments

Every scholar soon discovers he or she owes an immense debt to the faithful, interested librarians who tend to both the great and the little resources of scholarship. In my case, I want to give special thanks to the librarians who assisted me in using the manuscript collections at the University of Pennsylvania (Lewis Mumford Papers), Columbia University (Edith Wood Papers), Cornell University (Clarence Stein Papers), and especially at Dartmouth College (MacKaye Family Papers). I also wish to thank the librarians at the Cunningham Library, Indiana State University, who assisted me in a wide variety of ways.

In addition, I am grateful for the financial support that I received from Indiana State University and its Faculty Research Committee.

INTRODUCTION

The Regional Planning Association of America (RPAA) has long fascinated students of urban planning, regionalism, environmentalism, and intellectual history. Made up of some of the leading thinkers of its time, the RPAA involved numerous significant ideas and practices regarding metropolitan development; architecture and housing; the physical, cultural, and social environment; technology; and other aspects of a rapidly modernizing America during the 1920s and 1930s. Although it had little coherent organization, it was united by a shared ambition among its members to design a radically improved America.

I am by no means the first to deal with the RPAA, but I am the first to deal with it in all its fullness. More than thirty years ago Roy Lubove published a solid scholarly study of the RPAA's work in the general field of housing under the title *Community Planning in the 1920s,* and more recently Daniel Schaffer has ably discussed important aspects of the same subject in his *Garden Cities for America: The Radburn Experience.* They do not, however, give much attention to the RPAA's very important involvement in regional planning and regionalism. These aspects are covered in Carl Sussman's anthology of essays by RPAA members, *Planning for the Fourth Migration,* but this work, like most compilations, has numerous gaps in its coverage of ideas and activities.

Designing America has roots in my previous scholarship. Having a deep interest in radical social idealism, I published in 1988 my *Brotherly Tomorrows: Movements for a Cooperative Society in America, 1820–1920,* choosing these dates in the belief that the 1920s marked the end of century-long hopes of transforming society through voluntary cooperative societies. Some not especially attentive critics have taken me to task for ignoring post-1920 elements of social radicalism. This work on regional planning and the idealism that animated it is my answer to such criticism, my point being that the RPAA represents a much different kind of radical reform, featuring not cooperative communities but social management by technicians. In this scheme regional planning was a broad arena of operation and cooperation by a variety of

experts whose composite expertise was expected to provide wise management of social development. A critical weakness in this approach was
the general absence of any serious concern about the political means to
realize such hopes.

More than a decade ago I published a book on mid-nineteenth-
century New York, *The New Metropolis: New York City, 1840–1857,*
which dealt with both the realities of an emerging world-class city and
the efforts of planners and reformers to improve that city. I had hoped
in this present book to provide a somewhat similar understanding of
New York at a significantly later stage in its development, only to
realize that the RPAA, while based in the city and much concerned
with its problems, provided at best a narrowly selective view of New
York's realities. This was especially the case in its almost total aversion
to local politics, but even in the area of housing the understanding of
conditions by members tended to be abstract, the understanding of
outsiders—which generally they were. Not all was lost here, however.
If the result is relatively little about Gotham itself, there are, I think,
significant insights into the metropolitan area, into a new version of my
"new metropolis."

Similarly, I had hopes that I might build on my first work, *Ideals and
Politics,* in which I experimented with a multiple biographical approach
to the contributions a group of pre–Civil War New York writers and
thinkers made to social and political thought. My aim had been to deal
with this thought not in terms of abstract systems but as elements in
the lives of individuals in relation to themselves, to each other, and to
their times. Although the experiment was far from a total success, it
did lead me to believe that the approach might be applied to other
groups of individuals. In this present book, however, I have been forced
to recognize that, even within a definable group of individuals committed to the same general goals, the kind of intimate interaction that I
had hoped to find often is simply not there to be found.

What these disappointments do is not to scream defeat but to sug-
gest that every subject has its strengths and limitations to which the
historian must adapt. I have tried when possible to introduce the
living, personal element into the discussion of regional planning ideas,
ideals, and strategies, the actual result being determined by the availability of sources and the knowable positions of RPAA members at
varying points in time. Most essentially, this is a book that gives special
emphasis to four men who constituted the vital center of the RPAA,
each functioning in his own distinctive way.

Two of these men were architects, Charles Harris Whitaker and

Clarence Stein, both major forces in the architectural field, but each quite different in character and influence. Whitaker, the longtime editor of the *Journal of the American Institute of Architects,* in his discontent with the profession excited thought and created the opening for the formation of the RPAA. Stein, though himself committed to new ideas and approaches, made his chief contribution by turning the opportunities that Whitaker had created into practical accomplishments; he was the chief organizing force behind the RPAA and its activities.

The other two were basically philosophers attracted to the intellectual content of regional planning, but again in radically different ways. My personal hero is Benton MacKaye, a very practical intellectual who turned his experience in forestry into a grand vision that embraced the Appalachian Trail, the townless highway, the Tennessee Valley Authority, and a reinvigorated traditional America. He was the chief inspiration behind the RPAA, contributing little to its actual operations but much to its essential thinking. In contrast to MacKaye, who in character and situation was not a city dweller, Lewis Mumford was strongly influenced by his New York birth and upbringing; he was the only native New Yorker in the group. I started this work with a long-held admiration for Mumford as perhaps the most important American thinker of the twentieth century; greater understanding has substantially reduced this admiration, principally because it now seems to me that Mumford was far less an original thinker and that he owed a much greater intellectual debt to his colleagues than is generally recognized.

Whitaker, Stein, MacKaye, and Mumford do not complete the cast for the RPAA story. At one point or another, secondary characters played major roles: the architect, Frederick L. Ackerman, who brought to the group along with a disgruntled idealism a strong analytical mind, particularly useful in the calculation of construction costs. Henry Wright, noted for having an almost supernatural sense of terrain, was a genius at site planning, who taught his brethren much about creating a context for homes. Stuart Chase, although often absent from the group, contributed much to its appreciation of the strengths and weaknesses of urban-industrial society.

Two women, Edith Elmer Wood and Catherine Bauer, made substantial contributions to the development of housing policies, although often without the total support of other members. Alexander Bing and Robert Kohn were both practical men who offered little to thought but who played major roles in organizing significant housing activity, Bing in the private ventures at Sunnyside and Radburn and Kohn in government housing programs. And finally there was the husband-and-wife team of Robert and Martha Bruere, who gave the RPAA access to *Survey* magazine and who contributed significant understanding regarding the implications of electric power.

The composite picture furnished by this baker's dozen of actors and thinkers does not add up to a neat, coherent picture of planning thought and policy, but that, literally, is life. Although they were united by a common hope that they could make their professional expertise a force for social and economic change, they were too independent minded to form a "movement" that could be explained by some general thesis.

In writing this book I have been guided by numerous good examples, but two in particular stand out. One is Bayrd Still, for whom I once worked as a temporary graduate assistant, whose dedication to telling the truth in urban history has endured as a model of scholarship. The other is Zane Miller, whose *Boss Cox's Cincinnati* is not likely to be surpassed as an example of how to present a thesis that respects basic truth.

I

The View from the Octagon: Charles Harris Whitaker

In 1913 the Octagon remained one of the most architecturally and historically interesting buildings in Washington, D.C. Actually a hexagonal structure with a semicircular tower at one corner, it had been erected in 1800 by William Thornton, the original architect of the Capitol. After the burning of the city in 1814, the Octagon had served as the temporary presidential residence of James and Dolly Madison. Later, it housed a Catholic girls' school and then a department of government. Eventually left to deteriorate, it was saved from complete ruin in 1902 when it was purchased by the American Institute of Architects (AIA) as temporary headquarters. The AIA, the leading national organization for architects, intended to restore the building to its original grandeur as a residence and to construct a new and more convenient headquarters on adjoining property, but it was unable to raise the necessary money, and the Octagon continued to serve as its headquarters for many years.[1]

The old residence found expanded use in 1913 when it became the editorial office of the AIA's new journal. This monthly periodical marked an ambitious step forward for the AIA and the profession it represented. During the Progressive Era architects joined the growing number of professional people who sought to expand their influence on society by demonstrating that their expertise could, if given the chance, resolve fundamental social problems. In line with the City

1

Beautiful movement, the AIA hoped to find for architecture a public place where, freed from its usual dependence on private wealth, it could enhance the collective life of the people. The *Journal of the American Institute of Architects* (*JAIA*) was intended to promote this cause; in the words of its founders, to be especially "the authoritative publication in all that pertains to the great movements which are everywhere being set on foot and which have for their objective the betterment of the physical condition of our towns and cities."[2] It was an ambitious goal that required a special person as editor, and the AIA found him in Charles Harris Whitaker.

Born in 1872 in Rhode Island to an affluent family, Whitaker spent most of his formative years in Boston, where he attended the English High School. He did not graduate from the school, beginning a pattern of indifference to formal educational programs and degrees. Over the next years he studied art in London, Paris, Brussels, Berlin, and Leipzig, part of a cosmopolitan life that kept him out of the United States for more than ten years. Along with a broad understanding of architectural styles, he developed special expertise in the reproduction of artistic photographs, a skill that led to his accumulation of what became one of the world's most complete collections of photographs of classical Greek architecture. He made a final expression of his love for Greece when in his will he directed that his ashes be sent to that land.[3]

This cosmopolitan also was strongly an American aesthetic nationalist and an ardent supporter of the great but then-neglected American architect Louis Sullivan. In 1922–23, Whitaker paid Sullivan to write an autobiography for the *AIA*, an important step in reviving the latter's reputation; Whitaker took great pride in Sullivan's *Autobiography of an Idea,* proclaiming it "a masterly work" of American literature equalled only by Henry Adams's *Education.*[4] His interest in Sullivan's book enabled him to identify both with a creative element of the American democratic past and with a progressive future. Seizing on what he called Sullivan's "great idea" that form follows function, Whitaker urged his colleagues to reject defunct and useless architectural styles derived from Europe in favor of forms that, in obedience to aesthetic honesty, reflected the intended uses of the buildings in America.[5]

Having neither formal training nor employment as a practicing architect, Whitaker was free as editor to criticize, often with barely concealed contempt, the existing architectural profession. In 1916 he warned that schools of architecture were giving too much stress to architecture itself and not enough to music, literature, art, and other forms of culture—elements important not only for their power to expand imagination but for their connections with the real world. He warned that current practice tended to turn the architect into an "expert" isolated from practical reality, a disassociation that not only denied the profession its share of influence on society but also cut it off from the invigorating conditions of real life. Basically, he hoped to return the architect to the character of a craftsman, directly and honestly involved in creating structures suited to their intended purposes. Toward that end he proposed the creation of a "Society for Suppressing the Use of the Word 'Fine' in Connection with Art," convinced that the concept of fine art had helped to disconnect architecture from the realm of ordinary life, where it could do the most good for humanity.[6]

Although he was critical of the architectural profession, he shared with its more progressive leaders the confidence that it could become, as he put it in 1918, "a great and universal human service" when freed from its servitude to wealth "to serve the whole nation in its problems of physical development." These Progressive years brought a widespread effort of various professional groups to assert the importance of their expertise to the practical concerns of society. In his own special way, Whitaker was an important influence in this "professional revolution." During his decade and a half as editor, he made the *JAIA* a force for innovation and change. Later, Lewis Mumford said that he "did more to open the windows to the fresh currents that were stirring in architecture than perhaps any man in America."[7]

Much of Whitaker's early attention was on Washington, D.C., and also, in anticipation of regional planning, on its surrounding areas. In 1914 he advocated the creation of a national forest preserve between Washington and Baltimore, warning that the time had come for Americans to give thought to preserving their fast-vanishing forest resources: "A few years ago, the probable despoilment of our natural conditions seemed like an insignificant factor; now it looms large upon the horizon of our plans for the future." He especially argued that the Washington-Baltimore forest reserve would serve as an example for the nation, an "inspiration toward the possible development of a great national renaissance in art," making in his own way a familiar connection between nature and creativity, which his later colleagues in the regional planning movement could appreciate.[8]

Whitaker's concern that Washington set a good national example was especially evident in his strongly stated views regarding the public architecture of the city, views intended to make the *JAIA* what its directors proclaimed it to be in 1916: "an authoritative source in relation to questions of public buildings." Both Whitaker and the AIA lobbied for a strong public building commission to review all proposed new government construction and to prevent the many numerous building decisions that had, in their judgment, partly ruined L'Enfant's original plan for Washington.[9] Earlier in the century, much had been done to revive that plan, but the threat remained as in 1916, when the Treasury Department proposed building a huge central heating and lighting plant on the Potomac River. This megalith—with four smoke stacks each 180 feet tall—was to be constructed at a point where Whitaker believed it would "disfigure that beauty which L'Enfant, Washington, and Jefferson had in their mind's vision," and he joined with the other interested groups, such as the American Federation of Arts, to defeat the project.[10]

Whitaker was not opposed to government construction. In fact, he urged the erection of new public buildings to house various governmental offices that were then scattered among various rented accommodations in the city, some of which, he complained, were architectural blots on the city. Not only were such accommodations ugly and unduly expensive, he charged, but they involved a scattering of government functions, which increased the inefficiency of public operations. He supported a plan to construct a new building for the State Department as one that could contribute to the dignity and efficiency of the whole nation: "It is the imperative duty of the citizens of the United States to demand that its capital should be such a lesson in beauty obtained through the application of the principles of order and convenience that the smallest town or wealthiest municipality may there find the knowledge of how to plan for the future."[11]

To achieve that end, Whitaker argued the need for a systematic and comprehensive plan to guide the overall architectural development of the city. "Making Washington beautiful must be incidental to making Washington useful, orderly, convenient." In this connection, he lashed out at a tendency of architects employed in government programs to emphasize the merely monumental as a "crime," a failure to honor their "duty of planning and designing a building which shall give the maximum of convenience, comfort and efficiency at the minimum of expense commensurate with sound work and the dignified expression of the purpose of the building."[12]

Whitaker also took an interest in federal construction elsewhere in the nation. In 1916 he launched a sustained attack in the *JAIA* on the comprehensive Omnibus Public Works Bill being considered by Congress, attacking it as massive pork-barrel legislation motivated principally by the desire of congressmen to win favor at home and by the greed of local businessmen and land speculators. He proposed that the whole buildings program be placed under the direction of a supervising architect responsible for maintaining "the first elements of architecture—that the building shall be worthy of the purpose and the purpose worthy of the building." Whitaker's attacks brought a response from Congress, some of whose members charged that the AIA was concerned simply with creating a new demand for architects, but the editor typically refused to back down. In "An Open Letter to the Members of the Sixty-fourth Congress" he reiterated his contention that public buildings were a matter of national welfare requiring expert direction, and were much too important to be left under the influence of politicians. He received the support of his editorial board, which said, regarding the *JAIA*'s interest in public buildings, that it placed the AIA "definitely before the people of the United States as a body which is organized for the purpose of rendering a service to society."[13]

Whitaker was to continue his efforts to make government buildings an inspiration for better design throughout the nation. Eventually he was to have second thoughts about centralized control from Washington and came to advocate, under the influence of regionalism, the involvement of the people and architects of a locality in designing buildings that expressed local characteristics.[14] Before this occurred, however, his idea of what defined public architecture was given a dramatic turn by the entry in 1917 of the United States into World War I, which shifted his primary concern from public buildings to the much broader subject of adequate housing for all Americans.

The sudden outburst of government activity associated with the conflict put a great strain on available housing wherever that activity was concentrated. In less than a year, once sleepy Washington was overwhelmed by some 50,000 newcomers, with more arriving each day. The city grew "like a bonanza mining-camp," said one observer, and in the process acquired a New York–like crowding and energy that offered the possibility it might truly become the dynamic capital of the nation. Initially, Whitaker used the situation to illustrate the need for good planning, declaring that fifty years of inept management of public space had left the government ill prepared to deal efficiently with the complex demands of war.[15]

Soon, however, he was giving less attention to governmental efficiency than to providing decent housing for the rapidly mounting mass of war workers not only in Washington but in places dedicated to war industry. Observing that "a modern army is dependent upon industries at home," he warned that the war effort would be significantly hampered unless adequate living quarters were provided for workers. "War has given prominence to housing such as Peace could not give," he said in September 1917, arguing that the secret to Germany's military might was its mass provision for efficient housing. Later he would write that "the application of science and governmental aid to home-building for workmen in Germany was one of her vital steps in the great scheme of war preparedness."[16]

To learn the secrets of European war housing, he sent his colleague Frederick L. Ackerman to Britain to study the program there, making sure the reports that Ackerman sent back to America were quickly published in the *JAIA*. The main conclusion was that the national government should intervene to construct whole new towns for workers in the burgeoning plants and shipyards. Soon Whitaker's crusade for war housing helped persuade Congress to provide for government construction not simply of housing but of planned communities. Among the graduates of this experience with planned war communities were two of Whitaker's later associates in the Regional Planning Association of America (RPAA), Ackerman and Robert D. Kohn.[17]

The success of the war program intensified Whitaker's hopes that, as he put it in 1918, architects might be "invited to rebuild vast areas of dingy habitations," designing not simply good houses but whole communities for the great masses of people who lived in bad social environments. At times he dreamed of creating communities where cooperative organization would free men and especially women from the burdens of the household, places that would furnish heating and cooling from a central plant and where communal laundries and kitchens would eliminate domestic drudgery. Through such cooperative communities, "the home will be made richer and a better instrument for enlarging the field of life." For those who objected that such schemes were impractical, Whitaker declared that, thanks to the accumulated actions of supposedly "practical" men, Americans confronted an "era of waste, congestion, disorder and disorganization."[18] Why not then try the combination of idealism and skill that would be provided by architects committed to public service?

Like most students of the housing problem, Whitaker was especially concerned with the spreading slums of big cities, but he recognized that both the problem and its solution extended far beyond the metropolitan centers. In 1916 he had objected to the tendency of housing reformers to strive through building design alone to provide affordable good housing for the poor, pointing out that this generally led to large-scale project-type houses that would "forever commit us to the inevitable difficulties of transportation, crowding, recreation and child development."[19] In light of the radically new mobility afforded by the automobile, he wondered whether it would not be better to shift attention from the cities, where high land costs forced emphasis onto crowded projects, to the newly accessible fringe areas, where it might be possible to provide cheap, small houses that the poor could afford to own for themselves.

Whitaker also did not ignore rural America, where bad housing along with limited opportunity, he believed, drove people to the cities in search of a better life. The failure to upgrade rural living was producing a great drain on the countryside, which threatened future capacity to produce food and raw materials while adding new inhabitants to the overburdened city slums. It seemed necessary, then, to develop some comprehensive program of rehousing involving the construction of whole new towns for rural as well as city people. "Should we not organize rural life so that it would become attractive? Why not begin to think in terms of a multitude of communities where life could be lived under healthy and happy conditions, instead of trying to make a few communities bigger and bigger?"[20]

Much of Whitaker's attitude was influenced by the English Garden City tradition of Ebenezer Howard, but it also contained strong elements of native American thought, most notably that of Henry George. Although George is best known for his single-tax idea, it was his connection of land policy and land usage with overall social development that had the greatest effect on planning and reform. Although he had died years before, his philosophy was carried on by several disciples, none more devoted than Louis Post, for whose radical magazine, *The Public*, Whitaker wrote at least one article on the housing issue. Post, then assistant secretary of labor, and his wife, a leading feminist, were important influences for radical reform. While in his own *JAIA* Whitaker generally avoided references to George, elsewhere he emphasized the Georgist line that the private ownership of land by the comparative few would inevitably defeat even the best designed remedies for bad housing, since it inflated the costs of homes by radically increasing the cost of the land on which they were built.[21]

High site costs, Whitaker argued, led to efforts to house many people in a limited area, creating overcrowding and artificially inflating the value of surrounding land. With each attempt at improvement land prices rose, benefitting only a few landowners at the expense of real improvement. "To cope with them, we decrease, first, the size of the lot, then the size of the house, and then the size of the room." In order to prevent this "cancer at the heart of architecture," this process that led to congestion and slums, land had to be controlled for public use, preferably by way of some form of community ownership of the site and of surrounding lands. For a model of such land management Whitaker could point to the government war communities where planners like himself had been able to concentrate on creating a good environment without thought about maximizing land values.[22]

By 1920 Whitaker had convinced himself that only radical change could free Americans from their shoddy residential environments. That change, he believed, would necessarily involve some broad community plan that would embrace both cities and rural areas, a belief that predisposed him toward the new idea of regional planning. The return of peace, however, had taught him that he could not count on the special conditions created by the war emergency to foster government action. Some more enduring agency had to be created to extend the lessons of war into the time of peace.

Two years before he had helped persuade the AIA to establish the Committee on War and Post-War Problems to develop a plan that would make the profession "a great and universal human service." Subsequently, he served as secretary of the postwar committee, whose thirty-six members included Ackerman and Kohn, both key figures in the government's war housing program. Operating out of the Octagon, the committee attempted to organize not only architects but also all those involved in the building industry, making it thereby "the most important movement ever started by architects in this country." Before long, it announced its hopes of joining with other "brain workers" to create a "League of Professions," an organization of the diverse skills of professional men and women into a force dedicated to change and strong enough to overcome both inertia and opposition.[23]

Basically, Whitaker looked to the movement as a way of organizing the increasingly influential professional groups into a powerful counterforce to business and the profit motive. When some members of the AIA objected to this approach, he told them that it would increase the demand for architectural services and enable professionals to mobilize against the growing power of industrialism. "Is industry to go on until it devours us all, or are we to make it our slave and not our master?" The new industrial order had grown at the expense of craftsmanship and creativity, and the time had come for productive creativity to assert itself against mechanical routine and the domination of shortsighted selfishness. "Instead of a system where Business, Commerce and Industry can hire or buy all Knowledge, Science and Skill in order to make profits, we shall create a system where Science, Knowledge, and Skill develop, direct and control Business, Commerce and Industry, as agents for the welfare of mankind."[24]

It was a powerful social dream, one that led a young Lewis Mumford to say in 1920 that under Whitaker's editorship "there was more live sociology in the JAIA than goes into the American Journal of Sociology." By then, however, the great upswelling of cooperative effort evoked by the war had given way to uncertainty and conflict and to the hysterical reaction against radicalism raised by the Red scare. Although Whitaker clung to his hopes for some great coalition of architects, engineers, scientists, and others "to liberate the professions from the domination of selfish interests," he also was developing serious doubts about the willingness of architects to escape from the "house of prostitution" where the profit system had enticed them.[25]

At the same time, a major change took place in Whitaker's own life. In 1920 he abruptly moved the editorial office of the *JAIA* from Washington to New York City. In part this may have resulted from the collapse of hope for the continuation of wartime government, but it was also connected with a personal change, since during this period his wife, Celia, sued him for divorce, naming a young New York woman as the third party. By 1922 he had established his editorial office on East Twenty-third Street and his home on a farm in northern New Jersey, where he lived with his new wife, Eugenie.[26]

The move from the Octagon involved Whitaker in a more cosmopolitan and dynamic world than that of postwar Washington. Like numerous other Americans he disliked New York's dirt and congestion, but it was there that he was able to form a circle of interesting people. One of them, Mumford, who had first met Whitaker in 1918, said later that after the editor moved his office to New York he "brought together in friendly intercourse the group" that became the RPAA, the closest fulfillment of his dream for a coalition of professional talent.[27] While a few, like young Mumford, were native New Yorkers, most of these new associates had, like Whitaker, come from elsewhere, drawn to massive Gotham by its opportunities. Among them were several whose paths had also taken them through Washington and government service; these paths, too, had led to a disappointment with public life and to the search for new means of effecting change in America.

II

IDEALISM IN
PEACE AND WAR:
FREDERICK L. ACKERMAN
AND ROBERT D. KOHN

Whitaker's crusade to put architecture to human service received strong support from a few of his colleagues in New York City, no more so than from Frederick L. Ackerman. Born in 1878 in the small upstate New York town of Edmeston, Ackerman received a bachelor of architecture degree from Cornell University in 1901. After spending a year studying at the Ecole des Beaux Arts in Paris, he became a partner in Trowbridge and Ackerman, a professional relation that lasted until 1920. In 1915 he was appointed lecturer on the principles of architecture at Columbia University.[1] By this time, under the influence of Whitaker and others, he had committed himself to the effort to make architecture a force for social as well as aesthetic improvement, especially within the rapidly developing city-planning movement, which offered a broad basis for interprofessional cooperation.

In 1915, speaking to the students and faculty of the Cornell College of Architecture, he urged architects to prepare themselves for public service, especially for the improvement of "physical conditions within our communities." After noting that his own youthful idealism had grown over the years, he warned that idealism was helpless without an understanding of all the forces—political, economic and social, as well as aesthetic—that shaped the modern environment. Architects, he said, had become preoccupied with the City Beautiful movement and foreign aesthetic styles when they should be developing a "City of Common Sense" evolved from the real needs and possibilities of American society and guided by "a vital, indigenous architecture" rooted in American culture. Once they related themselves to reality, they would find plenty of allies, professional and otherwise, in the work of improving society.[2]

Ackerman dreamed of making architecture and planning a democratic movement aligned with an awakened citizenry. In 1914, as chairman of the AIA's Committee on Public Information, he urged the importance of educating the public, whose will was more important than abstract principles of architecture in determining the character of cities, a will that had yet to be guided by "sound social and economic ideas and good art." It was ignorance, not greed, that ultimately explained "the ugliness, the inadequacy of our surroundings." To prepare for fundamental improvement, then, required that architects exert themselves to reshape public attitudes toward planning, particularly to persuade Americans to subordinate their excessive individualism to the larger interests of the community to which all belonged. A reckless regard for individual rights and interests had produced a social environment oppressive to the great majority.[3] Borrowing from John Dewey's progressive educational philosophy, Ackerman proposed that city planning be taught in the public schools as a way both to educate children in the importance of their communities and to train them to evolve practical solutions from life experience. "Our schools consider things in the abstract only; the application is left to chance."[4]

While Whitaker's idealism in Washington led him naturally toward a concern with government architecture, Ackerman's dreams in New York City concentrated his attention on housing and overcrowding, leading him to take a special interest in the then new idea of zoning, which promised to give planners control over the use and development of urban lands. In 1913 he argued that there was little hope of improving even the appearance of American cities until a way was found that, like zoning, could prevent "intolerable conditions as regards congestion and a perfectly stupid loss of light and air," conditions especially intolerable on the island of Manhattan, where he had both his office and his home. He favored comprehensive controls over land usage and over the size and functions of buildings to prevent overcrowding and the development of slum conditions. Zoning was soon to become popular practice, but a guiding preoccupation with protecting property values disappointed Ackerman's hopes for a comprehensive plan in which "the rights of the entire community stand above and dominate the rights of the individual."[5]

Although Ackerman continued to hope for community-oriented zoning, his thoughts were redirected into new and seemingly more promising paths by America's entry into World War I. When Whitaker issued a call for architects to support the war, especially by contributing to the development of housing for war workers, Ackerman was one of the first to respond. As early as 1914 the New Yorker had urged architects to take an interest in improving conditions for workers, and so it was natural that, thanks to Whitaker, in late 1917 he went to England to study that nation's earlier efforts to resolve the same problem. There, supported by more than a decade of effort associated with the Garden City movement, the English government had built whole new communities that impressed Ackerman with the speed with which they had been constructed and with their healthy character as environments for living.[6]

Although recognizing that more than the Atlantic Ocean separated the two societies, Ackerman returned convinced that the English example was worth adapting to American circumstances. In early January 1918 he helped persuade the New York chapter of the AIA to pass resolutions demanding that the national government take all steps needed to "design and build communities." When Congress seemed ready simply to provide loans to stimulate housing construction, Ackerman attacked the plan. What was needed, he said, was a forceful government program that would quickly provide "a social and physical environment adjacent to war industries which will automatically create the spirit of integrated purpose which alone will produce our ships and munitions."[7]

Along with Whitaker and other architects, Ackerman lobbied for a government agency to initiate and control a wartime housing program, persuading the New York chapter of the AIA to issue a public declaration backing his proposals. He rejected any thought of temporary barracks-type housing for war workers on the grounds that such shoddy stuff would not meet human needs during the war and would be utterly useless afterward. Planned communities, on the other hand, would serve to meet housing needs in peace as well as war. He proposed a nonprofit government corporation to acquire the land needed for communities and to direct their actual contruction. Having learned from Henry George the importance of land values and the evils of land speculation, he insisted that the government maintain control over the land in and around the communities, taking any increases in value resulting from town construction and good planning for use by the new towns themselves. The more he thought about this plan, the more excited he became about its possibilities. "Let us be imaginative and visualize along our seaboard and wherever munitions plants exist communities of war workers organized as industrial divisions of our army."[8] In such communities, Americans might learn to subordinate their selfish individualism to the welfare of the community.

Congress responded by creating two distinct housing operations: the United States Housing Corporation, authorized to build housing for war workers in Washington, D.C., and elsewhere, and a more specialized housing division of the United States Shipping Board, intended to construct new towns to support the rapid increases in ship construction planned by the board. Ackerman was appointed chief of housing and town design for this second operation, giving him the responsibility for coordinating the work of architects and engineers into a massive effort quickly to produce effective designs for new communities. It was, as he said in August 1918, a demanding task that required immediate attention to "a multitude of extreme complex factors" involving not only the new towns themselves but their relationships with surrounding areas, an element of regional planning.[9]

Fortunately, Ackerman had an able ally in the man appointed to oversee the construction of the towns, a fellow New York architect, Robert D. Kohn. Born in New York City in 1870, Kohn had gotten his training as an architect at Columbia University and the Ecole des Beaux Arts. Beginning in 1895 he had established a successful practice in New York and had gone beyond that to become a respected leader in the effort to improve housing. Before the war he had served as the president both of the influential local chapter of the AIA and of the National Fire Protective Association. As a leading member of the Ethical Culture Society (the only significant religious connection of the RPAA), he also had important ties with the world of reform. Much of his attention was directed toward facilitating the construction of housing to meet the needs of New York's crowded population. For several years he had been a leading member of the local AIA's Committee of City Departments, formed, with the support of the construction industry, to rationalize municipal building ordinances in order to expedite the production of needed buildings. Kohn called it "a forceful committee in which architects, engineers, underwriters, and builders work together in a fine civic spirit."[10] This experience in coordinating diverse talents for constructive purposes helped make him an effective chief of housing production for the Shipping Board.

In 1918 the board organized a huge increase in ship building, and its housing division responded by initiating more than two dozen new communities to house more than 28,000 shipyard workers. Later, Ackerman recalled that his housing work was left relatively free from government meddling because Congress was preoccupied with the debate over whether to produce wooden or steel ships. Generally, the actual work of constructing these communities was done by private housing corporations financed by low-interest government loans and subject to general regulation by the Shipping Board. By April 1919 the board could report that it was close to completing twenty-four projects consisting of 8,774 houses along with 914 apartments and twenty-one dormitories. The preponderance of houses reflected what the chief of design believed were the preferences of most Americans. Ackerman in 1918 had rejected the then fashionable emphasis on multifamily dwellings as a way to resolve the housing problem. Such dwellings were contrivances designed by reformers for somebody else, he said, when most people actually preferred a single-family house, "a complete environment wherein can be gratified the idiosyncrasies of personality."[11]

Although Ackerman provided general oversight over planning and design, the detailed work was done by other architects under contract with the board. One of the most ambitious of the war projects, Yorkship Village, was designed by Erastus D. Litchfield, a New York architect. Located on some 225 acres a few miles south of Camden, New Jersey, Yorkship Village was billed as America's first garden city. Litchfield drew up an ambitious plan for a town of 12,000 people, with playgrounds, parks, and a shopping center. Much attention was given to site planning. "The tricks of the trade," wrote one observer, "are to make use of natural beauties, provide gentle street grades, guide traffic to a few broad through avenues and leave narrow residential streets that will be quiet and safe . . . make short closed vistas and winding roads, instead of the usual dull grid-iron street plan; and find the closest fit to the natural lay of the land."[12] Only a part of this plan was implemented before construction was terminated by the end of the war, but it and similar plans pointed the way to the improvement of America's rapidly unfolding suburban future.

These war villages seemed to prove that it was possible through large-scale, well-coordinated projects to provide adequate housing for America's workers. Lawrence Veiller, the housing expert, said in 1918 that the program offered a way to a slumless America. Although he had doubts as to the willingness of Americans to support a government program, he hoped that, at least, the national government would construct "Heroes Villages" to reward returning veterans when the war ended. John Taylor Boyd Jr., writing in the *Architectural Record,* declared that the program might well mark the beginning of a "great movement of benefit not simply for the professions concerned, but for American civilization," while Sylvester Baxter in the same periodical predicted that the "model communities" furnished an example of government effort that "cannot fail to have a lasting and beneficial effect in shaping the future of American domestic and social life."[13]

Congress, however, had enacted the program only as a temporary war measure; even the concern with good design was justified as making government housing more saleable with the return of peace. When the Great War ended in November 1918, therefore, both houses of Congress moved quickly to repeal the program. In the House of Representatives, the Committee of Public Buildings and Grounds, perhaps smarting under Whitaker's blasts against congressional architectural policies, condemned it as a refuge for "college professors and alleged experts." In late 1918 the Senate passed a resolution for the termination of construction on most towns, a step that a defender of the program saw as the beginning of a campaign to force the sale of war housing to private interests: "You can hear the predatory tread of real estate speculation." By 1920, responding to congressional directives, the Shipping Board had begun to sell off its projects at bargain prices, a process that continued into the early 1920s.[14]

For some of the principals in the war program, however, the idea lived on. For Kohn the project had demonstrated how the architect could involve himself in public affairs, fulfilling Whitaker's dream of service to the community. In 1919 he urged Americans to support the idea of completing the war-towns program, in the process coining a slogan for the later RPAA when he said that "to meet the housing need it is not sufficient to build houses—we must build communities." A year later, in regard to proposed projects on the slum housing of the central cities, he said that it would be wiser to build new homes in new communities located on the urban fringe where land was cheaper and the environment healthier.

The war towns had, for Kohn, also proven both the value and the feasibility of cooperative action among engineers, architects, and others involved in the construction of housing. Through the right organization as well as the right location, good housing could eventually be assured for all Americans. In 1922 he recalled that during the war "at one blow, the professional classes were recruited a millionfold"; the trick was to find a substitute for war as a basis for cooperation. Earlier, in February 1919, he persuaded the powerful New York chapter of the AIA to support Whitaker's postwar committee, declaring that the meeting at which this was done was "the most interesting held by this chapter in many years." After the failure of that movement, Kohn devoted himself to promoting professional cooperation and service within both the AIA and the building industry, aiming especially to rationalize construction practices and to prevent disruptive strikes by construction workers.[15]

Ackerman was too much of a loner to echo Kohn's cooperative ideal, but he, too, found in wartime service reenforcement for his own public ideal of government planning, one far broader and more radical than his colleague's. Success in the design of the war towns strengthened his hopes that humans could learn to create and maintain good environments for themselves, communities where "the home and its related communal features" would be protected from the threat of disruption and decay. For Ackerman, however, it was not enough simply to build communities but it was necessary to alter the whole character of society in terms of its values and organization. Not until this was accomplished, he warned, would there be protection from the kind of influences that, with the end of the war, were threatening the futures of the government's model communities.[16]

Early in 1919 Ackerman published a long article in the *National Municipal Review* calling for effective national planning to guide the development of the whole of American society. His call also served the cause of regional planning, especially in his dismissal of traditional political entities. "State boundaries," he stated, "are artificial boundaries which must be ignored in the organization of the physical plan for the economic use of the entire area of the nation." In the cities it was necessary to abandon "the old practice of producing ugly houses in ugly settings," but city planning was not enough: since urban and rural areas were intertwined, planners had to include the countryside as well as cities. The decay of rural society was leading hundreds of thousands of people to migrate to the overcrowded metropolises, and haphazard city growth was invading the countryside, threatening to consume the agricultural land needed to sustain future generations.[17]

As his chief planning tool, Ackerman looked again to zoning, expanding the prewar idea to include all land, rural and urban. Anticipating an important concern of the later RPAA, he said that the development of an effective national plan to determine how land was to be used required "the development of regional surveys," which could establish an accurate understanding of the physical and economic character of "each and every part of the entire area of the nation." To carry out the complex task of developing such a comprehensive plan, he proposed the creation of "permanent, central executive agencies" on every level of government, local, state, and national.[18]

Ackerman believed that such a plan could be made effective only by making a radical change in the manner in which Americans carried on the business of development, especially in promoting the growth of their cities. No longer should plans for "our industrial and agricultural areas be predicated upon the belief that we can go on expanding our cities indefinitely, massing together great populations engaged solely in commerce or in the fabrication of materials." To reverse this tendency, he proposed that there be public control over investment for purposes of development. Capital, for instance, should no longer be wasted in "building temporary buildings, temporary cities" destined to be torn down and rebuilt, but should be directed to creating the more stable and humane environment attained in the war communities and in the decentralization of population.[19] Presumably, a detailed national zoning plan prescribing land usage would be the chief road map for the flow of investment.

Above all, Ackerman believed, there had to be a radical change in the public values that ultimately governed development. Without such a change, even the best ideas and techniques would be of little avail, since they would be perverted to ignoble ends. In place of the dominant individualism, with its selfish concern for individual profit, he dreamed of cooperative effort guided by the faith that the improvement of the common society and environment in which all lived would be a benefit to all. Sharing Whitaker's Georgist outlook, he advocated the expropriation of increases in the value of land resulting from population growth and public improvement, the money to be used for the general good rather than for speculative profit.[20]

Soon after he published the essay on national planning in the *National Municipal Review,* Ackerman read two recently published books, *Modern Business Enterprise* and *The Vested Interests,* by the radical economist Thorstein Veblen, who became an important influence on his thinking. In 1918 Veblen had come to New York, where he soon contributed to the intellectual growth of several future members of the RPAA. Lewis Mumford, for instance, later recalled that Veblen had helped him to develop an interdisciplinary approach to understanding human society, an approach essential to regional planning. Ackerman found confirmation of his radical thinking in Veblen's ideas. Writing to Edith Elmer Wood, a conservative colleague in housing and planning matters, Ackerman said that Veblen had convinced him that there could be no effective public planning "so long as practically all governmental action is carried out in complete conformity to the principles which actuate modern business enterprise, which is, of course, nothing but activity actuated by the desire for profit rather than greater production to meet the needs of the common man."[21]

Ackerman recognized that this rejection of the profit motive might be seen as "rank socialistic doctrine," unacceptable to the American public, but he believed that real progress was impossible so long as "speculation" governed the situation. Any gains derived from good planning and zoning, for instance, would be diverted from meaningful improvement of the housing environment into higher rents and land values that, under the profit system, would bring a crowding of population. Thinking perhaps of Kohn's hopes for professional cooperation, he wrote in 1921, "The town planners, the housing experts, the engineers, the legal advisers, the organizers of moves in the interest of the common welfare are as a small force marching toward an objective upon a moving platform running in the opposite direction at a slightly more rapid rate than their own rate of advance." And so progress would be continuously sabotaged until the selfish interests of individual property were subordinated to the planner's ideal of public good.[22]

Such radicalism persuaded Whitaker in 1921 to declare that "it is only Mr. Ackerman who has blazed a trail through the economic jungle in which we are now lost." The trouble was that there were so few willing to follow the trail. The savage persecution of radicals during the Red scare following the war led Ackerman to complain that whenever someone suggested that the system should be changed so as to "aim at the production of goods rather than profits" he was condemned as an undesirable person to be investigated by Congress.[23] What, then, could be done? Given the conservatism of the times, there seemed no way but to engage in the slow process of reeducating the public.

In this Ackerman was at a notable disadvantage, handicapped by a wooden and convoluted prose style. Although respected by his immediate associates, he lacked the capacity to generate enthusiasm for his cause. By 1922, however, a new man of influence had appeared who both gave some popular appeal to the idea of national planning and expanded its meaning in a significant way. This man had, like Whitaker, Ackerman, and Kohn, followed a trail of public service that involved Washington, but his trail passed through the nation's forests and wilderness areas rather than through the congested cities of metropolitan America.

III

GREEN DIMENSIONS:
BENTON MACKAYE

The strivings of the new public-oriented professionals to make a place for their skills and ambitions took on various forms. As architects, Whitaker, Ackerman, and Kohn were in their own distinctive ways essentially urban in their concerns, concentrating on the housing and environment of the congested metropolitan centers. Although Ackerman gave much emphasis to the importance of rural areas in planning and zoning, even he focused his attentions on the problems and impact of the central cities. In the early 1920s, however, these architects encountered a very different personality who radically broadened their thinking regarding regionalism and regional planning, in the process opening the way for the creation of the RPAA.

Benton MacKaye, the new inspiration, belonged to the green, living world of nature and to the traditional society of rural communities. In the summer of 1914, MacKaye described his impressions of the city of Chicago, giving particular note to the "sardined humanity" crowded on the beaches and to the ranks of smokestacks looming above the steel mills of South Chicago, "each issuing a grim black cloud that streamed indefinitely across the prairie." The scene, he concluded, "made an exact diagram of play and work and commercialism in America. Here on the beach was the feeble attempt at obtaining Heaven; back in the phalanx of smokestacks was our titanic triumph in attaining hell."[1] It became his life's work to resist this metropolitan blight and to re-create what he believed was a radically better world rooted in the American past.

19

MacKaye came from one of America's most creative families. He was born in Stamford, Connecticut, in 1879, the fifth of six children. His father was James Morrison Steele MacKaye, a man of overflowing talents and ambitions. A painter, actor, playwright, theatrical producer, stage designer, and sometime inventor, Steele MacKaye (as he was generally known) wrote more than twenty plays during his fifty-two years, as well as building several theaters and establishing the first dramatic school in America. A driven man and a visionary, he spent much of his life trying to integrate his diverse talents into grandiose accomplishments, most notably into his "Spectorium," a giant theater that he designed to present, with special panoramic effects, a pageant on the discovery and development of America. Conceived for the Chicago World's Fair in 1893, it was never finished, costing MacKaye not only much money but his health, and in 1894 he died as he had lived, on the road—in Colorado on a train bound for home.[2]

Steele MacKaye left behind him not only his own accomplishments but also an accomplished family. Of his five sons, the second oldest and perhaps the most talented, William Payson, died in 1889 at the very beginning of maturity, leaving behind only numerous hints of a brilliant future never attained—but the others lived on to carve out successful careers. Harold Steele, the oldest, was a patent attorney and sometime novelist who, like his father, displayed a multitude of talents, being described as "an ingenious inventor, a clever amateur musician, painter, and playwright." James Medbury, the third brother, was an economist, engineer, and philosopher, who was to spend his last years as professor of philosophy at Dartmouth and defender of the Newtonian conception of the universe from the challenge of Einstein's theory of relativity. Percy, the closest to Benton in age and interests, was a popular dramatist and poet who helped create an interest in American folk culture. The youngest of the children and the only girl, Hazel, became an actress, director, author of pageants, and suffragist.[3]

Amid all this talent, Benton was able to find his own unique avenue of achievement. After spending most of his first eight years in New York City, he was brought to what became his true home when in 1888 Steele MacKaye moved his family to the small New England village of Shirley Center, Massachusetts. It was at Shirley Center, which Percy later described as *"our* little hamlet and haven in exodus from city wall and towers of perturbation," that the MacKaye family found its roots. In time, Benton MacKaye transformed himself into his ideal of a Yankee—a practical dreamer and an eminently rational eccentric. As a boy, MacKaye used the village as a place from which to explore the neighboring countryside, his first step toward his later interest in regional surveys. Forty years later, he said that his explorations had revealed to him a regional world of hill villages and factory towns well integrated into the green landscape, one where Mount Monadnock in southern New Hampshire served, like Japan's Fujiyama, as "the emblem of a unified homeland . . . the lofty pivot of an indigenous region and culture."[4]

Unfortunately for MacKaye this was a fading world abandoned by many of its people for the opportunities of big cities. Years later he was to write of New England that the typical village was "for the most part a deserted village," where the church remained, but with a diminishing congregation, and where the school graduated most of its students to the outside world. "The thirty dwelling houses have become thirteen— or three. The outlying fields have largely become brushlands."[5] Many Americans of his and older generations had expressed this same lament, but few went as far as MacKaye in making it the basis for a life's work.

As a young man MacKaye also left his homeland for a wider world of opportunity. In 1896 he enrolled at Harvard, where he studied under among others the philosopher Josiah Royce, who advanced his understanding of the relationship between man and the landscape, and the geographer William Morris Davis. Davis gave him a long-remembered lesson in the world's essential unity when in introducing a course he held up a six-inch globe and declared "here is the subject of our study—this planet, its lands, waters, atmosphere, and life; the abode of plant, animal, and man—*the earth as a habitable globe.*" Such influences helped develop a distinctly professional style that left little room for a romantic approach to nature. Later, MacKaye was to say that both he and his father were "visualizers," but, while Steele MacKaye visualized in terms of drama, he, as a regional planner, "visualizes chiefly by maps, charts and scientific statement." After graduating from Harvard in 1900, MacKaye's developing ecological awareness led him to commit himself to the new science of forestry, and in 1905 he received a master's degree from Harvard in that discipline.[6]

Soon after receiving his professional degree he joined the United States Forest Service, beginning more than a decade of sporadic but enriching involvement in creating and managing the nation's forests. From his graduate work, MacKaye had absorbed the view that forestry was a form of agriculture: the growing of trees and the careful management of timber production to meet society's needs. Now he was educated to a larger view by conflicts over forest policy, over what he later said was the question "could Uncle Sam as forester prevent the stealing of waterpower sites? regulate grazing? and control a dozen other uses of the National Forest—in addition to selling timber?"[7] He developed a strong sense of public service and a deep faith in government as an instrument of public purpose.

During his first five years, however, MacKaye was, as he noted later, "in and out of the Service," apparently because he was reluctant to leave New England. In addition to his public work, he took on varied temporary jobs, including teaching forestry at Harvard and organizing two private forest preserves. In 1910 he returned to Shirley Center, where he spent the next year and a half doing independent consulting work and writing about forests. Finally, at the end of 1911, when the service offered him more permanent employment, he moved to Washington, D.C. Although he spent most of the next decade in Washington, he was soon temporarily back in New England on a mission that opened his mind to new elements of regionalism and regional planning.[8]

In 1912 the Forest Service lent him to the United States Geological Survey to map the diverse forest cover of the several river watersheds in the White Mountains, an important step toward establishing the White Mountains National Forest. The year before, Congress had provided for public purchases of land that had an influence on river flow and navigation, a provision designed to get around constitutional objections to government purchases strictly for forest purposes. This work helped teach MacKaye two valuable lessons. First, he learned to appreciate the importance of watersheds and river valleys to land-use planning and development as he carried out studies that required that forests be treated as parts of a dynamic landscape. Second, he learned how to work as a member of a team with engineers and other technicians from the Geological Survey, an experience in the benefits of cooperating talents especially important for a man who was in his instincts very much an individualist.[9]

The White Mountains survey proved to be a prelude to an immensely enriching period of public activity when MacKaye returned to Washington to set up residence there. Some of it involved women. Benton's younger sister, Hazel, had become an ardent advocate of women's rights, supporting the cause by staging in Washington and elsewhere a number of pageants, popular dramatizations of woman's grievances. She also spoke for the cause, occasionally persuading her brother to pose as a heckler in order to attract attention and sympathy.[10]

It was through Hazel that MacKaye met his future wife, Jessie Hardy Stubbs, a widow who had come to Washington by way of Chicago in pursuit not only of women's rights but of world peace. Sometime after her marriage to MacKaye in 1914, she advocated that women "strike" for peace by refusing to marry or to bear children until warfare should be abandoned. In 1918 Ellen Maury Slayden—a Washington wife with little sympathy for suffragists—wrote in her journal that "pretty little Mrs. Jessie MacKaye" had rushed up to her on the street, "her face all lined with nervous strain and told me with delight that she had been arrested three times last week.. They go out from the headquarters in Jackson Place every night, make speeches and wave banners till they get themselves arrested, and march off to jail, handbags packed in advance with toothbrush and nightie, to revel in martyrdom."[11] Only later would it be recognized that here were signs of an unstable disposition that would lead to a tragic end.

MacKaye had his own intense commitments. In 1913 he joined the Hell-Raisers, a newly formed group of progressive intellectuals that included William L. Stoddard, Washington correspondent of the Boston *Transcript;* Art Young, the political cartoonist; and Stuart Chase, a radical reform writer and later member of the RPAA. Believing strongly in the benefits of government action, the Hell-Raisers gave special attention to Congress, drafting several bills intended less to be passed than to be debated, hoping that through Congress they could build public support for progressive policies. They were particularly interested in preserving the nation's resources in lands, minerals, and waterpower for public benefit. In 1913 the MacKaye-drafted Alaska Development Bill, providing for the planned settlement of America's last frontier, was introduced into both houses of Congress. Among other Hell-Raiser bills that MacKaye helped to draft was one in 1916 for the creation of a national Water Power Development Board, with authority over transportation, recreation, and flood control, as well as power in river valleys—a proposal that anticipated the Tennessee Valley Authority (TVA), created two decades later.[12]

MacKaye found his own special frontier in the hundreds of thousands of barren acres left by an unregulated timber industry, an example of timber mining, as opposed to the cultivation preached by the Forest Service. In 1914 he investigated the "stump country" created by lumbermen in Michigan, Wisconsin, and Minnesota and soon devised a visionary plan to redevelop and reopen such areas for settlement by communities of rural workers, a modern version of the old American tradition of new beginnings on new lands that had first produced the New England towns.[13] In late 1915 he noted that over the previous six months he had been advocating a plan to settle "wild lands," which would provide jobs for many unemployed Americans in the

development of the nation's natural resources. Soon after, in urging
support for his plan, he said that it was certainly better to spend
money "for helping men to build up the country than to help men to
kill one another."[14]

By this time MacKaye had drafted the National Colonization Bill
authorizing the Labor Department to take the lead in organizing a
government colonization project. In February 1916 this bill was introduced into the House of Representatives by Robert Crosser of Ohio but
it failed to get beyond a preliminary hearing, and the next year the
nation devoted its resources to helping men kill each other in World
War I. MacKaye, however, had won support for his plan, especially
from Assistant Secretary of Labor Louis Post, a leading disciple of
Henry George. In 1919, confronted with the problem of finding employment for returning war veterans, the Labor Department issued
MacKaye's first important published work, *Employment and Natural
Resources,* which presented colonization as a solution to that problem
and more.[15]

In some respects, MacKaye hoped to recreate a Jeffersonian world of
individual farms, where hard work would assure independence and com-
petence, but his means for doing so were distinctly non-Jeffersonian,
since they involved both government and communal settlement. While
Ackerman and Kohn were at work on their model towns for the Shipping
Board, MacKaye was envisioning planned farm communities to be constructed for settlers by a United States Construction Service, using the
labor of the unemployed; the service would clear land, build houses,
create marketing and credit facilities, and do whatever else was necessary
to establish a viable economic life, including especially the formation of
"ready-made" farms that could be put into immediate production.
While many of these communities would be planted in stump areas,
others would be established in woodlands as permanent homes for tim-
bermen, who would enjoy lifelong employment in the cultivation rather
than the devastation of forests, constituting what MacKaye later called "a
lumber empire based on sustained yield of trees and steadfast employment of men."[16]

Such a scheme was intended to achieve the dream long entertained
by social visionaries, who imagined communities where cooperation
would eliminate the social isolation and economic inefficiencies afflicting farms and thereby restore the vitality of rural society in a modernizing world. If the goal was essentially traditional, the means to achieve
that goal were so radical as to deny any chance of ready acceptance. The
key was not simply government intervention but public control over

the most basic of all resources, land—a substantial modification of private property rights. Having been exposed, like most of his future colleagues in the RPAA, to the ideas of Henry George, MacKaye was especially concerned about the effects of land speculation and individual property decisions on his communities. Public ownership seemed necessary in order to prevent those who had been settled in the new communities from selling land to monopolists and speculators or otherwise using the land in ways threatening to the community. Occupancy would be limited to those who actually used the land; any increase in land values would be reserved for public benefit. Although he was unsure as to whether it would be the individual community or the government that would own the land, MacKaye proposed that overall policy be set by a National Land Board, authorized both to reserve public lands from private sale and to purchase private lands for public use. [17]

MacKaye's colonization plan won some support. In April 1918 the *New Republic* endorsed it as an "able program for the social and economic rehabilitation of our national and agricultural lands" that would make the United States a world leader in the development of land-use policy. Writing at a time of public concern over the activities of the radical Industrial Workers of the World (IWW), the magazine's editor warned that timber mining and land speculation had done much to create the rootless, jobless proletariat presumed to be eager recruits for radicalism, a class likely to grow with the mass return of veterans from the war. Better, then, to enact a program such as MacKaye's, which by providing continuous employment would convert "the lumberjack from a hobo into a family man." Both Post's *The Public* and the *Monthly Labor Review* published articles written by MacKaye on colonization, and in late 1918 Representative Clyde Kelly of Pennsylvania submitted MacKaye's Workers and Soldiers Land Bill to the House of Representatives, where it was given a formal hearing. [18]

The prospects for effective public land and community development, however, quickly evaporated with the end of the war. Soon after the armistice in November 1918, he later recalled, "Washington went down like a circus tent," as programs like the one for wartime housing were abruptly terminated, introducing what proved to be a long period of retreat from active government. Unfortunately for MacKaye, his enthusiasm for colonization had led in late 1917 to his transfer, which he reluctantly accepted, from the Forest Service to the Labor Department, where he was left exposed to postwar cutbacks. At the end of June 1919 he lost his job, leaving him to make a fruitless struggle to support himself and his wife by writing. Finally, as a last act of public service, he obtained in October 1919 a temporary job as a "route agent" for the Postal Service in connection with the latest version of what he called his "utopias."[19]

This was a scheme to use the postal system to link the producers of food directly with consumers in the city in order to reduce urban living costs and to expand markets for farmers. Under his plan, farmers would be organized into cooperative "rural supply units," which would use the Postal Service's truck routes and post offices to provide food for "community units," without the expensive involvement of profit-seeking middlemen. Although he justified the plan as a way to reduce the cost of living, it was evident that his chief concern was with his colonization proposals, his hope being that the rural supply units would provide a basis for permanent farm colonies. Expanding on this, he dreamed that at least some of the supply units might evolve into garden cities with small factories: "A proper balance between the industrial and agricultural population . . . is perhaps the most potent means of withdrawing the surplus population from our congested metropolitan districts." To illustrate what could be done, he provided a sketch of a broad regional plan for Washington, D.C., and its related areas, including especially surrounding agricultural areas.[20]

MacKaye's "Plan for Cooperation between Farmer and Consumer" received some attention in 1920, but nothing came of the idea, and he soon lost his temporary postal job. For a short time, the loss of one utopia led him to thoughts of another: the Bolshevik Revolution in Russia, which radical idealists could still see as the best hope for reshaping the world. He briefly cooperated with two future colleagues in the RPAA, Stuart Chase and Whitaker, and in March 1920 these men, along with Jessie MacKaye, offered their services to the Soviet Union, noting that they had heard that the new Red utopia "would welcome the services of competent technical workers . . . in industrial and social fields, especially those who in their sympathies and convictions are in harmony with the aims of the present Russian Soviet Republic." They promised to recruit others for service and "to cross over into Russia and to report to the Soviet Government." In describing the work he personally would like to do in Russia, MacKaye wrote that he was "particularly interested in the opening of new country and resources through railroad development and in the utilization of land."[21] In those pre-Stalin days a willingness to participate in a foreign adventure perhaps is understandable, especially for those who had geared their thinking to public service, but it received no response.

This last disappointment to MacKaye's utopian dreams was soon followed by the worst period in his life. Having lost his place in government service he was forced to accept a job as a writer for a newspaper syndicate in New York City; by the spring of 1921 he and Jessie were living in an apartment on West Twelfth Street in Greenwich Village. This attempt to start a new life in the metropolis was soon brought to a crashing halt by Jessie's mental instability.

Before Jessie had married MacKaye and again in 1918 she had nervous breakdowns; in each case, she had recovered to carry on her work for peace and women's rights, but the basic problem remained, and after their move to New York she had a relapse. MacKaye said later that he took her from doctor to doctor to no avail, only then to see her apparently recover to the point where she began to smile and make jokes. Encouraged, he decided to take her to Croton outside the city for rest and recuperation. On the day of their departure (April 19, 1921), however, she had expressed a strong unwillingness to go, and when he got her to Grand Central Station for the trip she suddenly disappeared into a crowd. MacKaye hoped that she had gone to a hospital for treatment, but her lifeless body was soon found floating in the East River. At her instruction, her body was cremated and the ashes scattered over the hills of Staten Island, where she, an enthusiastic hiker, had once roamed.[22]

While MacKaye was able to find some consolation in the thought that, as he told a friend, she had escaped the "untold suffering" of a worsening mental state, he was emotionally devastated; he would never marry again, even though he would live on for more than a half century. And yet this loss was to open the way to what he would later call "a sort of golden epoch" of great personal satisfaction and accomplishment. It began when his friend Whitaker persuaded him to stay at his newly purchased farm at Mount Olive, New Jersey, to begin his recovery.[23] There, he conceived an idea that won the enthusiastic endorsement first of Whitaker and then, when it was published as "An Appalachian Trail" in the latter's *Journal of the American Institute of Architects,* of many leading Americans. Over the years, the idea opened the way for a long exploration that gave him a permanent place in the history of conservation and recreation planning.

It was with Whitaker's strong support at every stage that in October 1921 MacKaye published "An Appalachian Trail," which was significantly subtitled "A Project in Regional Planning." In it he proposed that the nation develop a trail some 1,700 miles long to run on the mountain ridges of the Appalachians from Mount Washington in New

Hampshire to Mount Mitchell in North Carolina. (As eventually completed the trail ran more than 2,000 miles, from Mount Katahdin in
Maine to Mount Oglethorpe in Georgia.) This plan owed much to the
work of others. During his days in Shirley Center, MacKaye had the
opportunity to use some of the extensive network of trails being developed in New England by several hiking clubs; by the 1920s he could
note that there were more than 2,000 miles of hiking paths from which
to piece together the New England portion of the Trail. The regional
aspect of his plan derived not only from his own earlier thinking but,
likely, from a proposal made shortly before by the Society of American
Foresters (of which he was a member) for the division of the United
States into "forest regions" to provide for the management of forests
without centralized bureaucratic control. [24]

MacKaye's Appalachian Trail article incorporated several elements of
his developing thought. One pertained to the need for recreation, a
matter of human health as well as pleasure, which had come to his
attention while he was with the Forest Service. In 1916 he had argued
that the national forests could play an important role in providing a
healthy antidote to the stresses of modern life. Now, he promised that
the Trail would open "a fairly continuous belt of under-developed
lands," accessible to all eastern urban areas, where it would be possible
to find a refuge in nature from urban pressures. He went beyond the
idea of the Trail itself to envision the development along its entire
length of "recreation camps," small communities designed to serve
those seeking revitalization. Such places might become health-giving
centers for those suffering from diseases such as tuberculosis and from
the kind of mental stress that had killed his wife. "Thousands of acres of
mountain land should be devoted to them with whole communities
planned and equipped for their cure," he said. Eventually these communities might acquire other functions, such as providing summer education, and could become permanent homes for significant populations. [25]

MacKaye also hoped that the Trail would provide a way to realize
his plans for farm and timber colonies. Earlier, Mrs. Louis Post had
called his attention to the economic potential of the mountains and
had suggested that grazing and stock raising could be added to farming and logging as the bases for colonies. Now he predicted that
whole valleys in the Appalachians could be opened for farming and
grazing, providing a basis for agricultural communities, while the
forests on the mountain sides could sustain "permanent forest camps,"
devoted to timber cultivation. Collectively, such communities could

reinvigorate the societies and economies of the mountain areas, reversing the flow of population to the crowded cities.[26]

In these ways traditional America would be made strong enough to resist the force of the metropolitan cities, restoring in the process what MacKaye believed were the real values of America, of pioneer social life in which "cooperation replaces antagonism, trust replaces suspicion, emulation replaces competition." In this dream he received the support of his brother Percy, a student of folk culture who was discovering the riches of mountain cultural life, finding there what he (Percy) called "the pioneer heart of my own people—America ancient and untamed," a popular idea in a time that often looked to the Appalachian region for a real American "folk" who had escaped the corruptions of modern life. Benton MacKaye rose to a new height of enthusiasm in an article written for the *New York Times* in 1923 in which he described the Trail as "the first step in the building of a people's Appalachian empire" that would stretch from New England deep into the South, reclaiming millions of acres for profitable use, enlivening valleys with "thriving communities" and reinvigorating the whole eastern part of the United States.[27]

MacKaye recognized that his newest utopia would not realize itself. Coining a term that was to have great significance a decade later, he said in 1922 that any reversal of the flow of population from rural areas depended on "some new deal" in the system of agriculture as well as forestry. In support of that new deal, he envisioned a system of planning embracing the technical skills of "the forester, the engineer, the architect, the agriculturalist," but he believed that technicians would accomplish little without the active involvement of the people. "The professional should guide but the amateur should do." He also thought that creation of the Trail might become a popular movement, the realization of William James's call for a moral equivalent of war capable of rallying "the primal instincts of fighting, heroism, volunteer service and of work in a common cause." In one of his rare speeches, he said that the movement "would stimulate a *vision* in the public mind—a vision of constructive National development."[28]

This optimism was partly validated. With the support of Whitaker and the AIA, the idea of the Appalachian Trail was widely publicized and served to unite the scattered hiking and camping organizations of America behind a common cause. It soon received endorsements from organizations such as the National Federation of Settlements and the Federated Societies on Planning and Parks, as well as from influential individuals. Among the individuals was MacKaye's history professor at Harvard, Albert Bushnell Hart, to whom he expressed the wish that the Trail would inspire "some form of pioneering activity among our younger people that would further such traditions of this country as I took from your classes years ago." By 1925 MacKaye could note that the project had been taken over by a permanent organization, the Appalachian Trail Conference.[29]

For one so deeply shy as MacKaye—and one so deeply scarred by personal tragedy—the decision to avoid public leadership made good sense. Leaving the work to others, he was able to avoid the centers of power in favor of the isolation and security of Shirley Center. There, at home, he set out to write a book developing the regional-planning aspects of his thinking. On the other hand, the loss of his direct involvement in the movement guaranteed that the original Trail idea would lose some its more idealistic features. Before long, thoughts of health camps and farm communities gave way to an emphasis on hiking and camping, and the plan to use the Trail as a device to work permanent change in social movement was replaced by the Trail as a temporary escape from civilization. By the time it was completed in 1937, the Appalachian Trail had long ceased to be the project in regional planning that MacKaye had presented in 1921.

Yet there was also notable success. Not only was the Trail eventually completed, but the original idea also soon opened the way for the development, along different lines, of an even more comprehensive vision of social change. Early in 1922, as he pondered the implications of his Appalachian ideas, MacKaye grew excited about its possibilities for widespread change. "The whole project grows vaster (as I knew it would) the more I get into it," he wrote to a New York friend, Clarence Stein. "I want if possible to launch it in a way so that I can give my future to the kind of work which I think I see here." How to launch the whole project? The attempt to answer that question was taken up by the group of idealists who had begun to form around Whitaker in New York, their aim being to incorporate the Trail into their own visions of regional planning.[30] Little was accomplished in 1922, in part because MacKaye was unable to get to New York, but the next year was to bring significant results, in the formation of the RPAA.

IV

CREATION: WHITAKER AND CLARENCE STEIN

The creation of the RPAA resulted from the convergence of the thoughts and needs of various idealists who sought ways to apply their special skills and talents in the service of radical social improvement. In the post–World War I era they strove to extend the Progressive tradition of public service that they believed had been elevated to new levels by the war. A few individuals in this varied group were especially important in the formation of the RPAA, notably Whitaker and two young associates, Clarence Stein and Lewis Mumford, all of whom lived in easy reach of each other in New York City and vicinity. Perhaps the most critical ingredient in the group's creation, however, was supplied by the one most isolated from the rest of its members.

In June 1921, some three months after his wife's suicide, Benton MacKaye retired to stay with his mother and sister in "a little country shack" a quarter mile outside of Shirley Center in north-central Massachusetts. He was then forty-two years of age and tired of the world, especially the crowded and frenetic metropolitan world of New York and Washington.[1] Supported by a small pension and occasional survey work for the Forest Service, he devoted himself to writing his magnum opus, the book eventually published under the title *The New Exploration: A Philosophy of Regional Planning.* In it he pointed out that there were many regions of the world like the great Appalachian region, each with its own unique problems and potentials, and each divided into numerous lesser regions. He hoped to promote not only creation of the Appalachian Trail but also extensive surveys of all the regions of the

United States, with the ultimate aim of promoting their development along regionalist lines. To initiate this process, in late 1922 he proposed the formation of "some permanent body for the purpose of carrying out our principles," an idea that some of his friends also were beginning to consider.[2]

Among the most active of the friends was Whitaker. Although he had relocated the editorial office of the *JAIA* from Washington, D.C., to New York City after the war, Whitaker shared MacKaye's preference for a life outside the big cities. In 1921 he purchased a small farm in rural northern New Jersey that he named Twelve Opossum Farm in a punning reference to the apostles. "Our farm is for fruit and chicks and you would adore the spot," he wrote in May when he offered the newly grieving MacKaye a place of refuge, "high in the mountains and with a brook, and not a soul in sight for miles."[3] It was there soon after that MacKaye broached the idea of the Appalachian Trail.

Whitaker hoped to find his own version of Shirley Center in the nearby hamlet of Mount Olive, located a few miles from Hackettstown. In 1922 he described the place as consisting of half a dozen houses, two churches, and a school—an old village that had seen better days. Like many rural places it was losing its young to the cities, since it could offer a future only of scanty rewards and hard living. If it suffered from its isolation from urban America, however, Mount Olive also was experiencing some of the influence of a spreading city population, a "foreign invasion of our mountains" that involved more than urbane expatriates like Whitaker. "There are Italians, keen, swarthy, laughing-eyed women who bear children with prodigality, and easy-going untidy men, who have evolved a new agricultural economy. We look askance at them and keep our distance, but many of us sell them milk to be made into those queer cheeses affected by the Italian restaurants in the city, the vast city that lies less than fifty miles away and is yet so distant."[4] It was one more lesson about the rapidly expanding influence of the metropolitan region, most of which Whitaker and his friends saw as bad.

Whitaker found an even more important lesson in the city itself. As editor of the *JAIA* in the postwar years, he continued his campaign to make architecture a major social influence on city development. He chose as his particular target the most pressing problem of postwar urban America: housing. In New York City in particular the chronic deficiencies of housing that had existed for more than a century had deepened into a major social crisis by the early 1920s. After 1901 the quality of apartment-house construction had been improved by state regulation, but this reform had served to increase housing costs, adding a new obstacle to efforts to provide decent homes for the poor, and the war and immediate postwar periods brought shortages of construction materials that intensified the problem. In a magazine article, "Wanted—Ten Million Houses," Whitaker warned that "along with the buffalo, the saloon, and the forest, houses seemed to be a disappearing species."[5] Without adequate housing, cities and city populations were sure to deteriorate in physical and moral character even more than they already had.

Why was the home becoming, as Whitaker put it in late 1920, "the vanishing sanctuary"? He found a fundamental cause in the short-sighted and selfish system of landownership that seemed to dominate every aspect of American life. As a disciple of Henry George, he attributed most of the trouble to a few monopolists who controlled the price and availability of land, appropriating for themselves the value added to land by society's improvements. The net result was high land costs, which inflated the overall expense of housing, forcing architects and builders to economize by producing for the average American—if anything—small, tawdry houses. Although Whitaker believed in the importance of good planning, he warned that even the best planning would be defeated by the existing private land system. It was time, therefore, to give up the old habit born of the frontier that treated land as an unlimited resource to be exploited for private profit in favor of the new view that land was a vital public resource to be controlled by the public for public benefit.[6]

Whitaker held that only radical change would bring significant improvements in housing and living conditions, but he was not unwilling to consider more limited solutions, especially as they related to regional planning. Over the years, he had come to see the big city as a "cancerous" growth on society associated with "the menacing problems of traffic-congestion, slum-gangrene, terminal disease, arterial sclerosis, alley-fever, tubercular ravages, infanticide (voluntary and automatic), and general decline." To resolve these problems required in particular some way of redirecting the flow of population from rural areas to the cities. In 1920 he proposed that this be done by constructing planned new towns in the areas around cities. "Why not begin to think in terms of a multitude of communities where life could be lived under healthy and happy conditions instead of trying to make a few communities bigger and bigger?" In these communities there could be such a combination of manufacturing and agriculture as to provide permanent employment for diverse populations, attracting people from the overcrowded cities and the underpopulated rural areas. Here, in this new world, land monopoly would be replaced by public ownership.[7]

With his limited interest in practical details, Whitaker contributed little to the developing art of urban and community planning, but for a time he did help shape the regional-planning movement in several notable ways. Against those who focused their attention narrowly on the city housing problem, he offered a holistic way of thinking that emphasized the importance of planning entire urban regions. Against those who thought only in terms of national uniformities, he urged the importance of local communities as the home of humanity. "The localities of the world, the places where our folk have lived their lives, are the sources of all that is worth remembering either in life or in art." Against those who accepted the unrestrained exploitation of nature's resources, he argued the need to learn "how to treat the land, how to love the land, how to organize the land." Against those in the architectural profession who were content to market their skills, he presented a vision of active service in which architects would cooperate with engineers and other technicians to direct future metropolitan development.[8]

In these respects Whitaker was the spiritual father of the RPAA, but in the 1920s his enthusiasm began to give way to an increasingly dyspeptic view of life that seriously limited his influence. In part the change began with the discovery that his New Jersey farm was hardly the way to health and happiness. In September 1922, while he was working at the farm, he hit himself with a sledgehammer, damaging his knee, and soon after he also began to develop respiratory problems. By November he could note gloomily that he was convalescing "from a variety of afflictions running from water on the knee to pneumonia." He seems never to have completely recovered.

Moreover, by 1923 Whitaker was encountering increasing hostility within the AIA to his management of the *JAIA*, ostensibly over its persisting failure to cover its costs, which brought him much anguish and led to its ceasing publication three years later. He wrote darkly of "powers" in the AIA associated with "Big Business" who were "determined to get my scalp and dangle it proudly wherever architects congregate." Eventually, a friend said that there were "two Charles Whitakers, the enthusiast in search of a better world that brought us together to help him disclose it—and later the sour, disillusioned Charles that turned his back on it."[9] By 1923 his fading leadership was supplemented and eventually replaced by that of one of his protégés, Clarence Stein.

Stein was born in 1883 in Rochester, New York, the youngest son of the president of the National Casket Company. Burdened by ill health as a boy, he had been denied regular schooling, but this had not kept him from entering the Columbia University School of Architecture. Initially aiming at a career as an interior decorator, he had, after a year at Columbia, moved on to a decorator's studio in Paris, only to decide to focus his professional interests on architecture and to attend the Ecole des Beaux Arts. In 1911 he found regular employment with the architectural firm of Bertram G. Goodhue, eventually becoming its chief of design for such projects as the copper-mining town of Tyrone, New Mexico, and the Marine Corps base in San Diego.[10]

Like his future colleagues in the RPAA, however, Stein was not satisfied simply to be a practicing architect. Even before joining the Goodhue firm he had been the secretary of the Young Men's Municipal Club, whose principal object was "to unite the young men of New York who aim to study and improve municipal conditions." Among these young men were two future members of the RPAA, Eugene Klaber and Alexander M. Bing. From 1915 to 1919 Stein was secretary of the City Planning Committee of the influential City Club of New York, where he worked with Bing, Robert D. Kohn, and Frederick L. Ackerman. Like them, he was activated to even higher aspirations in public service by the war. In late 1917 he had volunteered to serve as an officer in the Army Engineers but was turned down. A few months later he tried again, with the support of a letter from Bertram Goodhue, who wrote that for nearly a year "Mr. Stein has shown increasing restlessness and a general desire to get into the war." This time he was accepted as a lieutenant, but the end of the war soon brought his discharge.[11]

Whatever his actual involvement in it, the war strengthened his ambitions for public service. Early in 1919 he observed in his diary that he and some of his West Side neighbors were exploring ways of "conserving and using the abilities & energies that have been used in war work in civil life." Toward that end he joined with Whitaker and others in a call on the State of New York to form a special commission to deal with the housing crisis, emphasizing the need for a positive policy to provide new housing. At a meeting of the City Club he supported Kohn and Ackerman (who were reluctantly winding down their involvement in the national wartime housing program) when they denounced the prevailing emphasis on legislation to improve the quality of housing as worse than useless in meeting the needs of the poor. What was required was direct government involvement in the production of new housing. As part of the process, the club proposed that New York convene a meeting representing the various regions of the state to consider ways of developing effective regional planning; three future members of the RPAA—Stein, Kohn, and Ackerman—supported this proposal. [12]

When, soon after, the state created the Housing Committee, Stein succeeded in getting himself appointed its secretary, a position that enabled him to influence committee decisions. After making a study of the housing problem in New York City and elsewhere, in March 1920 the committee publicly endorsed the policy favored by Stein, Kohn, and Ackerman. This policy featured state support for housing construction through low-interest loans to private limited-dividend and cooperative housing corporations and possibly to municipal public housing bodies. Responding to the Georgist attitudes of men like Ackerman, the committee supported "community ownership and control of large tracts of land" in order to limit land costs and to deny private interests profits from land values created by public improvements. Finally, the report stressed the need for effective planning and recommended the formation of a Board of Housing and Community Planning in each city. The committee also expressed support for the developing idea of regional planning. "We can never hope to solve our housing problem until we have decentralized industry and limited the size of our cities." [13] The logic of this position led to some state-wide planning and control over land development.

Stein attempted to rally public support for these recommendations. Beyond publicizing the report in periodicals such as *Survey* and the *JAIA,* he helped organize the New York State Association, a lobby group that he described as being "interested in forward looking legislation," and he made a special appeal to women through Edith Elmer Wood, an expert on housing and a leader of the housing committee of the American Association of University Women (Wood was also destined to be a member of the RPAA). [14]

The state legislature, however, ignored the recommendations. Although Governor Alfred Smith eventually formed a state Housing and Regional Planning Committee, with Stein as its head, the hopes of using the experience and spirit of war to reconstruct America again were dashed. Referring especially to the obstacles posed by the widespread concern for protecting private property rights, Stein wrote in 1922 that the "legal difficulties that stood in the way of communities who wish to plan for the welfare of the many instead of the enrichment of the few land owners are apparently nowhere more severe as in this country." The lesson he learned was not to expect miracles of reform, especially when it came to efforts to regulate the use of property. [15]

If anything these experiences made Stein an even more effective force for idealism. By the early 1920s he had become a skillful organizer of reform effort. A slightly built man whose youthful appearance led some to underrate his power, he combined high intelligence with the patience, persuasiveness, and flexibility needed to lead men. He had taken to smoking heavy black cigars, probably to compensate for his seeming youth, perfecting the art of holding one in his mouth while talking. In image and skill he resembled the professional politicians who exerted great influence in the 1920s, but he retained the sensitivity and imagination that had led him into architecture. His friend Mumford remembered him as being capable of both smoking a cigar with Al Smith and admiring a Renoir painting purchased by a rich acquaintance, as being a politician and a connoisseur.[16]

Over the years Stein had acquired a host of influential friends. He had often worked with Kohn on matters of housing reform, a relationship that brought him into contact with Felix Adler's Ethical Culture Society, in which Kohn was a leading figure. Through this society he made a connection with the Hudson Guild (whose sometime president was Bing) and its Settlement House on New York's Lower West Side headed by John L. Elliot, an influential social worker. This connection introduced him to an interesting dimension of the emerging metropolitan regionalism. During the war the guild had acquired a five-hundred-acre farm near Netcong, New Jersey, which it converted into a cooperative camp where young city people could pay for a period of escape from the urban jungle by spending a few hours a day doing farm work. In 1920 Stein designed a dining hall for the farm, consolidating a relationship that soon was to make the farm a useful refuge and discussion center for him and his friends.[17]

Stein worked especially closely with the AIA. In 1918 he became associate editor of the *JAIA,* with special responsibility over its Community Planning and Housing column, and three years later he was appointed chairman of the AIA's Committee on Community Planning; both of these roles brought him into close association with Whitaker. Notably, the Stein-designed dining hall at the Hudson Guild Farm was only some ten miles from Whitaker's Twelve Opossum Farm.

Stein came to share, among other things, Whitaker's growing distaste for big cities—especially notable since the largely urban-oriented Stein had committed himself to live in New York City. Earlier, he had expressed some hopes for the redemption of the metropolis, but early in 1922, speaking before the New York Academy of Medicine, he declared that, because of the "disease" of concentration, the city had ceased to be "a fit place in which to live." A year later he would conclude that "as a result of their haphazard and planless growth, the gigantic cities of the old and the new world are becoming more hopelessly unable to carry on their work." The view that cities had ceased to be effective mechanisms either for living or for doing business he developed into his famous 1925 essay "Dinosaur Cities."[18]

Like Whitaker, Stein hoped to see the urban population relocated into smaller urban entities of limited size, such as the garden cities then being developed in England by Ebenezer Howard and his disciples. In December 1921 Stein described a plan devised by his Committee on Community Planning. He began by proposing that all future development of the areas around cities be guided by a transportation framework of highways and railroads designed to focus populations in planned new towns, each of which was to be separated from the others by open territory. Good planning would assure that all homes in the towns had adequate light, air, and privacy, with ready access to public recreational facilities. As a safeguard against land speculation the plan stressed community control over land development and values. To ensure the right use of land, it provided for extensive zoning both to protect residential neighborhoods and to guarantee the most efficient placement of economic activity, including "the placing of industrial districts in as close contact with housing areas as possible in order to reduce the human and financial waste of transportation."[19]

This was already familiar stuff for those who had worked with the Garden City movement and with the wartime towns, but by the end of 1921 another influence had entered to significantly broaden the picture: MacKaye's plan for the Appalachian Trail. Aside from Whitaker, the most enthusiastic proponent of the plan was Stein, whom Whitaker had introduced to MacKaye at his Mount Olive farm. Stein wrote the introduction to the reprint of MacKaye's article, made soon after its original publication in the *JAIA,* declaring that it "offers us a new theme in regional planning." And he used his influence to persuade the community planning committee of the AIA to endorse the plan.

In promoting the Trail the basically urban Stein tended to highlight its recreational side at the expense of MacKaye's environmental and cultural aims, emphasizing it as an escape from "being crushed by the machinery of the modern industrial city." On the other hand, he did appreciate its larger implications, telling his colleagues in April 1922 that "Mr. MacKaye's project is probably the biggest and most far-reaching undertaking in regional planning that our generation in America has known." This, he said, was no mere idea, because "leaders in the trail movement, in forestry, in community development, in landscape architecture in the East, have all shown a wide and helpful interest in the undertaking." Here was a great opportunity for architects to take a leading role in a professional coalition dedicated to the improvement of the human environment. "The technician is needed to plan, and the architect of all our professional men is best equipped to undertake the work, if he will only understand the problem and his opportunity and his ability to serve the community."[20] If only the AIA would take the initiative, what a world the new planning-oriented professional classes could make.

The truly regional and extraregional scale of MacKaye's plan dramatically expanded the boundaries and potential of regional planning, promising to break it free from its preoccupation with big cities and their contiguous areas. This expansion came at a critical time, since 1922 brought the first organization of another planning effort, which was more conventional but, in part for that reason, far more successful: the Regional Plan of New York and Vicinity (RPNY). The RPNY was an ambitious plan embracing more than 5,000 square miles within a 50-mile radius of the city. With substantial support from the Russell Sage Foundation, the organizers of this plan got off to a fast start, in part by persuading many of New York's leading architects to back it. Initially, three members of the future RPAA (Ackerman, Kohn, and Stein) agreed to participate, but they soon withdrew.

The project naturally came up for discussion in Stein's community planning committee, where, said Whitaker in September 1922, it was judged a colossal "scheme of centralization" that would facilitate the very congestion that ostensibly it was designed to remedy. "We all felt," wrote Whitaker, "that if the Sage Foundation was to lay out a plan for New York with 50,000,000 people, our job was to turn the thing so as to show the folly of such a dream."[21] And so began a rather one-sided quarrel involving the most ambitious planning efforts of their time, one that was to simmer for several years, finally to explode at the end of the decade.

How "to turn the thing"? To strengthen his forces, Whitaker recruited Mumford, a brilliant young New Yorker who eventually became the most powerful critic of the RPNY. In November 1922 he urged Mumford to meet with Stein at the latter's office on West Forty-fifth Street. "It will be wonderful if we could work out some plan to enlist your collaboration in our hazardous enterprise." Most of the actual organizational effort continued to be done by Stein. Already in March, encouraged by his success in promoting the Appalachian Trail,

Stein had written to MacKaye that "the time has come for us to get together and try to put our plan for development into a more definite form." For nearly a year this meeting was prevented both by MacKaye's failure to find the money he needed to get to New York and by Stein's own absence in Europe for part of the time. In December Stein wrote to MacKaye that he was thinking of forming a large loosely structured group, with most of the real work being done by a small group concentrated in New York: "That, of course, is the rub. Can we get together that group?"[22]

Finally, in March 1923, Stein was able to advise MacKaye, who was then staying at the Whitaker farm, that "we are slowly knocking the Garden City and Regional Planning Association into shape," adding that he hoped it would be big enough to contain the Appalachian Trail plan. On April 18 what was now called the Regional Planning Association of America was formally organized, the elimination of "Garden City" from the original name probably intended to acknowledge the importance of the Trail. At this organizational meeting—held in Kohn's office in the same building on West Forty-fifth Street where Stein had his—were Kohn, Mumford, MacKaye, and Stein and also Bing (a real estate man and builder), Nils Hammarstrand (a student of cities), Sullivan Jones (an architect with important connections to state government), and two architects much interested in urban planning, John Bright of Philadelphia and Eugene Klaber of Chicago. Of the last five, only Bing was destined to play a major role in the RPAA; on the other hand, missing from the group but already signed on were three key figures, Ackerman, Stuart Chase, and Whitaker.[23]

The decisions of this meeting were ratified and expanded by a larger meeting on May 19 at the Hudson Guild Farm in New Jersey. Mumford, who mistakenly remembered the month as April, recalled that the gathering coincided with a weekly square dance held at the farm by local farmers, a bit of folk culture in which the members participated and which they subsequently tried to incorporate into future meetings there.[24] Of special importance was a visitor who added an international flavor to the meeting, Patrick Geddes, the Scottish philosopher and regionalist, who was invited both because he was the special hero of members such as Mumford and because the group wished to dissuade him from endorsing the RPNY, whose promoters had reportedly brought him to America. Especially entranced by Mac-Kaye's thinking, Geddes strongly recommended that the RPAA focus its subsequent activities on the Appalachian Trail plan and also persuaded MacKaye to adopt the term "geo-technics" instead of regional planning to designate his approach to nature.[25]

The New Jersey meeting generated much enthusiasm in the group, but the serious work of actually creating an organization had yet to be done. In a series of meetings in Stein's office during the first weeks of June, Stein, MacKaye, Mumford, and Chase, acting as a program committee, sketched out the new association's mission and mode of operation. Here and elsewhere, it was evident that the organizers intended a loose association based on the voluntary cooperation of like-minded professionals. Although it had officers—originally Bing as president and Stein as secretary-treasurer—it had little formal organization, and no thought was given to incorporation. Members were expected to pay dues, but the dues were so low—$5 a year—that they contributed little to financing even the most insignificant operations. Of more financial importance was $1000 which Stein reported had been "received to be used in connection with the Regional Planning Work carried out by Mr. Benton MacKaye." This money, which seems to have been granted by New Jersey for the development of that state's portion of the Appalachian Trail, was put in a New York bank and used to finance some regional survey work in northern New Jersey and perhaps for other purposes.

The program committee gave some attention to sketching out the RPAA's mission and mode of operation. After urging that the planning of whole regions replace the haphazard growth of big cities, they declared that "a regional plan calls for new population centers where natural resources will be preserved for the community, where industry may be conducted efficiently, and where an adequate equipment of houses, gardens, and recreation grounds will enduce a healthy and stimulating environment." Subsequently they added that the development of these garden cities should be complemented by more local forms of planning, "a comprehensive plan for developing the region which, for industrial, economic, and general living purposes, is tributary to the site of such garden city or village."[26]

Beyond these general goals; the committee gave much attention to the question of how the RPAA would actually function, "whether the development of the Association should be that of a large propaganda organization or for the time should consist of a small group of technicians." Basically, the group confronted two distinct prospects: of creating a popular movement in support of regional planning, or of trying to find backing from established powers for their technical skills and plans. They failed to make any real decision except to say that the RPAA "will further its objects by education and practical promotion," a characteristic avoidance of any serious discussion of political action. Over the years to come, the RPAA vacillated between the two options, a situation that allowed members greater freedom to pursue their individual careers than they would otherwise have had but that also served to diminish the association's effective influence.[27]

If the program committee failed to provide a clear answer to this basic question, however, it did at least outline a significant program for future action:

> First. The Association will promote the study of housing, industrial decentralization, city planning and regional planning, through individual investigations and through general surveys.
> Second. The Association will aid the formation of associations and corporations designed to finance, control the land essential to planning, build and operate Garden Cities.
> Third. The Association will serve as center for information of technical aid to those who seek to erect houses, locate factories and build up communities on garden city lines.[28]

This was certainly enough of a program to begin their work, but at their next meeting on June 12 the program committee urged the RPAA also to take charge of the Appalachian project with the aim of developing it into "an exemplary regional plan." Hoping both to excite interest "in the regional approach to problems of living" and to promote the development of regional planning techniques, they proposed that surveys be conducted of key subregions within "the Appalachian domain," from the Berkshires in Massachusetts to—anticipating the later TVA— "the headwaters of the Tennessee River system." By this time, they could announce that one such survey was already being conducted, by MacKaye, of New Jersey's Columbia Valley, where the Hudson Guild Farm was located. MacKaye had begun the survey in May and, with the help of some of the $1000 that the RPAA had for the purpose, spent much of the summer working on it.[29]

There were at least two notable omissions in these deliberations. Having decided to join the Appalachian project (involving topography) with their basically metropolitan strategy of garden cities (involving man-made geography), the committee gave no attention to trying to synthesize what were two very different fields of operation. Eventually, the RPAA would drift away from its initial enthusiasm for Appalachia, until the creation of the TVA in 1933. Secondly, although it made a few references to cooperating with state and national authorities in conducting survey work, its program made notably little place for government and public policy, apparently in reaction to the collapse of the wartime hopes for a governmentally directed reconstruction of society. Without government, the RPAA program lacked a natural focal point around which to build a coherent policy position, undoubtedly one reason for the committee's failure to integrate its recommendations into one consistent whole.

Although it meant the absence of any clear-cut focus for action, however, this situation met the special needs of the RPAA as it actually developed. Whatever the hopes for creating a popular movement, the RPAA remained a small group of dedicated idealists, bound together by hopes of using their expertise to effect change but also determined to follow that line of regional planning best suited to their own talents and ambitions. The absence of a focused program was matched by the lack of a formal organization demanding adherence to a codified line of thought and action. In these ways the RPAA provided some basis for cooperation and collegiality but also allowed individual members to pursue their own special dreams. And it functioned in this manner throughout the 1920s.

V

TOWARD A GOLDEN DAY: LEWIS MUMFORD

The new RPAA was far less a professional organization than a society of like-minded friends. Even its occasional major meetings—held either at the Hudson Guild Farm or at the City Club on West Forty-fourth Street—were generally attended by fewer than a dozen members, making for informal decision making. More often, the meetings were sporadically held luncheon affairs, involving four or five of the core members, notably Stein, Kohn, Ackerman, Whitaker, and Mumford, and also MacKaye, when he temporarily left his refuge at Shirley Center for the big city. These lunch meetings made no formal decisions and left no records, but they seem to have served the dual purpose of strengthening friendships and promoting joint understanding. The strength of the RPAA, Mumford recalled in 1962, was "the looseness and flexibility of our relationships, in our respect for each others' individuality, with all our differences overcome and bonded together by friendship."[1]

The architects, who comprised the larger part of the membership, continued to follow their varied interests in housing and community design, and MacKaye pursued his explorations of forests, mountains, and traditional village life. Since these members preferred to be active in some specialized way, they created a place for someone who could function as the philosopher, publicist, and synthesizer of the group. From its beginning the RPAA found that person in its youngest and probably most brilliant member, Lewis Mumford, who became its secretary and principal wordsmith. If he lent his brilliance to developing and articulating the philosophical foundations of regional plan-

ning, Mumford drew much of his intellectual substance from his associations with the group and its work. He did not exclude himself when
in 1974 he declared, regarding the demise of the RPAA decades before,
that "we dispersed and none of us were as good after as we were
together."[2]

Mumford began his autobiography with the words "I was a child of
the city," adding that "not merely was I a city boy but a New Yorker."
Unlike the others, who had come to New York from elsewhere in search
of opportunity, Mumford had Gotham in his blood. Born in 1895, the
illegitimate son of a Jewish businessman and his German housekeeper,
Mumford took his last name from his mother's former husband, who
had disappeared from the scene years before Lewis was born. The nature
of his birth seems not to have been an affliction. Brought up in his
mother's extensive family, the boy had enough significant others to
promote his personal growth. Of his education, he remembered best
not his rather dreary formal schooling in what he later called "infantine
prisons" but the "spontaneous" learning that he first experienced on
walks with his maternal grandfather through New York's Upper West
Side. During his boyhood, he became an observant student of the city
and its life, eventually carrying out a systematic program of walking
though every one of New York's many neighborhoods.[3]

Mumford found a more stimulating intellectual environment at
Stuyvesant High School and, after his graduation in 1912, in evening
classes at the City College of New York. Deciding to become a philosopher, he transferred to the formal day program at City College, only to
encounter a more advanced stage of the dull schooling from which he
thought he had escaped. He dropped out and so, as he said later,
"Mannahatta in all its richness and variety" with its museums and its
manifold activities became "my university, my true Alma Mater." By
the time he was twenty he had determined to become a professional
writer, taking occasional courses at various colleges but continuing to
focus his learning chiefly on the urban scene. Although World War I
soon forced a different kind of experience on the young man—he spent
some ten months in the United States Navy as a radio operator—it did
nothing to deflect him from his writing ambitions.[4]

In early 1919 he graduated from the war into his first professional
writing job as a book reviewer and associate editor for the intellectual
journal the *Dial*. Although this employment failed to last the year, it
brought Mumford into contact with the thriving cultural world of
Greenwich Village, which included Thorstein Veblen as well as scores
of ambitious newcomers such as Van Wyck Brooks, literary editor of

the *Freeman,* an avant-garde literary journal located only a few doors from the *Dial* on West Thirteenth Street. Brooks and Mumford eventually became close friends. It was Brooks who later wrote of Mumford and his wife, Sophia (who married Mumford in 1921), "I thought of Lewis and Sophy Mumford as a new Adam and Eve with which the human race might have started, for one could scarcely have imagined an handsomer pair. I always felt as if they had stepped out of Utopia and were looking for some of their countrymen astray on this planet, who were also wanting to get home again."

By this time, Mumford had found his lifelong mission, which indeed did involve some effort to return to a lost utopia. Like many of his generation he had to confront the postwar disillusionment that characterized the so-called Lost Generation. The prewar optimism that had animated men like Whitaker and Ackerman had little meaning for the younger generation, who came of age during the war and postwar years. Chronologically, Mumford was at least as close to the younger generation as he was to the older, but he rejected the former's pessimism and cynicism in favor of the faith that idealism was a necessary ingredient of human progress. Convinced that the ideals that had governed the prewar period had lost their power, he committed himself as a writer and intellectual to establishing "fresh" (his favorite adjective) ideals that could revitalize the effort to achieve a better day.

Mumford found his inspiration in a source that he had discovered earlier: the writings of Patrick Geddes. He first heard the "new voice" of the Scottish botanist and biologist turned city planner in 1914, while he was at City College. From Geddes's *City Development,* he later recalled, he got his "first glimpse of the city as an age-old instrument of human culture." Geddes taught Mumford how to view the city, with all of its seemingly disparate diversities, as an organism, as a dynamic whole that drew its energies from its diversity. More, Geddes extended this view to the surrounding countryside, furnishing Mumford with his first glimpse of the city region. And he encouraged the development of what was central to Mumford's regionalism, the habit of viewing humankind in ecological perspective, emphasizing the dynamic relationship between human beings and their natural environment.[5]

On a more practical level, Geddes also proposed the means by which this dynamic whole could be understood: by a systematic, holistic, interdisciplinary "survey" of all aspects, human and natural, of the region. In making the region the field for a broad survey that employed a variety of skills and interests Geddes helped set his disciple's determination to become a generalist rather than a specialist, one who would concentrate his genius on synthesizing and organizing a rich diversity of human thought into a compellingly whole new design for human action.

In 1917 Mumford entered into a correspondence with Geddes. Under his mentor's influence, Mumford conceived an ambitious effort to understand New York City and its surrounding region, one that would enable him to build on his interests in sociology, philosophy, science, architecture, and literature. To help prepare for this, in 1917 he joined the American Geological Society and through it encountered the works of a school of French geographers who helped him to see the region as a geographic and cultural entity above and beyond the city.[6] The war interrupted the development of Mumford's regionalist thinking, but not for long.

During his months with the *Dial* in 1919 he tried to incorporate regionalism into several lines of thinking. In a short essay on government, for instance, he suggested as a model of government a confederation of city regions, which would replace the centralized state as the day-to-day reality for most of the population. In an essay on education, in which he argued for greater emphasis on concrete learning experiences over the arid generalities of book learning, he advocated the regional survey as providing a "first-hand, intimate, concrete acquaintance with the environment." In the *Nation* he argued that the postwar housing crisis could be resolved only by an integrated plan for change. "The housing problem, the industrial problem, the transportation problem, and the land problem cannot be solved one at a time by isolated experts."[7]

Mumford's interests in architecture and planning led him to Whitaker, a fellow admirer of Geddes. In 1918, hoping to publish his writings in the *JAIA,* Mumford initiated a correspondence with Whitaker in Washington. Before the end of 1919 he had won a place as a book reviewer for the *JAIA* and had published one article in it, "The Heritage of Cities Movement in America," in which he echoed Whitaker's hopes that architects would join urban planners, engineers, and other experts to guide "the reconstruction of American cities." In 1920 Mumford was able to make his first trip to England (where he missed Geddes but met Geddes's principal ally, Victor Branford) with the help of a commission from Whitaker to act as the *JAIA*'s correspondent on English architecture and planning matters.

Soon after Mumford's return to New York, Whitaker moved his editorial office there from Washington, and the relationship between the two ripened into a friendship. Early in 1921 Whitaker endorsed

Mumford's proposal for a study of the causes of urban centralization in the United States and otherwise supported the young man's strivings to find a position of influence. Eventually, he introduced Mumford to both Stein and MacKaye, whose combined zeal in support of the Appalachian Trail deepened Mumford's understanding of the potentialities of regional planning.[8]

Some of these influences were evident in Mumford's first major work, *The Story of Utopias*. The idea for this book had been suggested by Brooks as part of their common hope for a revival of idealism, but the original inspiration was supplied by Geddes, who had advocated utopianism as a holistic way of thinking about society and its potentialities. In 1921 Mumford suggested to the publisher Horace Liveright that the time for attention to utopian dreams was right, "for wishes and dreams are about all that we can salvage from the Great War." Once Liveright accepted the idea, Mumford set something of a record for creating a book, most of the writing being done in "a sort of desperate frenzy" during three months ending in early June 1922, and the book was published before the end of the year.

After finishing the book and shortly before boarding a steamer for Europe, Mumford told Brooks that he felt it was "a mixture of silk and shoddy." Later he tended to treat it as a youthful indiscretion. Yet it was an impressive debut, a book that expressed a powerfully imaginative as well as intelligent ambition to develop a strategy for constructive change. "I undertook this utopian inquiry," he informed Brooks, "because it seemed necessary to throw a rainbow into the sky at just this moment, if our generation, and the one that is on our heels, were not to become so sodden in spirit as a result of the storm through which we've passed."[9] For those who read the book, it did shed a bright rainbow of hope, although in a complicated way, since it was actually at least three works in one.

On one level it was a young man's somewhat casual and selective critique of utopian literature, especially that of the previous century. Eventually, Mumford condemned the utopian search for perfection as a threat to many of the diverse elements that made life worth living. "Life is better than utopia" became his credo. In the book, however, he treated utopian literature as an important source of inventive social ideas that could enrich efforts to improve society, among them being an emphasis on education and on some control over propagation as means of improving the human species. Utopias were by definition located nowhere, but Mumford insisted that "news from Nowhere is real news," furnishing ideas useful for confronting the challenge of social reality. The chief problem of utopias, he said, was not that they were too good for the world but that "they were simply not good enough" and so it was necessary to go beyond them. [10]

While Mumford intended his book to draw on utopias for practical ideas, he also projected a more ambitious goal: to argue the necessity of idealism as a factor in human thought and behavior. To those who scoffed at utopianism as fatuous and ineffectual, he replied that the influence of utopian thinking in some form was far more common than the skeptics realized. Basically, ideals were the ways by which humankind organized its strivings in a constructive way and by which it actualized its potentialities. "It is our utopias that make the world tolerable to us: the cities and mansions that people dream of are those in which they finally live. The more that men react upon their environment and make if over after a human pattern, the more continuously do they live in utopia." The power that science and technology were giving humanity to dominate its environment made guiding ideals ever more important. [11]

Even—and in some ways especially—those who proclaimed themselves "realists" hostile to idealistic thinking were themselves governed unconsciously by deeply buried utopian ideals. In his book Mumford entered into a prolonged discussion of what he called "collective utopias or social myths," which because of their widespread acceptance had actually shaped the social reality that modern man had created. He focused on two powerful and interlocking myths, each of which had helped create a distinctly dystopian reality. One was the Country House, initally a gentleman's isolated estate where the favored few had lived a life of material consumption. The popularization of this selfish ideal had produced the widespread reality of private living in isolating individual homes, which in modern society had undermined the sense of community and cooperation needed for the good life. Since the ideal stressed material consumption—what Mumford called the "goods life" as opposed to the good life—it assured the dominance of a second myth, that of Coketown, an emphasis on the production of material goods that had produced the human miseries and environmental degradations associated with the industrial age. [12]

Both of these dystopias had roots deep in the past. A third myth had a closer relationship with Mumford's own times. This he called Megalopolis, an ideal associated with the nationalism that had produced the horrors of the Great War and was continuing to threaten the peace and happiness of the postwar world. Megalopolis was the leading city of the nation state, intended to centralize national influence over life and to manage the complicated business of linking Coketown with the country house. For Mumford the Megalopolitan ideal demanded and got the subordination of the diverse realities of life to a uniform system that forced its members to think in terms not of life's concrete variety but of a few abstract symbols, most notably money. Its chief boast was its uniformity, its equal applicability to everyone without regard to the diverse histories and circumstances of real human beings. Basically, it was superimposing an artificial creation on the "natural regions," devastating local cultures and economies and concentrating populations in overcrowded, congested metropolises like New York.[13]

Having argued for the power of idealism, especially in its perverse and threatening form, Mumford was able to complete the development of his third and most basic theme, an argument for regional planning. Early in the book he made a distinction between utopias of "escape" and utopias of "reconstruction," the one involving a turning away from an imperfect reality into fantasy, the other more positively providing the guiding ideals by which people could re-create society in a better form. Throughout, he prepared the reader's mind for a new social myth that he believed could direct efforts to undo the damage done by the three dystopias, and he revealed that new myth, regionalism, in his concluding pages.

Part of Mumford's ideal involved a way of knowing opposed to the abstractness of the Megalopolitan mind, which he believed prevented the discovery of meaningful human truths. Borrowing heavily from his mentor, Geddes, he advanced the idea of the regional survey as a way to reunify the knowledge that had become increasingly disorganized with the progress of modern specialization. Science and art, he believed, had become disassociated from each other and from the human community, with the result that the power of science was left unguided by human values and the dedication to beauty of art was denied influence over common life. The answer was to abandon a fragmented, specialized, and abstract concern with things in general for a comprehensive survey of regional actualities. Such a locally focused effort would reunify fragmented strivings for knowledge—science, social science, art, and whatever else related to comprehending the human situation—into a cooperative understanding of real human situations that could be applied for tangible human benefit. On such complete understanding of the whole of local circumstances comprehensive plans could be made to realize the full potential of the locality.

The regional survey was an integral part of Mumford's social ideal, an ideal that featured not one standard social order no matter how perfect but a vital and diverse world of many distinct places. His utopia would not be one but many, a world of as many as fifteen million communities each rooted in its own special bit of nature and of history, each of whose inhabitants "will have a familiarity with their local environment and its resources, and a sense of historic continuity." Each would be a distinct habitat suited to the character and needs of its people, who would almost by instinct focus their energies on cultivating rather than exploiting their environment. Instead of the standardized world of impersonal relations and shifting ties, there would be a galaxy of stable local communities to which people would truly belong: "A cultivated life is essentially a settled life." In this world there would be no dominating nations and metropolitan centers; although big cities like New York would remain, their interests would be subordinated to those of the whole region to which they belonged. [14]

The Story of Utopias was an ambitious young intellectual's bold effort to reconstruct what he considered the all-important "world-within," the fundamental social beliefs that governed human social actions and ultimately the character of society. As he explained to Geddes, he had determined "to prepare the mind as well as the ground for the New Jerusalem." Much of that work involved the wholesale condemnation of every existing major line of social thought, not simply the unrealistic utopias of literature and not only the perverse utopias of capitalistic society, but also the proletarian myth that lay at the foundations of the attempted Soviet utopia. As Mumford said earlier in 1920, he believed there was little "difference between the paradise of business men called the United States and the utopia of bureaucrats called Communist Russia." It was necessary, he believed, to sweep away all such "fake utopias and social myths" and to build anew on the foundations of regionalism. By accepting this new ideal, with its roots in diverse reality, humankind could find the way to Mumford's version of utopia: not some unrealistic and sterile perfection but real life "pushed to the limits of its ideal potentialities." [15]

Undoubtedly, Mumford hoped his book would rally like-minded idealists around him. "I am quite sure that we could establish a fertile center of ideas in America," he wrote to Brooks shortly after he had finished the book, "if we could only find two or three capable people who are not afraid to live on short commons and look physical destitution in the face. The American notion that nothing can be done without gross subsidy is superstition. What we need is spiritual subsidy." At this time he was a member of the self-proclaimed Civilization Group, a coterie of intellectuals mostly associated with the *Dial* or the

Freeman. Little, however, came of either the group or the literary magazines, and *The Story of Utopias,* while it won respectful reviews, had disappointing sales and influence.[16]

On the other hand, Mumford's growing interest in the regional approach was opening a more promising avenue of influence. By 1922 he had deepened his friendship with Whitaker, who praised his book and persuaded him to spend some time at his Mount Olive Farm while he was in Europe. "Its a thousand feet in the air," Whitaker boasted, "and never a soul passes but the postman, and there's a fire and everything." Through Whitaker Mumford met Stein, and through Stein he soon met MacKaye.[17] By the time the RPAA was formed the next year he was ready to be a leading member, becoming its secretary, historian, and all-around publicist.

If nothing else, exposure to the influence of his new friends brought the young intellectual more directly into contact with concrete reality. Through MacKaye he acquired some understanding of the Appalachians and their embattled folk culture. Before the region was totally devastated by being "industrially developed," Mumford wrote in the summer of 1923, "my friend proposes to add rather to the human development; for he regards the region as a place of permanent human habitation and not as a treasure that must be quickly pillaged." What particularly impressed him was MacKaye's idea of reinvigorating folk culture by placing it on new economic foundations: the Appalachian Trail, with its appeal to the expanding recreational needs of urban Americans and its promise of revitalizing agriculture and timber culture.[18]

Through Whitaker's farm in Mount Olive, Mumford discovered a more immediate part of Appalachia and a new lesson in the threatening power of the Megalopolitan myth. In 1924 the *American Mercury* published his "Devastated Regions," which featured a gloomy view of the surrounding New Jersey hill country. In the article he stated that a closer view of what seemed to be a pleasant agricultural scene revealed that "the buildings around the farmhouse are palpably ruined, that the nearer trees are blasted and broken and that the stone wall which once properly bounded the pasture now gapes in a dozen places." Here was one particular case of the general trend that had drained the American countryside of its vitality in the interests of a few metropolitan centers. It seemed that perhaps the area was reverting back to nature, but this too was an illusion, as illustrated by the case of Whitaker himself: the countryside in fact was being repopulated by refugees from the arid life of the metropolis. What often appeared to be wilderness was being subjected to an accelerating invasion from New York City, an encroachment revealed in one place by an "obscene line of bungalows" that had appeared on a state highway and, more generally, by an increasing volume of automobile traffic "dribbling along the road on Sunday like stinking black molasses."

Like other members of the RPAA, Mumford saw positive potential in this change, if it was rightly guided. Noting that the streams in this hill area could be used to generate electric power, he dreamed that the decaying villages could be made to "hum again" with local industries that would provide stimulating new markets for farmers, whose present idleness had often led them to join the Ku Klux Klan "more out of boredom than conviction." And he saw some hope that the growing new population of refugees from the metropolis might support such a renewal when they finally recognized that the only way to get the life which they sought "consists in restoring our devastated regions—and, incidentally, in bringing back half the occupations and pastimes we have forfeited by our servile attendance on machinery."[19] To put the machine in its proper place and to resist the metropolis, however, required a fundamental change in attitude, especially the rejection of the dominating myths that had produced the existing mess. What could persuade Americans to abandon their infatuations with consumerism, industrialism, and metropolitanism?

For his answer, Mumford turned to history, doing what others, such as his friend Brooks, were doing: looking for what they termed a "usable past." As his subject he chose the domain of Whitaker and other friends: architecture. In December 1923 the *Freeman* published the first of a five-part series on American architecture, which opened with the assertion that early American architecture reflected the existence of a strong tradition of craftsmanship that in turn revealed the existence of a deeply rooted sense of community. "This community was embedded in villages and towns whose mummified remains even to-day have a rooted dignity that the most gigantic metropolises do not possess."[20] What had been might be again, if only the people were made aware of their forgotten inheritance.

By the time this article was published Mumford was deeply involved in turning his material on architecture into a major book, finally to be titled *Sticks and Stones*. He had the help of Whitaker, who in the fall of 1923 gave the manuscript a thorough and somewhat biting criticism, so much so that Whitaker wondered whether he had overstepped his bounds, only to hesitate, "for at present," he told his young friend, "I have such a slim hold on anything that values are hard to establish in my mind"—a revelation of a deep turbulence within him that was soon to reduce his effectiveness. In the book, however, Mumford acknowledged a heavy debt to Whitaker—and also lesser debts to Stein, MacKaye, and other members of the new RPAA.[21]

In his introduction Mumford said that he had tried to approach "our modern problems from their historic side, to criticize the forces that from one age to another have conditioned our architecture," noting that to facilitate this effort he had omitted illustrations, which would have focused attention on specific forms, "for a building is not merely a sight; it is an experience." Under the influence, perhaps, of his new friend MacKaye, Mumford singled out the early New England town as a utopian model of human community, at one point declaring that at its best it came close to being a "complete and intelligent partnership between the earth and man" and at another point identifying it with the garden city, the current ideal of the intelligently planned community.[22]

Much of *Sticks and Stones* attempted to examine, through its discussion of architecture, what had subverted this early promised land. Following along the lines already established by Whitaker and his hero, Louis Sullivan, Mumford cast an especially baleful eye on the neoclassical architectural style favored by the City Beautiful movement. He made it plain, however, that he was no cultural xenophobe hostile to all things foreign; his earlier discovery of European regionalism had alerted him to the existence in the Old World of some of the cultural virtues that had been identified in the New. The fault lay not in Europe but in the American metropolis, which had turned the neoclassical style into what he called the Imperial Facade, the face of an imperious striving to impose a sterile metropolitan uniformity on the diverse indigenous regional styles that had marked a creative architecture. It was "an architecture of compensation" struggling unsuccessfully through its bombast to compensate for the ugly and bleak realities that surrounded ordinary lives.[23]

The growing costs of building the "Imperial Facade" had slowed its growth, but this was little compensation, since the underlying attempt to impose a uniform style remained. In the age of the machine imperialism had produced the greatest symbols of Megalopolitan arrogance, the skyscrapers, whose "obdurate, overwhelming masses take away from the little people who walk in their shadows any semblance of dignity as human beings." Mumford was not opposed to the development of a modern style appropriate to the age and he praised many modern factories as being "clean and lithe and smart," but he believed that imperialism had suppressed much of modern architectural creativity, producing buildings that were neither beautiful nor conducive to human living. "There is so much beauty to the square foot in our old New England village, and so little, beyond mere picturesqueness, in the modern metropolis."[24]

To resist urban domination and to restore the indigenous local cultures that nurtured not only beauty and creativity but life itself, Mumford offered regional planning. It was necessary to correct the imbalance between the overcrowded city and the depleted countryside, and this could be done only when Americans had developed "an art which will relate city and countryside in a new pattern," ending the degradation of rural areas and reversing the flow of population to the metropolitan centers. This required that in land development, as Whitaker and Ackerman had already declared, profit striving and property rights be subordinated to human and natural interests until "the land be fully loved and cared for again." With community control over the land, it would be possible to develop a program of resource conservation, like that proposed by MacKaye for Appalachia, in the regions surrounding the cities, and also to implement a broad strategy for the decentralization of urban populations.[25]

The key to decentralization would be the creation of garden cities and villages that combined the best of the countryside with the best of the city. Once regional planning achieved effective control over the land, it could "provide a new framework for our communities which will redistribute population and industry, and revitalize the environment." Such a scheme would benefit from the rapidly increasing use of electric motors and gasoline engines, which made possible the decentralization of manufacturing in the form of small factories that could be located in the garden towns. With the scaling down of production, it would be possible to recover some of the old elements of craftsmanship, providing greater satisfaction in work and reviving some of the creative instincts that had been blighted by mass production.[26]

Mumford realized that his romantic expectations were only remote possibilities confronted by metropolitan power, but he closed his book with the declaration that if it had taken feudal Japan less than a century to adopt modern Western ways, "there is nothing to prevent our own civilization from recovering once more its human base—nothing that is, except our own desires, aims, habits, and ends." As an example of what might be done, he cited MacKaye's Appalachian Trail, which he called a bold plan for repeopling deserted mountain areas and decentralizing the congested populations of cities. To foster even more ambitious plans became Mumford's great mission in life. Leaving the technical details of planning to others, he concentrated on trying to transform the guiding ideals of Americans. He looked to the past for help. "The future of our civilization depends upon our ability to select and control our heritage from the past, to alter our present attitudes and habits, and to project fresh forms."[27]

Mumford looked especially to MacKaye's New England. In *Sticks and Stones* he had declared that the garden city was not simply an importation from Europe but a recovery of an American communal form most evident in the New England village. By the time the book was published, he was already writing a new work intended to deepen understanding of the life and ideals that had once animated that form. Turning from architecture to literature, he treated the pre–Civil War times of Emerson, Thoreau, and Whitman as America's "Golden Day," when culture had been most vital and creative. Although the Civil War and its aftermath had, in his rather simplistic view, devastated that culture, he believed that he had identified the heritage on which it might be possible to build a new golden day.

By the time he published his new study under the title *The Golden Day: A Study in American Experience and Culture* in 1926, he had had numerous reasons for hope, not only in New England but in New York State, where his friends in the RPAA seemed well along in the process of translating ideals into effective forces for change. Stein, the RPAA's principal organizer, played a leading role in this process, supported by several other recruits in what by the mid-1920s appeared to be an increasingly powerful regional planning movement capable of guiding urban America to a new and perhaps permanent golden day.

VI

PLANNING NEW YORK
STATE: STEIN AND
HENRY WRIGHT

When the RPAA was founded, regional planning was already a subject of rising public attention. In the July to December 1923 volume of the *American City Magazine,* for instance, the subject appears for the first time in that journal's index with five entries dealing with regional planning in New York, Boston, Milwaukee, and Los Angeles. In 1924 the New York Association of Real Estates Boards endorsed the idea, declaring that its members had committed themselves to "orderly development" of cities and towns, including their suburban subdivisions. A few months later the National Association of Realtors announced that a survey of its members confirmed this trend, one sign of a more general awakening of public interest in planning.[1]

The primary focus of interest was the RPNY. This plan for the city and its extensive suburban hinterlands in New Jersey and Connecticut as well as in New York State had been initiated in 1922 with a large grant from the Russell Sage Foundation. In 1923 the new chairman of the planning committee, Frederic A. Delano, announced that the committee had gathered most of the information it needed to begin the preparation of a plan for the territory within a fifty-mile radius of New York City. By the end of the year Thomas Adams, the director of planning, had begun to describe his vision of a future city embracing 5,500 square miles and some thirty-nine million future inhabitants. Not all New Yorkers believed a plan was necessary, including one who, in a letter to the *New York Times,* declared that the city was already "perfectly adapted to its habitat and associations," but it had the support of the *Times* as well as numerous influential New Yorkers.[2]

This development brought little joy to Whitaker and some of his associates in the RPAA, who had already concluded that the plan, despite promises to the contrary, leaned strongly toward a dangerous centralization that would make New York even more congested and inefficient than before. In 1923, however, the RPAA could anticipate the eventual victory of other forms of regional planning better suited to their ideals. By then MacKaye and Stein, with Whitaker's support, had mobilized powerful backing for the Appalachian Trail, which they hoped might help unite leaders in recreation, forestry, community development, architecture, engineering, and social science in a broadly conceived effort to rework the physical and social environment. Moreover, 1923 also saw the formation of a potentially powerful new public force for the same end, the New York State Commission of Housing and Regional Planning headed by Stein himself.

This new commission had grown out of the earlier attempts to resolve the postwar housing crisis. In 1920, as secretary of the Housing Committee of the Reconstruction Commission appointed by Governor Alfred Smith to study postwar problems, Stein had declared that the housing crisis stemmed from causes more fundamental than the war and therefore required radical new solutions. Especially fundamental was the speculative exploitation of land, which had so inflated land values, and thereby housing costs, as to force a large part of the population into slum conditions. There could be no solution to the housing problem that did not include the subordination in land development of private profit to public good. To establish public control over urban and suburban land, Stein advocated that the state encourage the creation in every city and town of a Board of Housing and Community Planning that would put together a comprehensive local plan of development. Beyond that he also urged that the idea of comprehensive planning be extended to metropolitan districts and even to the whole state.[3]

The state legislature ignored these recommendations, but the idea of comprehensive planning was kept alive, particularly in Stein's Community Planning and Housing column in the *JAIA.* "This is the age of immense cities," he wrote in 1922. "Yet future generations will be stunned and dismayed that these gigantic productions of our time came into being without plan." Finally, in August 1923 Governor Smith appointed a new five-member state commission of Housing and Regional Planning (CHRP), with Stein as chairman, the other members being chosen to represent business and labor. The CHRP's primary responsibility was to determine whether a housing emergency continued in the state, but it was also given a broader, albeit vaguely defined, mandate to study the whole housing situation in cooperation with planning groups and representatives of business and industry throughout the state. Technically, the official focus of such activity was housing, but nothing prevented the commission from broadly interpreting its mission, a freedom that Stein exploited from the start. At the first meeting the new commissioners concluded, according to the *New York Times,* that "the housing problem could not be separated from the problems of city and regional planning," leading them to launch "a series of investigations in regard to these more permanent problems."[4]

In explaining this decision Stein argued that the housing problem was deeply rooted, extending back to the beginning of the industrial age, and involved far more than housing itself. Because the cost of dwellings included not only the house but its site—the land, streets, and needed utilities—decent habitation could be provided only by comprehensive planning embracing all the elements required for the creation of a good residential neighborhood. And this, said Stein, could not be limited to neighborhoods or even to whole cities:

> These problems are tied up with those of neighboring centers of population and neighboring farm land. Our housing problem can not be met in our big centers unless we find new and better ways of distributing industry among the working population. It is only by such planning that it is possible to prevent large centers from becoming unmanageable and only thus can we meet the congestion of homes, of streets, of transit lines. Regional planning is the art and science of planning a physical region in such a way that industry, farming, housing, transportation, recreation shall all give the maximum return. Regional planning cannot be carried out by any separate community. It is a function that must be stimulated and assisted by the state.[5]

At the time, Stein had reason to believe that the government of New York State would in fact assist effective regional planning. Governor Smith had a strong interest in the matter, and with his support Stein and his committee began to organize a statewide effort. On June 9, 1924, they convened the first New York State Conference on Regional and City Planning in Buffalo, involving officials, technical experts, and business people. The *American City Magazine* observed that this was the

first time in New York that representatives of cities and towns had
gotten together with state officials to discuss the development of effective planning. In his introductory speech Stein again stressed the need
to extend planning beyond the limits of cities, noting that the existence
of suburbs and satellite towns and a dependence on outside sources for
essentials meant that "no city is master of its own destiny." He intended the conference to create a basis for permanent cooperation
among various existing planning agencies, an aim at least partly realized by the formation of the New York State Federation of Planning
Boards.[6]

Less than five months later, Stein's CHRP convened another conference in the Buffalo area, this one at Tonawanda, to initiate effective
regional planning for the whole Buffalo region by organizing all the
municipalities in the region for common action. "The potential importance of the region to the future of the whole State," said Stein, "indicates how meaningless are the artificial boundaries of village or city."
This second conference created the Niagara Frontier Planning Association, an informal group that proceeded to lobby the state legislature
until it created New York's first official board to develop a regional
plan, the Niagara Frontier Planning Committee, which consisted of
public officials from Buffalo and other municipalities situated on the
Niagara River. Over the next years, the committee drafted a comprehensive plan for the region.[7]

Further east, at the state capital, Stein's commission won another
victory for planning when in late 1924 it organized a conference of
officials from Albany, Schenectady, and Rensselaer counties, from
which came the formation of the Capital District Planning Association.
Thus, by 1925 New York State could count three significant regional
planning efforts, including the RPNY. In that year the state legislature
also passed a bill sponsored by the CHRP authorizing counties and
municipalities to form and fund boards "to study the needs and conditions of regional and community planning and zoning." This act
merely allowed for the creation of such boards, but it provided some
basis for hope that New York would take the lead in the regional
planning movement—which it did, first under Governor Smith and
then under his successor, Franklin Delano Roosevelt.[8]

Smith especially deserved credit for providing enthusiastic support
for the movement during its formative stage. In an address, delivered
by the then new-fangled radio, from Albany to the first conference at
Buffalo, he had declared that "the planning of the State is probably the
greatest undertaking we have before us. It is the making of the mold in

which future generations will be formed." His act in speaking over the new electronic medium itself called attention to the changing scope of urban life and planning brought by the twin dynamos of the new age, electricity and the automobile. In 1925 Smith spoke of the need for "seeing a state whole" so as to understand and control all the influences that shaped life in any particular locality. "There is a direct relationship," he said, "between the development of the natural resources of the state and the relief of the congestion of its big cities," if only because what was done to create opportunities outside cities would have a powerful effect on the flow of urban population. The relative health of agriculture, he recognized, would be a strong influence on the crowding of the rural poor into the big urban centers.[9]

That this was more than simple planning piety became evident in 1925, when Stein's commission reported a comprehensive regional survey and preliminary plan for the entire state. Begun in 1924, this report was finished in time to be unveiled informally at the International Conference on Town, City, and Regional Planning in New York City in April 1925. A writer for the *New York Times* called it "a concrete plan for a sort of research magnificent" dealing with the affairs of the state. Several members of the RPAA were involved. Stein supported it with his organizational skills, and Mumford contributed to its substantial historical sections.[10]

Even more appears to have been provided by MacKaye, although not as much as he implied years later, when he told a friend that "back in 1924 I made a plan for a plan for New York State." During this period he was active in promoting the opening of the New York sections of the Appalachian Trail, in the fall of 1924 organizing "an expedition" of friends to walk the trail route between Bear Mountain and the New Jersey border; later, he offered a plan to open the Trail east of Bear Mountain as far as the Massachusetts border to the Taconic State Park Commission, then headed by Roosevelt. In May 1925 he outlined a scheme for the development of waterpower, parks, and planned rural communities in New York, one special feature of which was a proposal for the development of a "St. Lawrence-Mississippi waterway" as the first step toward "the diversion and decentralization of industry generally." MacKaye's chief contribution to the state plan was as a consultant on topographical matters, helping to map the state, as he recalled in 1932, "into industrial regions in lieu of counties."[11]

The most directly involved was Henry Wright, a comparative newcomer to the New York scene and to the RPAA, who was becoming both Stein's professional partner in planning and architecture and an important source of new ideas for regional planning. "He was an original," Stein would later say of his friend, "an unusually active mind—an inquisitive analytical mind—that constantly drove him from one problem to another, and from one solution to a still better solution." Although frequently stubborn in his commitment to what he believed, in the words of another associate, he was simply "a nice man to know," a man of quiet confidence who was willing to listen to the ideas of others and to explain his own to them with clarity and patience. [12]

Wright was born in Lawrence, Kansas, in 1878. After graduating in 1901 from the University of Pennsylvania with a degree in architecture and after completing his apprenticeship with a Kansas City architectural firm, he established a practice in St. Louis with George Kessler, the prominent planner of parks and boulevards. Wright soon developed a special interest and skill in site planning, demonstrating what Stein called "a supernatural sense of site" regarding the best way to relate buildings to the land. Another associate, Henry Churchill, later recalled that Wright could walk a fifty-acre tract of land and then, simply on the basis of his memory, make an accurate sketch of its contours.

In 1913, after he had established his own firm, Wright achieved some national recognition when an article in the *Architectural Record* favorably reviewed his design for a residential subdivision, Brentmoor Park, to be constructed on thirty-five acres outside of St. Louis. Noting that there were many good plans for individual houses but few that adequately related a group of buildings to their site, the article presented Wright's plan as a rational model for community site development. Given the task of subdividing the site into fifteen mini-estates in a way that would assure the "greatest degree of beauty and community advantage," Wright created a plan centered on a long narrow park separating the two principal roads in the development. [13]

In 1918 Wright joined Kohn and Ackerman in planning the worker villages of the Emergency Fleet Corporation, working chiefly to develop site plans for projects at Newburgh, New York; Bridgeport, Connecticut; and Camden, New Jersey. This opportunity to plan communities for more than the rich broadened his social interests and prepared the way for his later successes in designing the model communities of Sunnyside and Radburn.

With the end of the war, Wright returned to St. Louis, where he served as consulting architect for the City Planning Commission, but he had outgrown both the city and his previous ideas. In attempting to devise for the commission a program to regulate the subdivision of suburban land, he came to conclude, like Stein, that city planning was not enough to prevent the incoherent and wasteful land development that threatened the urban future. Moreover, he was making new friends, especially Whitaker and Stein, who introduced him to the AIA's community planning committee and then to the RPAA. When in 1924 Stein looked for someone to draft a preliminary exposition of the proposed New York State plan, his natural choice was Wright, with whom he was already working on a model community, Sunnyside Gardens, on the outskirts of New York City. [14]

With the assistance of his friends in the RPAA, Wright was able to complete the essentials of his report on the state plan in the early spring of 1925. His final version, dated May 7, 1925, was not intended to be a definitive plan. Rather, he tried to establish a basic direction for future planning, beginning with an effort to "ascertain and measure the forces which have shaped the present state and to evaluate the many forces which are now altering the present mould." With the understanding of basic forces, a plan could be devised, but this would not be the end of the process, since even a good plan had to be constantly updated "as a result of changing habits and economic relations of men, and their ability . . . to harness nature to their need." To sustain this work, the report proposed the creation of a permanent state planning board to consist of the heads of all departments responsible for public improvements and, significantly, representatives from local regional planning groups such as those in Buffalo and Albany. [15]

Aside from the planning process, Wright's principal concern was with the concentration of population in New York City and the towns occupying the relatively narrow strip of land in the Hudson and Mohawk Valleys, the great L-shaped area that dominated New York's topography as well as its economic and social development. Wright attempted to demonstrate that this concentration, far from being permanent and irreversible, was simply a phase in the state's growth. Prior to 1840 the dominant trend, in fact, had spread New York's population widely over its inhabited areas until there was "almost complete noncentralization with small, self-sufficient communities scattered throughout the state." With the Industrial Revolution, however, the influence of steam power had caused the crowding of the population in a few urban places and a corresponding decline of the old rural society, with its independence and self-sufficiency. The net results were bad living conditions and wasteful economic organization, which cancelled out the benefits of modern life. [16]

Luckily, a new set of forces had appeared that made it possible to reverse the centralizing trend. By the 1920s electricity was rapidly displacing steam as the dominant form of energy, providing an inexpensive form of power that could be delivered almost anywhere, allowing both for a decentralization of industry and for a basic improvement in the conditions of rural life, brought about by the new amenities provided by electrical power. Moreover, steam-powered railroads were giving way to a more flexible system employing automobiles and trucks, which promised an end to rural isolation and a diffusion of population and economic activity away from the great population centers. Although the opportunity for healthful decentralization was there, however, it would not be realized without the guidance of the right kind of plan.

Wright's report culminated with an argument for regional planning as the only sure way to a better world, city planning being presented as little more than an imposition on suburban space of a scheme designed to sustain the overcrowded city. Undoubtedly thinking of the RPNY, Wright emphasized that regional planning had a much different objective than that of the city-focused "metropolitan" variety, and then quoted his friend Lewis Mumford: "Regional Planning asks not how wide an area can be brought under the aegis of the metropolis, but how the population and civic facilities can be distributed so as to promote and stimulate a vivid, creative life throughout a whole region—a region being any geographic area that possesses a certain unity of climate, soil, vegetation, industry and culture."[17]

Much of the planning, Wright emphasized, would be done by the kind of local regions that were being organized for planning purposes in the Buffalo and Albany areas, but he ended with a special hope that such local efforts would evolve into statewide planning and a state plan rooted in local realities. In consultation with government departments and private interests, New York State could establish rational control over its future under a blueprint designed "to develop logically the undersettled regions, to give aid to farming and lumbering, to prevent further overcentralization of cities while assisting economy for the manufacturers by the proper use of hydroelectric power, to consolidate water supply and to furnish a proper basis for local action."[18]

Wright expected the practical details to emerge with the continued growth of regional planning. In 1925 he could look to the expansion of efforts from the New York City region at one end of the state to the Buffalo-Niagara region at the other. Planning was becoming, he hoped, "a living and growing thing," sustained by the increased involvement of public agencies and private concerns. Moreover, there were encouraging signs of growing public interest in the regional approach. In April 1925, for instance, the *New Republic* strongly endorsed the idea. It summed up what it took to be the main aims of New York's "geographical strategy," namely the establishment of permanent forest regions, the location of farms near urban markets, the decentralization of industry, the development of protective greenbelts around cities, the comprehensive planning of housing and recreation, and the construction of planned garden communities. After listing these elements of the overall strategy, the editor concluded that "such a goal would be a fantasy unless it lies in the direction of the main technological and economic trend. Apparently, however, it does lie there. What we need is the social machinery to realize it."[19]

By the mid-1920s the RPAA had some reason for believing that it was helping to construct that necessary social machinery. Although the national government continued to be dominated by the apparent do-nothingism of the Coolidge administration, New York State had its activist executive in Governor Smith, and even New York City Mayor Jimmy Walker had turned to Kohn for help in developing a progressive housing program. Moreover, other members of the RPAA were making headway on their own. Some were much involved in the successful development of the model community Sunnyside Gardens, and others were expanding the range of their influence, having won an ally in the influential social journal *Survey Graphic*.[20] It would be only a matter of time, then, before government and the public would make regional planning a reality. Or so it seemed in 1925 to the already converted.

VII

GIANT POWER: STUART CHASE AND ROBERT BRUERE

By the mid-1920s the idea of planning had acquired a strong hold on the thought and imaginations of idealistic professionals like the members of the RPAA. Planning appeared to be a powerful instrument of social change that did not depend on the whims of popular politics. Founded on an understanding of essential realities divulged by studies and surveys, planning would embody a kind of objective potential, something realizable because aligned with manageable geographic, economic, and social forces. Moreover, it promised to be the field on which skilled professionals could unite their specialized understandings and talents in cooperative support of plan making and implementation. Architects like Whitaker and Ackerman, conservationists like Mac-Kaye, organizers like Stein and Kohn, and intellectuals like Mumford could join with engineers, social workers, and other "brain workers" (as Stein termed them) in creating a powerful alternative to the business community as the guiding force of progress. If the RPAA had room for Mumford's stress on the influence of myths and ideals, it also had a place for the dream that rapidly developing modern mechanical powers could be rationally organized into one giant power for human betterment. This technocratic dream was the special contribution of Stuart Chase and Robert Bruere.

"The horn of plenty is overflowing, but a dead hand reaches up to seal its mouth"—that was Chase's basic belief. Born in Somersworth,

New Hampshire, on March 8, 1888, Chase shared with MacKaye a profound reverence for the New England town. In 1931 he wrote that the sight of a village green brought tears to his eyes. "This is where I was born, my homeland, the place I love." As a young man, though, Chase was even more eager than MacKaye to seek the opportunities of a larger world. The son of Harvey Stuart Chase, a distinguished engineer and the head of a prominent Boston accounting firm, young Stuart attended M.I.T. and then Harvard, graduating cum laude from the latter in 1910 before joining his father's firm.[1]

Chase's specialties were economics and accounting, conventional skills harnessed to an unconventional idealism. Like most of the future members of the RPAA, he fell under the influence of Henry George. In 1911 he read George's *Progress and Poverty,* whose economic ideas and social visions overwhelmed his past beliefs and shut "the door forever on money-making as a profession," leaving him hungry for something worthy to do. In an article written for *Forum* magazine in 1914, he announced his goal: "I want to know what I am and why I am, in order to determine the things most fitted for me to do—not as an individual greedy of success but as a sharer for a time of the life and sunshine upon this little whirling sphere in God's vast universe." What should he do? There was no easy answer. The old creeds and ways that had guided men in the past were falling to pieces around him, victims of rapidly changing times.[2]

World War I gave him something worthy to do. Like the other members of the RPAA, he was drawn into government service, employing his accounting skills under the Federal Trade Commission (FTC) and the Food Administration to help limit price gouging in the meatpacking industry. Organization for war excited his hopes for a radical improvement in economic affairs. "The war has given us the unique opportunity to revolutionize the whole economy," he informed readers of the *Independent* magazine in 1917, "to destroy the vicious, to encourage the necessary, to make wholesome and strengthen immeasurably the goods of the nation." By then he had begun to form the hope that would animate his remaining years, the hope for a rationally organized economy that would meet all human needs.[3] He even thought briefly that the advances of the war could be maintained in peacetime economy—only to be disillusioned by postwar realities in a particularly disturbing way.

Earlier, in his idealism, Chase had identified with radical causes. Besides his open identification with the single-tax ideas of Henry George, he had spoken out in favor of women's suffrage and of birth control. In 1918, while living in Chicago in connection with his investigations of meatpacking, he had formed a club dedicated to the cause of Fabian socialism, and the following year joined with his friend MacKaye in offering his services to the new Soviet regime in Russia, listing John Reed as one of his references and noting that he hoped to help the Russians develop "schemes of adapting production to national requirements through scientific budgeting."[4]

Chase's accounting skills never found employment in Soviet Russia, but they did become entangled with radicalism in America. In 1919, during the postwar "Red scare" and while he was scrutinizing possible price gouging in the meatpacking industry for the FTC, he was attacked by Senator Watson of Indiana as a dangerous radical who had made his government office in Chicago into "the rendevous of a number of men devoted to the destruction of property, overthrow of Government and the consummation of the ideals of Socialism." Less than two years later, after moving to Washington and after he had antagonized a corporation in which a powerful senator had an interest, he was fired from the FTC, ending any hope for government employment.[5]

Chase, however, soon found a new form of public service. Moving to New York City, he joined the Technical Alliance, a group of engineers and other technicians who had adopted the technocratic doctrines of Veblen. The alliance fell apart in a short time, but he was able to create his own replacement, the Labor Bureau, a research organization of economists, accountants, and engineers intended especially to provide technical services to labor organizations. By October 1922 he was able to tell MacKaye that the "persnickety Labor Bureau" seemed to be taking hold: "I like the work profoundly. I think it will become a permanent fixture." It was undoubtedly Chase's group to which MacKaye was referring when in 1922 he wrote to Stein that he was pleased by "the present contemplations of a certain crowd of young technicians who seek to plan portions of the earth's surface and to meet the 'challenge of waste,'" although MacKaye felt obliged to add he was not satisfied by their lack of what he believed essential for success: a guiding social vision and the support of the people at large.[6]

By this time Chase had tasted independent creative life and wanted more. Living was not simply existing, he wrote, but a vital existence free from routine, monotony, and restraint. He estimated that perhaps only 25 percent of his time was engaged in true living, but he concluded that this was more than average and that "my ratio of living can only grow with that of my fellow-men." Chase's dedication to improving the ratio of living for all men drew him to the cause of regional planning, and in 1923 he helped found the RPAA, serving as a member of the program committee, which drafted the constitution and statement of objectives of the association. He saw in regional planning the means to eliminate the wasteful congestion of overcentralized cities in favor of a decentralization of production in the form of small factories. This would restore the vitality of rural society and open the way for fundamental improvements in urban life. In 1924, recovering some of his prewar enthusiasm, he spoke to the metropolis: "Men reared you and men shall tear you down, and yet build a city where life runs free and beauty dwells."[7]

Regional planning for Chase was part of a larger strategy. Some years after he had moved to New York he compared his life there with that of his great-great-grandfather at Newburyport in 1800 and concluded that there had been little real progress. "Why is it, in the face of unparalleled technical improvement and engineering development," he asked, "that my standard of living in terms of vital values, is so little better if indeed better?" His answer was simple: that modern technical power had not been placed under the guidance of human intelligence. What was needed was rational planning directed by enlightened technicians: "Where are the engineers and statesmen to dig with hand and brain into this roaring wilderness—so finely wrought in isolated detail—and bring from it ordered cities, impounded waters, terraced and tended forests, the sweep of great transmission lines, clean rivers, workshops planned with the dignity of cathedrals, and the end of grime and poverty and despair?"[8]

Chase was confident that the technical talent already existed to create what he called a functional society. Under the management of technicians, the economy could be planned to more than double existing living standards, in large part through a more efficient organization of existing productive facilities. In 1925 he published *The Tragedy of Waste,* the first of a series of well-selling books that popularized the gospel of technical efficiency. In it he catalogued the forms of waste that were depleting the powers available to humankind for its liberation from poverty. Among them was one that reflected MacKaye's thinking: the abuse of the nation's timber resources. At the rate of present cutting, Chase estimated, American forests would be wiped out in about thirty years, leaving barren soils, eroded lands, and polluted streams. As the antidote to this he offered MacKaye's plan for timber culture associated with permanent forest communities, citing it as an example of the method of "the engineer" intent of a rational use of nature.[9]

If natural power could be engineered for human good, so could a developing man-made power. By the mid-1920s Chase had joined with numerous others in crusading for what they called Giant Power. Originally conceived in Pennsylvania soon after World War I as a way to modernize the coal industry, the scheme had special appeal to those concerned with energy conservation. In 1925 the Federal Conservation Board estimated that the nation's petroleum supply would be exhausted within the next six years at the current rate of consumption. Even earlier a deeper concern over the dependability of the leading source of energy, coal, had been precipitated by a long strike in the coal fields. The answer to this impending energy crisis seemed to lie in the efficient development of the newest and most promising form of energy, electricity. One great rational system of electrical power production and distribution could bring cheap energy even to isolated rural areas, thereby contributing to the efforts of regional planners to decentralize economic activity.[10]

To make that possible, Chase and others dreamed of locating giant generating stations at the coal mines, thereby eliminating the waste of transporting coal and providing for its efficient use. Coal-generated electricity would be supplemented by the efficient development of hydropower, less than 15 percent of which, by Chase's estimate, had been developed. From the dams and the mines electrical power would be delivered by well-coordinated systems of high-voltage lines running to every part of the country. In 1925 Chase was enthusiastic about the benefits of this system:

> Giant Power is one of the bravest and most exhilarating glimpses of Utopia which engineers and scientists have ever dreamed. It not only saves coal and oil, it electrifies the railroads, lightens the traffic burden, abolishes smoke and soot and grime, makes . . . for industrial decentralization, for less congestion in the cities, for more life and vigor in the country. One's eye follows the sweep of the great high voltage lines as they charge the hill and drop to the valley—straight and true and infinitely powerful—and for an instant one glimpses the end of meanness, poverty, disorder; a world set free.[11]

Chase's pursuit of this industrial dream received strong support from Robert Bruere, a more marginal member of the RPAA. Bruere was the oldest of the group, having been born in St. Charles, Missouri, in 1876, but he shared some of the same hopeful enthusiasm for a better world. In 1927 he said that "I belonged to a reforming generation, to a generation of 'causes'; we wanted to 'reconstruct the social order' after some design of our own." Before the war his idealism had brought him to New York City, where he taught at the Rand School of Social Science, served as general agent of the Association for Improving the Condition of the Poor, and, beginning in 1917, was the director of the Bureau of Research. Like Chase, Bruere's idealism was changed by wartime hope and postwar disillusionment. In 1922, for instance, at the close of a period of labor unrest, he took note of labor's demand for a "living wage," agreeing that it was a necessary ingredient of social progress but arguing that it could be obtained only by the rationalization of production to enhance efficiency.[12]

Although his involvement in the RPAA was only occasional, he did play a significant role in promoting the group's goals in 1924 and 1925 as an associate editor of *Survey* magazine. This magazine was ideally suited to the effort to promote the cause of planning. Financed by a cooperative association that included numerous social reformers like Jane Addams, Paul U. Kellogg (its editor), and Graham Taylor, and directly descended from the late-nineteenth-century *Charities Review*, it aspired to be the leading popular journal of "constructive philanthropy," with a special mission to publicize those reform ideas that had been ignored elsewhere. In order to broaden its appeal, its owners, Survey Associates, began in 1921 to supplement it with a special illustrated monthly version, *Survey Graphic*, which by the mid-1920s had more than 20,000 subscribers.[13]

Even before Chase began to promote the Giant Power idea, Bruere had proclaimed it in 1923 "the key to our liberation not only from the coal problem but the dead hand of our inherited machine equipment." In March 1924 Bruere published a special Giant Power issue of *Survey Graphic*. By this time the idea was winning significant public attention. In Pennsylvania the old conservationist Gifford Pinchot had submitted a plan for a state-controlled electrical system oriented around Pennsylvania's coal industry. In New York, Governor Smith was beginning to take an interest in the matter from the angle of waterpower, particularly that of the Niagara and St. Lawrence Rivers, eventually urging the creation of a State Power Authority to devise a comprehensive plan for the efficient development of all the state's power resources. In 1924 Robert LaFollette, candidate of the Progressive Party, came out in favor of a "national super-water power system," a forerunner of the TVA.[14]

Bruere introduced the special issue with a perceptive overview of the character and significance of the new power scheme, which he defined as "the conversion of all our primary energy sources into electricity and their pooling in regional systems which will then be integrated into a nation wide federation of systems." Although the technical side of this scheme was already being developed by engineers and other technicians, he believed that it was necessary to find a corresponding class of social engineers who could control Giant Power for human good. Beyond cheap, available power, the primary question was whether the new system would be directed toward a healthy decentralization of society, meeting the energy needs of farms and small communities, or whether it would further intensify the development of "mass production in already overcrowded and slum-dwelling areas."[15]

In support of Giant Power, Bruere assembled a team of reform advocates that included his wife, Martha Binsley Bruere. A prolific writer of magazine articles and an ardent feminist, Martha Bruere advocated Giant Power as in influence for liberating women from domestic servitude. In 1923 she wrote that the chief problem for women in modern times "is to take their places in the new industries of a new world while still filling their old place as the center around which the family units have been organized to revolve." With electrical appliances to reduce their home workload, women could find the time to pursue worthwhile careers in the outside world. And the extension of electricity to rural areas would lessen the pressure on farmer's wives to move to the towns, thereby helping to reverse the flow of people to the overcrowded cities. In the special issue Martha Bruere contributed a glowing article on the effects of a well-organized hydroelectric power system in Ontario, Canada, especially on one town where thousands of people lived "in domestic ease through a plentiful supply of power at low enough rates so that they use as much of it as they choose."[16]

Martha Bruere's article was followed by MacKaye's "Appalachian Power: Servant or Master?" which Robert Bruere had solicited in the interest of promoting "big ideas" like that for the Appalachian Trail. Probably because he was engrossed in efforts to finish his book, *The New Exploration,* MacKaye provided only a two-page article to the issue, but it was enough to lead Kellogg, chief editor of the *Survey,* to tell its author that "you have handled a big theme in small space with rare craftsmanship."[17] After linking his thoughts to his original article on the "so-called 'Appalachian project,'" MacKaye reminded the world that Giant Power involved not only industrial and technical efficiency but ultimately "social efficiency," the conversion of energy into the maximum possible human welfare and happiness. To achieve social efficiency it was necessary to use Giant Power to help build a decentralized world much like the one he had been advocating for years, a world of compact, democratically administered communities that combined modern industry and conveniences with manageable social scale and immediate access to nature.

Having stated this now-familiar ideal, MacKaye got to his main point, which was to urge attention to developing Appalachia. He divided the eastern United States into two distinct civilizations: one, located in the "super-populated belt lying between the cities of Boston and Washington," was modern and cosmopolitan, while the other, occupying a "sub-populated belt" along the Appalachian range, was "colonial," that is, a traditional society inhabited by "the purest form of original American Anglo-Saxon stock" devoted to the traditional ideal of individual freedom, "the freedom of higher living," in contrast to the organized toil of the metropolitan world. Although MacKaye never stooped to any nativist attack on the immigrant populations of the big cities, it was evident that he had a strong idea as to who were the most American of Americans. Rather than strengthening a "toiling commercial America" suffering from overcrowding, Giant Power should be used to support "the tradition, the folk, the land, and the resources left over from colonial days." Although MacKaye did not detail the nature of the support, he did make note of the fact that Appalachia had great amounts of coal- and waterpower to be developed along Giant Power lines, electrical energy to be delivered cheaply to the local people so that they could compete with the overcrowded metropolis. [18]

The special Giant Power issue of *Survey Graphic* in March 1924 was one of the most popular issues of that magazine and a special triumph for Robert Bruere, its initiator and editor. He continued to take some interest in the subject, in May 1925 again urging that the new system—which would alter "the technical and social framework of American life"—be directed by "human engineers" along lines dictated by regional plans. Eventually, though, he drifted away from regional planning and the RPAA, concentrating his attention on labor issues. In his pursuit of industrial efficiency he became an advocate of company unions as instruments of enlightened labor management, and in 1927 he was appointed the secretary on industrial relations of the J. C. Penney Foundation. [19]

The success of the Giant Power issue of *Survey Graphic,* though, did open the way for what looked like an even greater opportunity for the RPAA to shape the future, since the issue undoubtedly inspired the famous regional-planning number of the *Survey Graphic* in 1925, which Bruere supported both as associate editor and as a writer. With the publication of that issue and following the success of Giant Power, it seemed possible to anticipate a progressively growing influence for the RPAA. Unfortunately for the cause of regional planning, however, what had been a modestly triumphal march uphill toward significant influence reached a peak in the mid-1920s, only then to falter in the face of disappointments and troubles.

VIII

UPS AND DOWNS, 1925–1926: MUMFORD ET AL.

The mid-1920s first would feed the hopes of the RPAA for eventual success in reshaping America and then would introduce several disappointments that shook the progress of the organization. After its flurry of early activity in 1923 the RPAA rarely held formal meetings, but its leading members did make a notable effort to cooperate in sustaining their momentum and their confidence in the eventual success of their cause. In September 1924 Stein, newly returned from Europe, met briefly with MacKaye and gave him some material regarding European planning, which MacKaye soon told Mumford indicated a "widespread desire of the people abroad for a fundamental new way of approaching modern problems. It seems as if they are thinking along the same lines as you and I have been talking. So perhaps we are not the only damn fools."[1] Indeed, even during the presidency of Calvin Coolidge these regional planning advocates found other evidence that they were not the only "damn fools" to dream of a radically better world, one such proof being the success of the Giant Power issue of *Survey Graphic*.

It was natural that the RPAA should conceive of a new special *Survey Graphic* number devoted more directly to regional planning. With some encouragement from Chase, MacKaye discussed the idea with his friend Bruere. Then, in mid-September, Mumford, Stein, Whitaker, and Ackerman—all present in New York—met with the journal's publishers and worked out a tentative arrangement for the number, which, it was agreed, would be "an extra-large issue." When the RPAA yearly meeting convened in October at the Hudson Guild Farm in New

Jersey, the Appalachian Trail remained at the head of its agenda. Mumford described the gathering as "an Appalachian revival meeting," one of whose chief activities was a walk over a nearby portion of the Trail. As Mumford also noted, however, the members "spent long hours threshing out the contents of the Regional Planning number," finally turning over to him the responsibility of editing it, a logical choice since he was then serving as the editorial secretary of the AIA's Committee on Community Planning.[2]

By December Mumford had begun to complain to MacKaye about the "damned regional planning number," especially about a shortage of the right kind of articles. Although he was confident that MacKaye and possibly Bruere would join him in providing an understanding of regional planning in its positive form, he feared that most of the other contributors would give too much attention merely to making negative criticisms of existing planning or to presenting technical answers to technical problems. "People will never be stirred out of the rut of their habits by a technical report," he warned. What he wanted was something that would excite the human spirit and imagination, something that required a strong emphasis on the kind of cultural regionalism that had developed in parts of Europe. "We must start a regional movement in America before we can have regional planning."[3] Without the guiding inspiration of regional cultures, rooted in traditionalism rather than in the rationality of the metropolis, even the best-intended plans would become like the RPNY, servants of the metropolitan needs of the central city.

Mumford, however, had to take what was offered him. When the special issue appeared in May 1925 it consisted of twelve articles by eleven different authors, all but two of whom were members of the RPAA—the exceptions were Governor Alfred Smith and C. B. Purdom, an English expert on garden cities. Governor Smith's contribution was an aptly named short essay, "Seeing a State Whole." The RPAA contributors were introduced as "a group of insurgents who, as architects and planners, builders and rebuilders, have tried to mold cities in conventional ways and, finding the task a labor of Sisyphus, have pinned their faith boldly to the new concept of the region." In their efforts to develop "a new plan for relating masses of population to the land," they were described as having a personal stake, each in his own way trying to overcome the "fractured lives" associated with metropolitan society by reconciling "the means to live with a way of living."[4]

Mumford, introduced as "one of the most ingratiating and informing interpreters of the regional planning idea," contributed two articles.

The first, "The Fourth Migration," set the tone for the rest of the issue. After noting the inadequacies of three earlier migrations of restless Americans, who sought the good life through farming, industrial production, and metropolitan life respectively, he offered the hope that the new technology associated with the automobile and electricity would bring a final movement of population to a permanently satisfying life. Utopia could be realized if those who controlled the situation would "utilize the land intelligently, relate industry to power resources and market, and provide an adequate 'human plant' for the community at large."[5]

In his second article, "Regions—To Live In," Mumford tried to describe the basic human dimension of regional planning as opposed to the merely technical. In obvious reference to the RPNY, he declared that true regional planning asked not how best to promote the growth of metropolitan centers but how to distribute population so as to stimulate a "vivid, creative life." He said that no society should be tolerated that took "the joy out of life" in favor of some stultifying mechanical routine, and he called for "a higher type of civilization" embracing all people. Underscoring the essential conservatism of his insurgency, he called regional planning an "industrial counter revolution" that would "realize the gains of modern industry in permanent houses, gardens, playgrounds and community institutions" and also achieve a "new conservation—the conservation of human values hand in hand with natural resources . . . permanent agriculture instead of land-skinning, permanent forestry instead of timber mining, permanent human communities."[6]

When it came to describing what he meant by a region Mumford was notably general, defining it as "any geographic area that possesses a certain unity of climate, soil, vegetation, industry and culture." A more concrete and more dynamic depiction came from MacKaye in his article, "The New Exploration: Charting the Industrial Wilderness." For MacKaye, modern industrialization had created a chaotic system, "a rough hewn organization," which could be effectively integrated only through regional planning. Each part of this system consisted of a metropolitan "mouth region," the marketing, manufacturing, and consuming part of the system, and a provincial "source region," which supplied the raw materials. The best way to explore the whole system, said MacKaye, was to start with the source areas and to follow the streams of commerce to the metropolitan centers. Good planning should begin, then, with the farms and forests.[7]

Having established the primacy of the provinces, MacKaye was free to emphasize what he had long stressed: Appalachia and the importance of conservation-oriented agriculture and resource extraction, most notably his old scheme of timber culture and permanent forest communities supplemented now by an emphasis on the effective development of hydroelectric power. Although he was willing to concede the importance of the metropolitan areas, it was evident that he believed the key to the future was in the mountains and valleys. He selected as an example the Somerset Valley of the Upper Deerfield River in Vermont and western Massachusetts, whose future development he believed would inevitably affect Boston, New England's metropolitan center. To provide the basis for a stable community life in the valley, a lumbering area in the nineteenth century, he urged careful attention to both forest culture and the full development of hydroelectric power; most of the population was to be settled in two of MacKaye's logging communities. Out of the dedicated cultivation of such valleys throughout the nation, he believed, would come the salvation of modern urban society.[8]

Mumford and MacKaye best summed up the essence of regional planning in the special *Survey Graphic* issue, but the other members of the RPAA added important details. In what became the most reprinted article in the collection, "Dinosaur Cities," Stein declared that the congested metropolitan centers were obsolete entities doomed to break down from their growing inefficiencies; efforts to resolve urban problems, then, should be concentrated not on the centers but on the regions. Typically, in "Coals to Newcastle" Chase chose to attack what he insisted were the great wastes in unnecessary transportation and exchange that resulted from the failure to develop strong, largely self-sufficient regional economies; effective regional planning would not only eliminate such wastes but eliminate the dinosaur cities they sustained. In his "Giant Power—Region-Builder," Bruere presented basically the same picture in advocating his scheme for the generation and distribution of electricity to promote the decentralization of population and industry.[9]

The other articles by RPAA members were even more specific: Bing's "Can We Have Garden Cities in America?" Wright's "The Road to Good Houses," and Ackerman's Georgist attack on land speculation as the cause of urban problems, "Our Stake in Congestion." One of the marginal members of the group, James K. Hart, an educator, in his "Two Generation Communities" condemned cities for denying youth the opportunity to develop their full potential: "The treasures of youth and beauty cannot be saved unless men can find room enough, once more, on the face of the earth for two generations, youth and age, to live side by side." This room was to be found in the form of relatively small-scale communities.[10] The issue ended with an emphatic declaration of difference from conventional city planning: "For the regional planner makes bold to discover the truly economic use of wide areas of land, rural as well as urban, and then seeks to stabilize the drift of population by bringing people permanently into the most productive relationship with these areas. . . . The regional planner calls for a right about face; his only hope of a hearing is that he has, on his side, reason—and whatever is left of hunger and love for the land."[11]

This battery of articles was intentionally timed to identify the RPAA with an organized international movement, being issued only shortly after the annual conference (the first in America) of the International Town, City, and Regional Planning and Garden Cities Federation in New York at the Hotel Pennsylvania in late April. In announcing this connection, *Survey* described the gathering as bringing "together in New York, town, city, and regional planners from the four corners of the globe for an international conference that shall break new ground for America." Stein had attended the previous conference in Amsterdam as a vice president of the Federation and representative of the AIA; likely, he had influenced the decision to hold the next meeting in New York. Since the conference was planned with the help of the National Conference on City Planning and was held jointly with the fifty-eighth annual meeting of the AIA, it promised to be a momentous event, one that the RPAA hoped to exploit to its advantage and at the expense of its rival, the Regional Plan Association of New York, which had one session of the meeting especially devoted to it.[12]

Both planning groups mounted exhibits at the conference, and both had speakers, but the RPAA benefited first from the welcoming address of Sullivan Jones, the state architect and Governor Smith's appointed representative, who quoted the governor as saying that the goal of regional planning was "to make the life of every man, woman, and child a fuller and finer life." After declaring his own view that the aim of planning should be to "satisfy man's physical, intellectual, and spiritual wants," Jones boasted about Stein's Commission of Housing and Regional Planning, observing that "we are beginning to plan the region of which the city and towns are only parts" and citing as evidence of growing public support the progress in creating local regional planning commissions and a statewide federation of planning boards.[13]

Stein and Mumford also spoke, both at a joint session with the AIA headed by Kohn. Stein complained of the difficulties New York City's narrow streets and crowded conditions posed to the architect's strivings for good design. More generally he denounced big overcrowded cities

and praised Wright's state-planning report as a start toward ameliorat-
ing their "inevitable breakdown." Mumford condemned the prevailing
"checkerboard" or gridiron pattern of planning. Later, in summing up
the conference, he said that two diametrically different forms of American planning were evident: "One assumes that technical ability can
improve living conditions while our existing economic and social habits
continue; the other holds that technical ability can achieve little that is
fundamentally worth the effort until we shape our institutions in such a
way as to subordinate financial and property values to those of human
welfare." Mumford believed that there had been at least some tilt in the
conference toward the second form, favored by the RPAA.[14]

Weeks before the New York meeting began, the RPAA had decided
to follow it with their own special gathering at the Hudson Guild Farm
in New Jersey, a meeting to which the foreign delegates to the conference were invited. "We have thought," wrote Stein, "that this would
give them an opportunity to see something of American country life,
and us a chance to meet them in a more leisurely and informal way." On
the weekend following the conference, the RPAA rented a special car on
a Lackawanna Railroad train to get its members and guests to Netcong,
the two leading foreign guests being Ebenezer Howard, the president
of the federation as well as the father of the Garden City movement in
England; and Raymond Unwin, the leading British city and regional
planner. The weekend was a memorable one. MacKaye recalled that on
Saturday night they had a square dance, a bit of American folk culture
that enticed Unwin into action, "with coat off and vest on, prancing to
the tones of the bull fiddle," and on Sunday the members went for a
walk, with " 'Uncle Ebenezer' [Howard] roaring jocosely how to plan
our little valley."[15]

The joy of this social gathering summed up the mood of the RPAA
in the spring of 1925. It was a time of triumph, not only because of the
conference but also because of the publication of Wright's report—
which Mumford praised in the *JAIA* as providing, if not a plan, at least
a "diagram that indicates realistically what a thorough-going plan
would attempt." And the special *Survey Graphic* number soon won
praise from several planning authorities, including Howard, who said
of it that "light is poured upon the world's great problems of reconstruction."[16] In the two years of its existence, the RPAA had, through
multiple exertions, seemingly made a giant step toward its aim of
educating the world to the nature and value of regional planning.

In fact, however, the triumphant uphill march soon began to falter. It
was not long before it became apparent that the *Survey Graphic* special did

not seriously alter the world's consciousness, nor did it have the effect of lessening public support for the RPNY, which, with the backing of powerful people, was relentlessly developing into a strong influence on planning decisions. Moreover, the members of the RPAA were losing some of their earlier focus on the cause. MacKaye was wrapped up in the effort to complete what he hoped would be his masterwork, *The New Exploration,* while also taking an interest—along with Stein and Wright—in a scheme to teach the Soviet Union the advanced land-utilization and agricultural techniques developed in the United States. [17] Wright was spending much of his time in St. Louis, and Robert Bruere had become increasingly involved with labor matters.

Also, a special situation developed around the two youngest members, Chase and Mumford, which weakened the sense of unity in the group. Although Chase continued to take an interest in the RPAA, he was becoming increasingly engrossed in his writing career as a crusader against waste, achieving enough success to lead Mumford to say a little enviously that "Stuart has a reputation with a capital R to administer." For his part, Chase may have become a little resentful over Mumford's rising influence, probably the reason for his gratuitous attack in 1928 in the *Nation,* where he went out of his way to complain regarding *The Golden Day* that Mumford "tells us frequently . . . what he is against, but only rarely does he let it be known what he is for" and then to place him among "a great array of critics" who worked assiduously to point out society's shortcomings without providing clear-cut alternatives. [18]

During these years Mumford was also becoming distracted. Not only was he deeply involved in completing his works on American culture, first *The Golden Day* and then a biography of Herman Melville, but he was having family problems. In 1925 he and his wife, Sophia, had had their first child, a son they named after Mumford's hero Patrick Geddes. Geddes Mumford proved to be a sickly child, demanding of his parents' attention, and then in October 1926 Sophia had a miscarriage followed by a period of ill health. Partly exhausted, Mumford wondered about the connection between health and creativity, observing to a friend that "fatigue and bad spirits always show up in my writing." Finally, he was becoming increasingly uninspired by Geddes, recalling later that the letters that he received from his old mentor saddened him by "the repetitiveness of their ideas and suggestions and, even worse, their irrelevance." [19]

Stein, too, was distracted, especially by his ambitions as a practicing architect. In July 1925 he told MacKaye that he was trying to spend more time at his drafting board. One result was a plan to provide affordable homes for "brain workers," especially teachers and professors, this at a time when he was also much engrossed in the planning of model communities, first Sunnyside Gardens and then Radburn. Another result was the plan, with Kohn, of the Ethical Culture Society's new Fieldston School in Riverdale, a day school designed to educate the next generation of professionals on a small group basis. The architects hoped that their plan would point the way to the construction of "small, convenient regional schools in each suburb instead of the present huge, central, specialized education factories."[20]

Not surprisingly, Stein lost some of his earlier enthusiasm for the RPAA, an important development since he was the Association's principal organizing and directing force. "I have no clear idea as to what the Regional Planning Association is going to do," he told MacKaye in 1925, adding that "I sometimes wish there were no such thing as regional planning and that I could put all my time into the thing which I find the most fun." Other members apparently were experiencing some version of the same thing, since he complained that "it is difficult to talk things over with anyone," most of his colleagues having temporarily dispersed to one part of the country or another. Finally, in June 1926, he was able to convene a meeting at the City Club in New York—which only seven members, including himself, attended. He proposed that the RPAA prepare a series of brochures to bring together "in a definite and scientific manner" the facts of regional planning; no such series was ever prepared.[21]

Mumford had similar concerns with similar results. Engrossed though he was by family concerns and his growing literary ambitions, he did try to do his bit to keep the group active. He missed the June 1926 meeting, having decided to spend much of the summer near Amenia, in a rural surrounding well away from the metropolis, a prelude to what eventually became a permanent move out of his native New York City. He was doubly appreciative, therefore, when in December he was finally able to meet with Stein, Ackerman, Chase, and Wright at Stein's New York apartment, but he told MacKaye that little had been accomplished except to agree that the RPAA "ought to get out a short creed." Although he remained hopeful about the future, he concluded that "the good old meetings are dead for the present, the spirit of 1924 and 1925 is missing." When in April 1927 the RPAA held its fourth annual meeting at the City Club in New York, Mumford was there, but he was one of only seven to attend.[22]

The years 1926 and 1927 also brought two major failures in the effort to promote public understanding of regional planning. One came in 1926, when Stein's CHRP, fresh from its success in issuing Wright's report on state planning, was suddenly put out of business by the New York state legislature. Early in 1925 Governor Smith had commended the commission as a useful public agency, especially in promoting an awakening of regional planning throughout the state, but it became entangled in a bitter controversy over housing. From the beginning, one of its primary functions was to monitor the state's postwar housing needs, especially to determine whether wartime rent controls should be continued. In 1925, after extensive hearings, the commission concluded that, at least in New York City, a crisis continued to exist, a conclusion that led it into conflict with the state's powerful real estate interests who wanted controls ended.[23]

Ironically, Stein and his fellow commissioners had also decided that rent control was no solution to the housing problem. In their report for the year, they declared that there would be no remedy until the costs of housing could be radically reduced, and that required substantial reductions in the cost of credit. To illustrate the point, Stein estimated that, on the average, more than 50 percent of a month's rent in New York went for interest charges, and calculated that a reduction in interest to 4 percent on loans for housing could reduce the average rent of $12.31 per room to $7.73, a reduction that would bring affordable housing into the reach of thousands. Convinced that private enterprise worked to keep costs high, he and the commission recommended the creation of a state housing bank to provide cheap credit to limited dividend private housing corporations and also a state housing board to encourage and guide construction projects by such corporations.[24]

This program, declared the commission, would provide for a truly "constructive housing policy," the only way to eventually conquer the chronic slum problem of New York and other major cities. Such a policy, however, seemed especially designed for New York City and ran into the opposition from powerful upstate interests, especially in the Republican Party. The proposal for a state housing bank was denounced as "socialistic" in the legislature, and in 1926, when the Republican legislative majority passed a housing bill, there was no provision for such a bank. Instead, the legislature created the State Housing Board, basically a fact finding agency, but in the process also repealed the section of the 1923 housing law that created the Commission on Housing and Regional Planning.[25]

Notably, there was no outcry against the termination of a major public driving force for regional planning. The reasons for this silence were complex, but they involved strong conservative opposition to both the commission and the idea of regional planning, coupled with the partly contrary fact that, in New York, regional planning seemed to be taking hold, in the form not only of the RPNY but of a new state law that encouraged the formation of regional planning agencies like the Niagara Frontier Planning Association. Perhaps the decision factor, however, was more personal: the attitude of the chairman of the commission.

From the inception of the commission, Stein had been the driving force, but by 1925 he was growing tired of the effort. In September, on board a train taking him home from California, he wrote to Mumford that his trip had gotten him to think about architecture and to realize that "form and color mean more to me than all the rest—economics, sociology, regional planning—yes—but I am an architect—or at least I used to be." He spoke of resigning early in the following year, admitting that his resignation "will give up the advantage of publicity for what we have to say," but then concluding that perhaps it was time to stop in order to develop more fully what had already been accomplished. Soon after, at one of the commission's hearings, he became embroiled in a bitter public quarrel with the president of the United Real Estate Owners' Association over rent control.[26]

In 1926 Stein made no protest when the legislature eliminated the commission, even though it meant the end of the one public agency that could sustain and direct the forces favorable to regional planning in the interests of the whole state. One result was to strengthen the influence of the privately dominated RPNY, an increasing anathema to the RPAA because of its apparent concern for promoting the growth of New York City at the expense of the proper development of the surrounding region.

By 1927 hopes for promoting real regional planning were further dashed when the cause was deprived of its original driving force, Whitaker and his *JAIA*. During the mid-1920s Whitaker suffered from both physical and mental exhaustion. His move to his Mount Olive Farm had not brought much health or contentment. He lapsed into periods of depression, as in the summer of 1923, when he wrote that "all I see hope in is in the breakdown of the industrial order and the revival of the craft traditions, by forcing men to depend on themselves and not upon machines." By 1924 he seemed on the verge of a mental breakdown. In November, writing to Mumford under the mistaken impression that he was expected to edit the *Survey Graphic* special, he explained that his mind was in such turmoil that he could not do the job. "I live from day to day in confusion worse confounded. The wiles of my enemies assume new forms every morning and resolve themselves into a dark shadow every night."[27]

In the previous two years, Whitaker had sustained himself psychologically in part through a noble friendship with the great American architect Louis Sullivan, then all but forgotten. For Whitaker, Sullivan was a heroic exception to a profession that had been dragged into "a house of prostitution" by those who treated the art of building as no more than the art of making money. Having persuaded Sullivan to write his autobiography for the *JAIA,* Whitaker spent much time on its publication, in the hope that it might have some redeeming effect. Early in 1924, while struggling with a bout of sickness, he succeeded in getting the autobiography published as a book by the AIA Press in time to get a copy of it to Sullivan as he lay dying in Chicago; in 1924, the American Institute of Graphic Arts chose it as one of its fifty outstanding books of the year.[28]

Despite its quality, the book further complicated Whitaker's relationship with leaders in the AIA. For years, there had been rising complaints about the cost of publishing the *JAIA,* which had not succeeded in paying for itself, and Whitaker's often eccentric radicalism had not made it any easier for conservatives to agree to provide support for it. In 1925 Whitaker hoped that the Sullivan autobiography and other books published by the AIA Press would make enough profits to subsidize the *JAIA,* but, as he complained to Mumford, this new effort increased his work load, "so now I am a book salesman."[29]

The new distractions weakened the quality of Whitaker's work as editor. In 1926, hoping to take advantage of Mayor Jimmy Walker's appointment of a great committee of five hundred citizens to consider ways to improve New York City, he initiated a series of articles on the city in "its numerous aspects," declaring that cities mirrored "our careless philosophy,—our faith that beauty must be deferred until pecuniary elements are satisfied." In September he opened the series with an oblique attack on the RPNY as an example of planning by "big-cityists" who were content to promote further urban congestion, and he closed it in December with the rather curiously phrased conclusion that "the increase of population is reaching a point where the means of giving it an adequate human sojourn will not be found in the old method of appropriating unsettled areas or the wholesale destruction of life through war."[30]

Although the series included articles by several RPAA members, it was weak and did nothing to save Whitaker's editorship. In 1927 the

AIA adopted a resolution that required that the *JAIA* henceforth be
"edited, published, and distributed by and from the Octagon" in Washington, D.C., and soon after, Whitaker was fired. In 1928 the *JAIA*
was itself replaced by a monthly, the *Octagon,* which had little of its
predecessor's crusading character. In August 1927 Whitaker wrote to
MacKaye with some relief that "after fifteen years I am momentarily
foot loose and fancy free," adding that his work had "been a cruel grind,
and has about worn me to a frazzle." It was the beginning of a whole
new life for Whitaker. In October the sage of Twelve Oppossum Farm
announced to MacKaye that he was uprooting himself from Mount
Olive and was soon to sail for Europe. "Maybe we'll start a T.O. Farm
in Europe somewhere and you will come over and we'll have at least a
dress rehearsal of the chapter that has passed—for we won't admit that
it has come to an end."[31] Although he was eventually to return to the
United States and was to loose one last blast on the architectural profession, his great days had passed.

The loss of two major public rallying agencies was a major defeat for
the cause of regional planning, but this loss was followed by some major
triumphs, both in theory and practice. In 1925, when he had contem-
plated retirement from the regional planning commission, Stein had said
that he was inclined to agree with the opinion of Wright, who had gone
to St. Louis, that it was time to temporarily step away from the cause and
then to "come back to it with a refreshed and critical mind."[32] Although
he and Mumford each had sensed a slowdown in the momentum of the
RPAA, they had no thoughts of abandoning it, and neither did Benton
MacKaye. Significantly, the years 1928 and 1929 brought a new spurt of
activity for these three men and some of their associates that seemed to
indicate that regional planning was entering into a second, even more
effective phase in its efforts to remake America.

IX

THE SAGE AND THE SIEGE
OF SHIRLEY CENTER:
MACKAYE

While Mumford, Stein, and most of the other members of the RPAA carried on their crusade for a regional strategy amid the intense lights and shadows of the metropolis, the one who perhaps had done the most to inspire their efforts labored quietly in the obscurity of a small New England village. After the tragic death of his wife, Jessie, in 1921, MacKaye had found his refuge and roots in his adopted home community of Shirley Center, and would rarely leave it over the next decade. He did have his temptations, especially in 1927, when he became involved, with Stein and Wright, in the planning of some experimental collective farms in Soviet Russia. He dreamed briefly that he might visit the new radical world to which he had unsuccessfully volunteered his services at the end of the war: "a trip there," he told Wright, "would certainly be a great experience, and the application of our ideas would very likely have a better chance there than elsewhere." It was Stein, however, who in the summer made a "perfectly bully trip" to Russia in these pre-Stalinist days when hopes remained for the Soviet utopia.[1]

By the mid-twenties MacKaye lived in a "little country shack" about a quarter mile north of the village common. In appearance and behavior he was becoming, as Mumford would soon describe him, "the archtypical Yankee, tall, lean, wirey, tough," a man often taciturn among strangers but a warm and colorful conversationalist in the company of those whom he considered his friends. He lived with his sister, Hazel, who was retiring from her career as a maker of reform-minded dramatic pageants; one of her last productions was an Equal Rights pageant given at three widely separated locations in 1923–24. In 1928, after years of emotional distress following her mother's death, Hazel suffered a nervous breakdown, forcing her to resort to a rest home in Great Barrington.

While their brother James assumed most of the cost of her care, Benton's limited resources were further diminished. He had already written to Mumford that he was "living here on a cave man standard with wood and water and light and every other primal element to be extracted from its source." Mumford was later to say of him that "he did not waste his time in making a living, but subsisted like Elijah, on such fodder as the ravens brought him." In fact, he struggled to support himself through a combination of writing and consulting work in forestry, often resorting to odd jobs to piece together a small income, at least once considering going "into the backwoods in search of a good job as a lumber-jack."[2]

He often urged his New York friends to visit him at Shirley Center, where "we can talk things over under real regional conditions," a reminder to his city friends that they had little direct experience with the provinces. To tempt Mumford, he offered the hope that if "we could have that 'jaw', the face of the future earth (within our own Utopias at least) would be different for it." In 1927 he dreamed that the whole RPAA might meet in Shirley Center. But he was not on the world's well-beaten track, and few came to talk. Although he spoke frequently of visiting New York City or the Hudson Guild Farm in New Jersey, he generally lacked the money if not the time to do so. "I am perhaps the richest man on earth in terms of the 'unearned increment' of wonderful friends," he wrote to Wright in 1928, "but in terms of lesser value it is different," meaning that he lacked the money even to visit his sister at Great Barrington.[3]

With the exception of money, though, he was a rich man, living an active, creative life of his own choosing. He occasionally received encouraging words from friends, including some from his old boss in the Forest Service, Raphael Zon, who wrote: "I am interested in your Regional Planning, and thank heaven that at least you can afford to remain impractible, footloose, and a free spirit. You may still achieve something in your life if you live long enough." If he were a free spirit, he could also believe that he had sunk his roots deep into the local soil. Shirley Center, as he told Chase, gave him the advantage of viewing "the industrial wilderness from a secluded perspective," and it also provided him with an immediate sense of the past. In the summer of 1927, borrowing from his sister, he was planning a pageant to revive local popular interest in the traditional culture, the leading event being "a colonial costume dance" at the town hall—this even though he had no great liking for colonial dresses on women, believing that "the present costume is the finest thing to date in history." Two years earlier he had revealed a less parochial side to his life by attending a conference on international peace; he liked the peace group so much that he hoped to get it "connected up somehow with our bunch."[4]

MacKaye continued to invest much of his time in the Appalachian Trail, an idea whose time had plainly come by the last half of the twenties. In 1925 the first Appalachian Trail Conference had met in Washington, D.C., and selected a committee to promote the development of the trail, and MacKaye committed himself actively to the effort. On more than one occasion, he led a group of students from nearby Bridgman School into the mountains, where they cut a broad trail up to a panoramic point. In 1926 he proposed to the Taconic State Park Commission, then headed by Franklin Delano Roosevelt, a plan to create a 120-mile section of the Trail from southwestern Massachusetts to Bear Mountain, attempting to organize a hiking party in support of the plan.[5]

At the same time, he continued his efforts to persuade the public of the virtues of the Trail, proclaiming it "a new approach to the problem of living, a development of outdoor community life, as an offset from the various shackles of commercial civilization." He appealed to the concern of many thinkers in the 1920s that modern civilization was subverting the freedom and the vitality of the human race. In a speech before the Blue Mountain Club in 1927, he said that the special role of his great pathway was to activate the "psychologic horsepower" that he believed had become largely dormant in most people. The same year, at the New England Trail Conference, he declared that he hoped to make the Appalachians "the site of a Barbaric Utopia," a vitalizing force against an effete civilization.[6]

Although he took a great interest in developing trails, MacKaye refused to be contented with them alone, never having lost the social side of his idealism. Writing to Mumford in 1927 regarding trail-making efforts from Virginia northward to New Hampshire, he said that he was hopeful for "a 'coup' of some kind to put the northern half of the Trail upon the map," but he added, "I want to start something on the maps besides a trail. I want to plant the seed at least of an 'activity.'" In the broadest sense, the activity was regional planning. In 1925 he had proposed to the RPAA six different planning activities relating to such things as waterpower, parks, and model communities, most associated with efforts to decentralize population away from the congested cities. Two years later, he tried unsuccessfully to get public support for a regional plan that he had drafted for New England, the key to which was, as he explained to Stein, "the conversion of surplus flow of water and the constructive flow of waterpower toward a more equitable distribution of industry."[7]

MacKaye's greatest effort was directed at completing what he intended to be his major work, *The New Exploration,* significantly subtitled "A Philosophy of Regional Planning," a work that, he said in 1923, grew "more fascinating and expansive the more I go on with it," As early as November 1922 he informed Stein that he had finished the first draft of a book on "the philosophy of our Appalachian project," meaning the importance of nature and of recreation as a refuge from the ills of what he called the "industrial wilderness." He took some special interest in recreation in its most basic sense, calling it "essentially the business of living." In 1922 he told Stein that in the book he intended to give some attention to industrial development in the hope of helping to realize the potential for release from toil furnished by machinery: "We must seek not only more space for *recreation* but more *time.*"[8]

Beyond philosophy, MacKaye also was striving to provide a more practical dimension by including a regional survey of the region he knew best, Appalachia, especially the Upper Deerfield Valley, hoping to develop "a cross-section" of the resources as well as the contours of that area. He was convinced that, along with his expertise, he was developing a vision of what society might be, one that he believed most technicians needed in order to guide their talents toward humane ends. By combining theory and practice, he hoped to provide a guiding vision that might mobilize the technicians into a phalanx for change.[9]

He had intended to complete the book in 1923 in support of the opening of the campaign for the Appalachian Trail, but it was to be another four years before he finished, during which time he was able to incorporate in it some of the new ideas, such as Giant Power, that were developing around him. He was able to benefit from Mumford's expanding work on American culture, especially in regard to the relationship between cultural and geographical influences. According to Mumford, MacKaye had confessed that it was not until he had read *The Golden Day* that he thought of reading the writings of his great predecessor, Henry Thoreau. Possibly. At the least, he did not refer to Thoreau until 1927, when he said that he was reading *Walden* and finding it wonderful. In the preface to *The New Exploration,* he noted that Thoreau and Mumford were the most frequently quoted authors in his book, declaring that the former's ideas were "the fragments (the precious stones, if you please) for building some day a structure of philosophy, for remolding human outlook on earth." Delay also exposed the book to the influence of Oswald Spengler, whose *Decline of the West* excited his interest, especially for Spengler's distinction between "culture"—something youthful, creative, and inspiring—and "civilization," the deadening final phase of a society's rise and decline. [10]

Then, too, the extra years allowed him to give more thought to regional planning itself, especially to what he meant by a region. Regional planning, he told Mumford in 1926, involved two realms. One was the realm of "play," basically the local area in which people spent most of their lives, a territory roughly within the radius of one day's drive in a motor car; his own personal realm for living was "the little region" around Shirley Center. The other realm was that dedicated to work, the realm of modern production and consumption. In contrast to the little local regions, the economic region was becoming by extension "part of an endless chain reaching to the four corners of the earth." In explaining his book to Mumford in 1927, he wrote that under the influence of industrialism civilization had "become a sort of barb-wire entanglement reaching around the world," one that threatened cultures everywhere. It was the object of his book to propose ways by which American cultures might resist the withering influence of the worldwide economy. [11]

MacKaye had first given his work the innocuous title *Regionalism* but, as he explained to a woman acquaintance, he soon retitled it *The New Exploration* "to imply action as well as comprehension." The world into which he ventured was, as he had already explained in his article for the *Survey Graphic* special, the industrial wilderness that modern man had created for himself. In an article for the *Nation* in 1926 he wrote that "industrial civilization has conquered the wilderness, but civilization turns out to be itself a wilderness," the new challenge for a new kind of explorer. Although he was aware of the larger international context of industrial development, he limited his exploration to the United States, observing that it was actually two nations in one, making it a "double-barreled" industrial power facing both East and West. One was Pacific America, stretching westward from the Rocky Mountains to California, which he mentioned in order to focus on his favorite America, the Atlantic, ranging westward to the Mississippi Valley. In his eyes, Atlantic America was becoming the world's mightiest industrial empire, with Appalachia as its great powerhouse, the source of its energy and mineral resources. It was basically the relationship between this Appalachian powerhouse and the urbanized portions of Atlantic America that MacKaye chose to explore.[12]

Environment was MacKaye's key interest, being, as he saw it, "the breadth of life" for humankind, "the pervasive source of man's true living." Ideally, it was the habitat that not only provided for man's physical needs but nurtured his spiritual development. Environment was especially the product of geological and human forces, "the contour of the landscape, the arrangement of its vegetation, the visible marks of man's clearings and fences and farms and gardens and cities as well as in wild forests and mountain areas." The true basis for civilization was what MacKaye called the "indigenous environment," which embraced both the "primeval" (physical nature) and the "colonial" (man's traditional culture), the ideal being the New England village, like Shirley Center, a human community directly in touch with nature. The indigenous was broad enough to include not only forests and farms and villages but even cities, for "the city is a community *par excellence* . . . the village grown up." It was the indigenous that gave spiritual form and force to civilization as well as providing the material energy. So long as it maintained its health, human society would have both the creative energy and physical power needed to resolve its problems and to create the basis for individual happiness and virtue.[13]

Unfortunately, the indigenous was being threatened by the invasion of an antagonistic environment, the "metropolitan," which was spilling out from the congested, overblown urban centers. Where the indigenous was harmonious and quietly suited to man's nature, the metropolitan was "unnatural, cacophonous." Where the indigenous was a multiverse of distinct local environments suited to man's diverse nature, the metropolitan was a mechanical, standardizing influence that threatened to reduce everything throughout the world to one dead level of "monotonous, standardized, mechanized uniformity." The metropolitan environment was evident not only in the overblown cities but in their drab suburbs and in the strands of commercial ugliness along the highways that radiated from them, a blight spreading into the once isolated indigenous world of Appalachia. Even the national parks were not safe. In 1925 MacKaye suggested that the RPAA take a hand in an upcoming survey of Shenandoah National Park, agreeing with a friend's warning that, without the right program, "we shall have not an Appalachia but a Coney Island."[14]

For MacKaye, the principal task of regional planning was to repel the metropolitan invasion and to restore the health of the indigenous world. Typically, he saw this task as basically an engineering effort to redirect the dominant forces of the times. As an early example of regional engineering, he pointed to the work of the United States Forest Service, where experts had not only developed a system of forest culture but had tried to control the flow of water within their domain. The metropolitan invasion, in his view, was a flow to be contained by regional planners, especially the flow of population. In a general way, the rate of flow could be controlled by reducing the birthrate—he had long been interested in birth control and he agreed when a friend declared that his whole thesis could be reduced to it, but he decided not to emphasize it in the book in order to avoid getting entangled, as he explained privately, "in a web of sex and eugenics discussion." Instead, he warned that the most immediate task was to protect what remained of the indigenous world from the "flood suddenly set loose from a thousand ruptured reservoirs," that is, from the metropolitan centers. [15]

Assuming that population, "like water, follows the channels that have been laid for it," he proposed that its movement be limited and directed by the construction of the equivalent of dams and levees, using the existing topography of an area whenever possible. Hill and mountain lands were to be protected from development by reserving them for forestry and recreation along the lines of his plans for the Appalachian Trail. Since metropolitan population tended to follow the roads and highways laid in the valleys, its flow was to be restrained by creating a series of "open ways" along the major road systems, actually strips of land closed to any kind of metropolitan development. [16]

More positively, MacKaye proposed that steps be taken to absorb the spreading population into indigenous settings, especially by developing what he called "regional cities," explaining that the term was intended to denote a combination of "the natural region and the true city." In its hypothetical form, each would consist of a central city of some 40,000 people surrounded by as many as sixty villages, where more than a third of the regional city's population would live with the comforts and opportunity made possible by electricity to be furnished by Giant Power. With its intervening hills, rivers, and lakes, each regional city would constitute a semiautonomous local world of numerous community units strong enough to resist the metropolitan invasion and to provide a healthful environment for modern Americans. [17]

He was willing to declare that his aim was "making a utopia of reconstruction—the remodeling of an unshapen and cacaphonous environment into a harmonious and well-ordered one." If the aim was utopian, the means were practical, social equivalents of the techniques he had employed in stream and forest management. *The New Exploration* was intended to be a practical book that laid out a system of what he viewed as "regional engineering," which, more pretentiously, at the suggestion of Patrick Geddes he was coming to call "geotechnics."[18]

As ever, he tried to bring philosophy into local action. In 1927 he spoke of a project embracing both Shirley Center and the Wampack Mountain Range some twenty miles away, viewing the two as "complementary halves of a complete whole." Much of this would encourage activity on the local portion of the Appalachian Trail, facilitating the development of what he called "outdoor culture," while much of the rest of the project would involve efforts to revive the communal culture of Shirley Center by renewing the town's consciousness of its unique history. With the right tools employed by skilled men under the right philosophy, it would be possible to regulate and stabilize the relationship between indigenous and metropolitan America, answering the basic question of "how may man's work upon the Earth's surface be rendered more pleasing and less vile?"[19]

Like most authors, MacKaye hoped that his book would convert the world to his manner of thinking and, like them, he achieved considerably less. The handful of reviews of it were generally positive. Most reviewers praised it as both timely and original. "Coming as it does upon the heels of change in American life from a rural to an urban economy," wrote one, "the book offers a stimulating and interesting introduction to the problem of comprehensive planning." MacKaye's friend and fellow RPAA member Chase best appreciated its practical character, declaring in the *Nation* that it was "not the cry of the back-to-nature prophet. Modern technology is accepted; the machine is regarded as something to be tamed rather than banished. It is the first large-scale attempt that I have seen to plan an environment where genuine culture and recreation may flourish." MacKaye was especially pleased with Chase's conclusions and also with the comment of his old friend from the Forest Service, Raphael Zon, that his philosophy was "nothing else but a working plan applied to entire communities."[20]

The New Exploration, however, did not catch fire either with the general public or with the planning profession, being too abstruse for the one and too remote from the practical problems of city planning for the other. Still, MacKaye could find glimmers of hope, not only in Wright's New York State report but also in a Massachusetts plan to control the metropolitan flood then being worked out by the Governor's Committee on the Needs and Uses of Open Spaces. The principal task of the governor's committee, he wrote, was to locate future public parks, forests, and other kinds of public space so as to form a series of "dikes" to control the metropolitan flow from Boston and other centers of population. In the work of this group he saw the beginnings of "a war map" that would ultimately govern planning decisions throughout New England.[21]

In late 1928 he thought that he might be able to persuade the Naugatuck Valley Chamber of Commerce in Connecticut to employ him in drafting a regional plan. Declaring that the valley furnished strong opportunities for effective planning, he proposed that public parks and forests be developed on its hillsides and that future construction, limited to the valley floor, be regulated. He realized the importance in a democracy of public consent, and so he proposed that any plan developed by him be submitted first to the chamber of commerce and similar organizations for their consideration and then, following a campaign of public education, the final plan be put up for popular vote. His offer was ignored, but he pushed on, ever willing to advance public appreciation of geotechnics. He even expressed the hope in 1929 that the new president, Herbert Hoover—"our first engineer President"—might be persuaded to provide a positive answer to the question "can the vision of the engineer control the excesses of science?"[22]

The immediate future brought few victories for his big idea of regional engineering. On the other hand, he did capture some popular interest in one special element of his planning, an element that, like the recreational aspect of his Appalachian Trail plan, was practical and focused enough to catch the public eye. This was the "townless highway," a plan that anticipated the interstate highways of a later time, although typically, when it was finally implemented, it produced results directly contrary to what MacKaye had intended. Eventually, these highways would complete the dismantling of the old America, whereas MacKaye developed his plan out of his own deep interest in preserving one special bit of the indigenous world, Shirley Center.

In his more optimistic moments he could say in reference to places like Shirley Center that "the New England community is yet a potent force," one he hoped to revitalize. In May 1927, writing to Mumford in regard to *The New Exploration,* he declared his intention to restore the town's "communal environment," researching its history and using the result to create a series of activities, including a folk play, that would deepen the devotion of the people to their common locale. As he explained to a fellow Yankee planner, Edward T. Hartman, "if we would build up an indigenous setting we must first build up an indigenous psychology." Before he could mobilize the forces of traditionalism, however, the metropolitan invasion reached Shirley Center in the form, as he told Mumford, of "two or three prospective bungaloes." The threat that some "bungaloed agglomeration" might soon overwhelm the old town convinced him that he and his neighbors must act to defend their environment. Was Shirley Center, he asked, to be "Babbitted or salvaged"?[23]

The key to this problem was the automobile, a rapidly spreading threat for all manner of planners. The auto seemed to be everywhere, often simply as useless junk. Chase said that in one rural area north of New York City, "in half a mile of what was once a wild, primitive backlane, lovely with cliffs, hemlock and birch, I counted twenty-six abandoned cars, each with its encircling sprawl of tires, torn curtains, shattered glass." Wherever there were highways, he wrote, junk was accumulating, and "the whole country is crossed and double-crossed with these scabrous trails." In varying ways, said MacKaye, "the centuries-old balance of environment was being upset today by the invasion of the motor-car." It was the car, with its unequalled mobility, that provided the unprecedented means for the metropolis to spread its influence, especially in the form not only of "bungaloes" but of gas stations, roadside stands, and advertising billboards.[24]

MacKaye was not as antagonistic to the automobile as were his friends Whitaker, who agonized over its "barbaric invasion," and Mumford, who resolutely refused to learn how to drive one, but his concern over the metropolitan siege of Shirley Center led him to give special attention to means of controlling the auto's effects. Initially, he looked to zoning, which during the 1920s seemed to have much promise as a planning tool. In *The New Exploration* he had made note of a proposal in Massachusetts to zone the state's highways so as to control such "malignant growths" as filling stations and billboards, and he thought of persuading Shirley Center to require builders to "erect structures in harmony with Massachusetts and not with Florida." More broadly, he said that every town's growth should be guided by a plan shaped to its own special character, which for communities like Shirley Center meant "symmetry, simplicity, hominess, not stragliness, complexity, 'Main-Street-ness.' "[25] In the late 1920s, however, his hopes shifted from zoning to something more dynamic: an equivalent to the Appalachian Trail designed to control the movement of the automobile.

He laid out his thinking in a notable article, "The Townless Highway," published by the *New Republic* in March 1930. Basically, towns like Shirley Center were to be protected from the metropolitan invasion by routing major highways around rather than through them. The idea of bypass roads was nothing new, but MacKaye developed the idea in a significantly new way. He began by declaring that the existing highway policy was founded on the wrong premise: that highways were simply new forms of the old roads for carriages and wagons, when in fact they should be viewed more as the equivalent of railroads, that is, thoroughfares to be separated from any kind of activity other than the transportation of people and goods. The automobile was a new kind of locomotive whose power of speedy movement was to be facilitated by the removal of all obstructions from its path.

In practice, this meant the elimination of all grade crossings and the limitation of the number of points of access to the highway. It also meant strict zoning to eliminate any sprawl of service stations and other roadside facilities that not only disrupted traffic flow but defaced nature. Rights-of-way were to be landscaped on either side, and roadside facilities were to be limited to specified locations, much as were stations on a railroad. Ideally, MacKaye wanted the construction of separate roads for passenger and freight traffic so that the one form of movement would not obstruct the other. Although this concern for facilitating traffic was real, he also maintained his primary interest in turning back the metropolitan invasion. Existing towns like Shirley Center were to be protected by running the main roads around rather than through them, allowing them to survive as indigenous environments. To provide for the population expected to spread out along the highways, new planned towns were to be constructed off the highways, each separated from the other so that each could function as a real community and not become part of the metropolitan smear.[26]

Soon after he first published this plan, MacKaye wrote privately that his aim was to provide a defense against "the tendency of towns to flow together through the modern motor route and to form throughout the country one standardized metropolitan framework." As a defense, he hoped to create a "wall" around every town, "a sharply defined zone of open territory and having a 'thickness' measured if possible in miles: motor routes would cross this territory but all buildings thereon would be confined to carefully limited groups around 'stations.'" In an article published in the same year by *American City Magazine* he gave a more local focus to his thinking by urging Harvard, Massachusetts, to reverse its decision to allow the construction of a main highway through its center. Harvard could either elect to turn itself into a junction,

"thus helping her decline as a home neighborhood and her transition as
a second-rate emporium. Or else she can definitely separate these functions and obtain excellence in each."[27]

The townless highway idea excited MacKaye's ambitions. In 1930 he
tried to turn his article into a book, inspired by the hope that he could
persuade the federal government to support his highway policy. The
year before he had told Stein that his new plan was a complement to the
Appalachian Trail and more: "There is only one place for an Appalachian Trail but there are several places on the map for an experimental
Townless Highway," including projected routes from Chicago to Boston and from Boston to Washington, D.C. "The whole point is to make
use of the Federal-aided public roads to control future policy in laying
out State highways."[28]

A few months after the publication of his *New Republic* article he sent
Stein a copy of a complex bill he hoped Congress would enact as an
amendment to the Federal Highway Act of 1916, the basis of national
highway policy. If the bill had been enacted, it would have radically
altered the future course of urban development, having a strong influence both on land usage and on population distribution. "My conception of the Townless Highway," MacKaye told an inquirer, "is of a
means primarily of migration and only incidentally of transportation."
Among the bill's various provisions detailing his plan was one that
typified his most basic thinking, declaring that any lands, "the use and
value of which is affected by the federal road, shall be laid out in
accordance with some suitable plan or plans having in view the growth
of distinct communities as distinguished from linear roadside development, and the architecture of all buildings (commercial, industrial,
residental, or other) erected within such settlements or developments
shall be considered an integral element of any such plan or plans." His
prewar hopes for government-constructed logging communities had
acquired new and more complex forms.[29]

To strengthen his cause MacKaye enlisted the support of Mumford
who, when he first learned of the idea, had written that "my imagination already sees you down in Washington, switching the highways."
In 1929 Mumford had publicly complained of the perverse magic that
had transformed "an era of bad roads that led fairly often through
interesting country, into an era of good roads that began in one big city
and get lost in the jumble of the next." He responded to MacKaye's
urgings by joining him in writing a new article on the townless
highway, which appeared in *Harpers Magazine* in August 1931. The
article began with a lamentation over "the vast sprawling metropolitan

slum of multiple gas stations and hot-dog stands" and ended with a call for the federal government to apply the principles of the townless highway so as to assure that its money would be spent in "weaving together a national system" founded on "a genuine recognition of the motor revolution."[30]

MacKaye's new crusade, however, had less effect than his previous crusade for the Appalachian Trail. He thought he had won the endorsement of Charles Davis, president of the National Highways Association, but just at that time Davis was seriously injured in a traffic accident. Beginning in late 1930 MacKaye tried to persuade Congressman Robert Crossner to submit his highway bill to Congress. Since this was the same congressman who had introduced his colonization bill fifteen years before, he had reason to expect some action on his new proposal, the real point of which, he told the congressman, was "to guide the population's distribution, and hence the rebuilding of the country." Crossner, however, could not be convinced that the idea had compelling importance at a time of deepening depression, when people were starving to death.[31]

MacKaye tried to carry on his propaganda campaign, hoping both to finish his book on townless highways and to sell enough articles on the subject to, as he told Mumford, keep him in "shirts and sandwiches," and as late as November 1932 he was able to publish a short piece in the *Survey Graphic* advocating a scheme to turn abandoned railroad rights-of-way into highways that would allow people to "go safely, speedily, and without nuisance" from Boston to Atlanta and elsewhere. He had little success. Although he continued to campaign for a townless highway around Boston throughout most of the 1930s, the depression years virtually extinguished his dream of creating a great national system governed by his principles.[32]

In 1929 MacKaye had declared that the "combined movement of things and folk is nothing less than the flow of a particular species of civilization" and had proclaimed the control of that movement "the greatest of engineering problems." The townless highway and the Appalachian Trail were important instruments in regional engineering for the attainment of larger ends than traffic movement and hiking. Ultimately, the great end was to preserve and revive a strongly traditional world, scaled to human size, one that resembled the timber communities with which he had started his social dreaming years before:

> Thus the timber cut each year would be reduced to the growth each
> year; cattle on the hoof would be reduced in numbers to retain a grass

sod which would support a steady yield of milk and beef; electric
power generated in modest voltage from obscure and minor dams
could turn the wheels of obscure but efficient smokeless factories. Such
slow but sure economy, based on up-to-date machinery, might become
the basis of a series of small unobtrusive and truly lovable communities into which the "backflow" of population [from the big cities]
might be guided.[33]

Along with New England towns like Shirley Center, such communities formed the ground of MacKaye's social imagination, but he also
was attuned to the larger urban world through his friends in New York.
There, his fellow members of the RPAA were working out their own
version of the same dream to fundamentally alter the urban landscape.
This version too promised success—only to be defeated by the Great
Depression.

X

SUNNYSIDE AND RADBURN: STEIN, WRIGHT, AND ALEXANDER M. BING

Stein had a personal reason for acquiescing to the abrupt disbanding of the Commission of Housing and Regional Planning in 1926. Although it had been a rewarding experience with significant results for regional planning, his chairmanship of the commission had detracted from his work as an architect, which he was anxious to pursue. After 1925 Stein developed a diversified practice, listing among his works two hospitals in New York, buildings for the California Institute of Technology, and the Lavenburg Homes, a privately funded low-income apartment complex in New York. He also was involved with his partner Kohn in developing ambitious plans for the Fieldston School, the million-dollar school complex for the Ethical Culture Society to be located in Riverdale on the outskirts of New York City. In the mid-1920s, Stein also gave time to developing plans for model farms in the Soviet Union.[1]

Whatever he did, however, Stein remained true to his earlier concern for New York's chronic housing problem, a problem that stubbornly refused to go away. By the mid-1920s, even after a spurt of housing construction in the city, many New Yorkers lacked access to decent housing. In 1925 Frank Mann, the tenement-house commissioner, estimated that there were some 30,000 vacant apartments in the city but that their rents were too steep for the 69 percent of city families who had incomes of $2,500 or less. A year later, the new State Housing Board said that under existing conditions new dwelling units could not be built at less than a monthly rent of $10 per room, beyond the incomes of 60 to 70 percent of families. As Stein pointed out, this problem was not limited to the poor and working classes, since many members of the middle class, including teachers and other professionals, were being forced out of Manhattan by their inability to find affordable housing there.[2]

For people like Stein, it seemed evident that the problem demanded some radical solution, but what could be done? For those who had hopes of turning utopia into reality, the matter of means was an important question. In the past those who sought to remake society had often adopted communitarian means, the creation of voluntary cooperative communities, but by the 1920s faith in this approach had been seriously weakened.[3] New means had to be devised, ones especially suited to the strivings of the professional and technical classes as they worked to gain significant influence over their changing times. For the RPAA, the question was complicated by its ambiguous attitude toward government and business, the two great forces for change.

Regarding government, the RPAA's emphasis on comprehensive planning pointed strongly to some active governmental presence to implement the plan. On the other hand, their suspicions of politics and politicians isolated them from the decision-making process. The ideal was implementation through state-appointed commissions like Stein's housing and regional planning commission—agencies designed to be insulated from politics—but the CHRP at least was not insulated enough to prevent its termination by the state legislature. Regarding business, the RPAA believed that a shortsighted, selfish profit motive was the essential cause of modern miseries. And yet in the 1920s, as at least some members recognized, business was proving itself the most powerful and creative force for change.

What then could be done? For answers, the RPAA looked to Europe, but not always in the same way. Edith Wood, a leading authority on housing, urged the United Stated to follow the lead of European governments in developing a "constructive" housing program, furnishing what was needed both to clear away slums and to make good housing cheap enough for the all of the working classes to afford. Although she did not completely ignore regional planning, her main interest was in providing a direct public solution to the housing problem under existing circumstances. She helped prepare the way for the New Deal housing program of the next decade.[4]

Most of the RPAA, however, leaned toward solutions that were both more conservative and more radical than Wood's, being less willing either to trust government or to work within the existing order. In the early 1920s, for instance, Stein had tinkered with the already well-worn attempt to design "model" apartment houses to be constructed by private enterprise. In 1920, convinced that slum housing was not being replaced fast enough, he had supported a competition for the best plan to remodel existing tenements. In the same year he had drawn up a plan for a garden apartment complex in the Bronx that would house six families on a 65- by 150-foot lot, providing each apartment with its own entrance, thereby preserving, wrote an observer, "the old American idea of individuality and privacy." He had also worked up a plan for a larger garden complex to house ninety-two families on one city block. Such large-scale projects promised to be cheaper to build than piecemeal construction by small builders, and they opened the way for the more efficient use of building sites.[5]

Stein, however, had little confidence that good design alone would provide decent homes at prices most New Yorkers could afford so long as housing was subject to speculation and an uncontrolled profit motive. Building houses to sell rather than for living had produced both shoddy construction and the inefficient use of land and materials. The situation had been made worse by the high interest rates demanded on private loans for construction.

As his preferred solution, Stein dreamed of organizing those who needed housing to provide their own homes through cooperative action. Workers, for instance, might organize to build large-scale housing projects that they would own and operate collectively. Such efforts would not only cut housing costs but reduce the burdens of housekeeping for women by way of cooperative laundries and "meals cooked at a central point." Unfortunately for this dream, few people seemed willing to make the sacrifices required for a successful cooperative. In 1925 Stein wrote that one group to whom he had advocated cooperative action "seemed impressed for a moment with the opportunity of cutting costs, but then one of the members asked 'Will the houses sell well? If we build cooperatively can we sell and make our profit?' "[6]

He found greater hope in the English Garden City movement, which emphasized large-scale, well-planned projects by way of limited-dividend private corporations backed by government. By limiting dividends, it seemed possible to eliminate the speculative impulse from housing while drawing on the profit motive. By 1924 the limited dividend company that before the war had built England's first garden city, Letchworth, was ready to pay a 5 percent dividend to investors, leading Stein to conclude that a similar project in America would "make a tremendous success."[7]

In 1923 Stein and Wright began to draft a plan for a community of 25,000 people to be located in South Brooklyn on a square mile of land, nearly a third of which was devoted to parks, recreation, gardening, and industry. Housing consisted of a mix of apartment houses and row houses supported by shopping and social facilities. They were especially proud of their success in substituting for the conventional grid street plan a layout that reduced the area required for streets from one third to one quarter of the whole acreage. Before the plan could be implemented, however, the land was acquired for private development under the ordinary profit system.[8]

Disappointment, however, soon gave way to success, beginning with the creation of an effective instrument for garden city development. The Brooklyn project had brought Wright and Stein into close association with Alexander M. Bing, a successful real estate developer. Semi-retired from Bing and Bing, a million-dollar development firm, Bing was persuaded by Stein to lend his talents to efforts to resolve the housing problem. Bing was one successful entrepreneur who supported the interests of workers. In 1921, during a time of reaction against organized labor, he advocated trade unions, collective bargaining, and the minimum wage as the basis for industrial peace. Bing had little interest in regional planning per se, but he provided the RPAA with some important skills it lacked, especially in the raising of money. He was accustomed to financing big projects. In 1922, for instance, his firm began a fourteen-story apartment house on Park Avenue and Eighty-fifth Street. In 1924 he pondered the bankruptcy of the National British Building Guild, which he called "the largest modern experiment in worker control of production outside of Russia," and concluded that the failure resulted from inadequate managerial skills.[9]

Like other housers, he took an interest in European developments, eventually becoming a vice president of the International Federation City and Town Planning, but he believed that foreign examples had to be adapted to American conditions, notably the absence of strong habits of cooperation among American workers, higher expectations regarding the size and quality of housing, and resistance to common ownership of land. He also recognized the greater American hostility to government, but during the governorship of Alfred Smith he did hope to persuade New York State to provide private limited-dividend corporations with low-interest loans and the power to condemn slum properties.

Using his business skills and contacts, Bing took the lead in forming the City Housing Corporation (CHC), a limited-dividend company incorporated in March 1924 to build "better homes and communities." Among its members were Felix Adler, head of the Ethical Culture Society (of which Kohn was a prominent member), the noted progressive reformer Richard T. Ely, John Elliot of the Hudson Guild, Eleanor Roosevelt, and several investment bankers. As president of the CHC Bing promised that the new company would operate "along strictly business lines," but that business was the idealistic one of creating "the Future Garden Cities of America."

Those who purchased its $100 shares were to receive a share of the profits limited to 6 percent. Bing expected this limited-dividend approach would substantially reduce the interest charges on money borrowed for construction—a major element in overall housing costs—thereby making it possible for the CHC to meet the need for good inexpensive housing. There were numerous investors in the corporation, including RPAA members Ackerman, Bing, Stein, and Wood, and it was soon able to raise more than $1 million through the sale of its shares, the largest sale being $150,000 worth in 1925 to John D. Rockefeller.[10]

The CHC moved quickly, in 1924 acquiring a seventy-acre tract in Queens from the Pennsylvania Railroad. Although it was not large enough for a complete garden city, the tract, located within fifteen minutes subway ride of downtown New York, was suited for large-scale residential development, not the least because, having been originally zoned for industrial use, it did not include any constricting residential zoning requirements. Unfortunately, the CHC was forced by the city to impose the grid system of streets and rectangular blocks on its property, limiting its freedom to plan, but Bing had assembled a team of talented designers headed by Stein and Wright who made the best of the situation. The result was Sunnyside Gardens.[11]

Stein and Wright were a complementary pair of dedicated planners. Stein took charge of designing the buildings, a mix of one-, two-, and three-family row houses and some apartment buildings based on his preferred cooperative principles. He believed that a good planner could anticipate what people wanted even when they did not know themselves, a belief that was soon challenged by a general lack of enthusiasm for his cooperative apartments. Wright concentrated on the context for Stein's buildings, especially the layout of the land, streets, and supporting utilities, driven by the conviction that bad site planning wasted much space and inflated the cost of housing. In 1921, in Whitaker's

JAIA, he proposed replacing what he called "the old stupid prosaic way of lining up our houses in monstrous rows" with an imaginative plan for urban housing that provided both variety and extensive open space. In the summer of 1924 he and Stein spent three weeks in England, devoting most of their time to studying the garden cities, and returned, as Stein put it, "more enthusiastic than ever about the possibility of developing a Garden City here."[12]

By the end of 1924, the two men and their associates (who included Ackerman) were able to complete the first phase of Sunnyside Gardens, and two years later the CHC could report that it had constructed a "complete community with homes for 650 families." Although it did not include affordable housing for the truly poor, it did provide for much diversity: there were one-family houses for sale at $883 down and $66.78 a month, along with two-family houses for $1180 down and, after subtracting the rent the owner could expect to collect, $29.87 a month. For renters, there were similar houses as well as apartments. These places tended to be rather small, reflecting the effort to reduce costs, but in compensation they covered only 30 percent of the tract, leaving the rest to be developed as open green space. "Instead of unsightly backyards cluttered with clothes poles and fences," boasted the CHC, "a new block plan provides artistically landscaped central garden courts." Each block of homes looked inward on a central court with a playground, lawns, and gardens, a miniature neighborhood especially designed for families with children. For the whole community there were tennis courts and a three-acre park, the latter dedicated in May 1926 by Mayor Jimmy Walker. And all of this was within fifteen minutes of downtown Manhattan.[13]

Sunnyside Gardens attracted especially young middle-class and professional people fleeing from the crowded conditions of Manhattan and Brooklyn. In early 1926 a study revealed that of 168 residents, 108 had incomes between $2,000 and $4,000, with the rest equally divided between those earning less and those earning more than those figures. Among the settlers were Mumford, his wife, Sophia, and his young son, Geddes, who arrived in September 1925, among the relative few to take a cooperative apartment. The Mumfords enjoyed the sense of community that developed between them and their fellow pioneers, and they took much pleasure in the green open spaces. Mumford recalled that in the fully developed site "you might follow a footpath through a network of gardens and green lawns for almost half-a-mile, with all sorts of charming vistas." Even before Mumford had moved in, he had taken MacKaye on a walk through early

Sunnyside, leading MacKaye to proclaim to Stein that "you have planted the seed of a new era."[14]

Sunnyside did not persuade MacKaye to abandon Shirley Center, nor did it keep the Mumfords from eventually moving to a rural village out of the city. However, it did attract numerous buyers and renters, making it an economic success sufficient to excite Bing and other members of the RPAA to dreams of creating a full-fledged garden city shaped to American conditions. In less than five years, a corporation that began with less than $1 million in capital was able to build and sell nearly $8 million of good housing. It was in reference to the CHC that the *New York Times* declared that "the desert that man has made in the environs of New York needs some all-powerful colonizer who can enjoin on those who reclaim it the necessity of planning today for making each community into a little oasis bright with lawns, flowers, trees, and parks." Soon, the *Times* could also say that, benefitting from economies of scale and from new construction techniques, the CHC was able to redeem the wilderness and make money in the bargain. In little more than a year, sales of Sunnyside houses (with the exception of the cooperative apartments) were good enough to produce a small profit and to persuade the CHC to increase its total capital from $2 million to $5 million.[15]

Bing was a man of big visions and great enthusiasms. He was so busy with Sunnyside in the summer of 1925, reported Stein, that "it was impossible to talk with him about anything else." He gave some attention to matters of design, at one point urging efforts to reduce housing costs by developing "a machine-made house," but his special interests were in finance. As early as the special regional-planning issue of the *Survey Graphic* in May 1925 (the same month in which the CHC had decided to more than double its capital), he had asked "can we have garden cities in America?" and he had answered "yes." He acknowledged that there were formidable problems to be resolved, especially how to acquire the $10 to $25 million required to build such a city, but he was convinced that the money was there, and he was determined to get it. At one point, he proposed that philanthropic endowments, which he estimated as involving some $3.5 billion dollars, be invested in limited-dividend housing; at another, he urged insurance companies to set aside 5 percent of their $18 billion in assets for the same purpose.

Bing actively sought the direct cooperation of the RPAA in developing a scheme for a complete city. Although the CHC and the planning association were distinct operations there were close ties between them. Bing had served as the first head of the RPAA as well as president of the

CHC, and three members of the RPAA (Stein, Wright, and Ackerman) were his chief designers. In addition, Ackerman, Bing, Stein, and Wood held stock in the CHC, while Ackerman, Kohn, Stein, and Wright all served on its board of advisors, and Mumford lived in its first creation, Sunnyside. Bing could count on their support, especially from Stein, who told Wood that he was convinced that Sunnyside had provided the experience needed to make an authentic garden city: "I feel certain that we can make a tremendous financial success of the Garden City, if that were the object. Socially, I think we can do much to improve conditions."[16]

In June 1926 Bing convened a meeting with MacKaye, Whitaker, Wright, Bruere, Chase, and Stein, held in the City Club, and spoke of the need for greater understanding of the problems arising from the construction of a new town. It was agreed they would launch an investigation of the matter, initiating what was described in the RPAA minutes as an analysis of the "physical equipment of the garden or regional city," including not only housing but "buildings for industrial, governmental, educational, cultural, recreational, religious, and social purposes." Little seems to have been done, however, until 1927, when in April Bing informed the RPAA that the CHC was searching for a property large enough for a major "new housing development" and had not been able to find a site within New York City.[17]

Later in the year, on October 8 and 9, Stein convened a special meeting of the RPAA at the Hudson Guild Farm in New Jersey primarily to discuss the characteristics of a garden city. This was to be an informal conference that would not be expected to produce definitive answers. Twenty-two people attended, both regular members and their wives and several invited guests prominent in the housing and planning fields. Stein opened the discussion by asking a leading question: what was best, a "satellite city" heavily dependent on some great metropolitan center for its needs, including employment, or a largely autonomous "regional city" with its own businesses and jobs?

The conferees soon agreed not to make a definite commitment with the aim of "playing it safe in the first large venture in the direction of the garden city," but their inclinations were plain. Convinced that a massive decentralization of economic activity as well as of population was necessary to resolve the problems of modern urban America, most wanted the regional city. Much of the discussion focused, therefore, on the cultural and industrial composition of the project. How, for instance, to make it a culturally interesting place that could counter the attractions of the metropolis? It was suggested that a small college be established and that there be at least one movie theater as part of a general provision for popular entertainment, but no one seemed to have clear answers and the subject soon was dropped.[18]

Far more interesting to the group was the matter of establishing industries to provide internal employment opportunities. Here was the key to preventing the city from simply becoming a dependent dormitory suburb available only to the more advantaged classes. Concerned that low-wage industries would attract poor people and lead to the creation of slum conditions, however, the conferees emphasized the need to introduce skilled industries paying a wage scale "adequate to the garden city standard of living." Stein argued the importance of skilled jobs to good housing conditions, as did Mumford, who warned that with low-wage industries, "the garden city would have a shanty-town on its outskirts." The stress on the desirability of skilled labor introduced the question as to whether the new city would be open to labor unions or not. Mumford warned that to make it an "open shop town" would be to convince labor leaders that industrial decentralization threatened their interests and so "would lose the cooperation of the very groups needed to make the garden city industrially successful."[19]

The overall social composition of the new city was a major theme of the conference. The group seemed to agree with Wright when he said that ideally the population should number no more than 50,000 in order to avoid the need for an expensive mass-transit system, but they were less certain as to who would constitute the population. At a time when northern cities confronted a huge migration of black Americans from the South, it was not surprising that the question of race should appear. The all-white group was inclined against the admission of blacks in the beginning, but John Elliot of the Hudson Guild declared that it would be a "great mistake" if such an exclusion were made permanent policy. This in turn raised the question of racial segregation within the community, but Mumford soon shifted the discussion to the more comfortable question of class: was there to be class segregation by creating neighborhoods designed for different income levels?

Wright announced that he was opposed to any clearly defined class segregation, arguing that since, ideally, all houses would be substantially built and well-designed, differences in income would be much less a matter of exterior appearance than of interior appointments; that is, with some exceptions, there would be a general mixing of classes. In this discussion there seemed to be general agreement that, with the exception of the poor, several classes would be included; that the community would not be for workers alone. Stein was later to say that some more affluent residents were needed there in order to pay for the schools and other public services.[20]

Beyond the matter of social composition, the conferees gave attention to three interlocking matters of general policy. One involved the question of landownership and control. In England the land occupied by the garden city was owned by the community and directly subject to public control, but in America public ownership, especially of land not used for public purposes, was likely to be ruled unconstitutional. It was decided, therefore, that initially the CHC would own the land, leasing it to house owners, until a way to municipal ownership could be found. The second matter involved the nature and timing of popular involvement in the governance of the city. Although all agreed that the CHC would eventually have to turn political control over to the people, there was varied enthusiasm for the idea, some arguing that effective democracy would encourage inhabitants to take a responsible role in the experiment, while others thought that it might lead to conflicts over company policy and to what one member called a "sacrifice of efficiency."[21]

Even more basic was the question of how to maintain the integrity of the original design over the long run, with or without public ownership. How to protect the garden city from the destructive influences of human greed and social change? Wright argued that the very virtues of a good layout would work to maintain it, especially if they were reinforced by the right zoning requirements. Another member wondered, however, whether it would be possible to preserve the design in a changing world without eventually creating "a static or dead city." Ackerman replied that most changes in a growing city originated not from functional needs but from the desire to make speculative profits, his argument being the essentially Georgist one that the exclusion of any opportunity to make money through speculation in property was the best way to assure stability. Virtually all conferees agreed that some kind of regulation to protect the experiment was needed, but it was evident that they did not agree on what actually would be required.[22]

The conference produced no great overarching vision, but it did at least confirm three basic policy assumptions. One was that the traditional garden-city form, derived from the English experience of the late nineteenth century, would have to be radically revised in an American society being revolutionized by the automobile. Another was that earlier hopes for providing a place for the truly poor would have to be abandoned; in the absence of any public subsidies the experiment would have to be limited to those who could pay. The third assumption was that, without the poor, a garden city was feasible under existing conditions.

The October conference was soon followed by a major decision. In the summer of 1927 the CHC had secretly begun to buy up a tract of truck gardening land in the Borough of Fairlawn in northern New Jersey, using money derived from the sale of some 20 acres of its Sunnyside property that it had decided not to develop. In January 1928 it announced that it had succeeded in purchasing 1,005 acres for its projected city, which was given the concocted name of "Radburn." The land was located only ten miles from New York City and three miles from the industrial city of Paterson. The cost of the new development was estimated to be between $50 and $60 million.[23]

Not everyone greeted this announcement with enthusiasm. Although he had been one of the most active participants in the October conference, Mumford did not like the project. In February 1927 he had already stated his view in the *JAIA* that the money and effort demanded by the actual construction of a garden city could only be at the expense of the larger movement to convert the general public to support garden cities and regional planning. Such an effort, Mumford warned, would likely fail, because it would be an isolated act of defiance against the existing way of thinking about society. When he learned of the land purchases, he told MacKaye that he did not expect "much good to come out of the new venture," adding that it seemed ironic that good land for truck gardening should be sacrificed to an effort to build a garden city. Years later, he would say that, when the RPAA turned to practical experiments like Radburn, "with my lack of professional status I could only be an understanding outsider."[24]

Even Mumford, however, could soon proclaim that the project was at least "a very useful stopgap" and an advance over existing city planning. And others expressed greater enthusiasm. The *New York Times* said that Radburn could be "a pioneer of the 'new city' to which many minds have been turning as a cure for the congestion of centralized industry." Chase, who could claim to be an objective observer since he was one RPAA member who paid little attention to garden cities, declared that the character of Radburn both as the first major experiment in decentralization and as a town planned for the Motor Age "makes it perhaps the most significant undertaking in community planning which this country has seen." The project also won the endorsement of Thomas Adams and others involved in developing the RPNY.[25]

The CHC moved quickly. Since Bing expected no public financial support for his $60 million project, he concentrated on raising the necessary capital from private investment sources, eventually persuading

John D. Rockefeller Jr., Arthur Lehman, and several other capitalists to underwrite most of the initial construction costs. Hopeful of making Radburn a true regional city, the CHC mailed out circulars to some 5,000 manufacturers in the metropolitan area, detailing the advantages of relocating their skilled operations. By early 1929 the CHC had launched an advertising campaign to attract buyers for its first homes, which were nearing completion, making a special appeal to select groups such as the faculty members of New York universities and colleges. It promised the public that it would develop its lands "in accordance with a harmonious plan for the design and selective location of single-family and multi-family dwellings, garages, stores, factories, streets, walks, parks, playgrounds, and other structures and areas, so as to create a community to be known as 'RADBURN,' providing the greatest possible degree of health, safety, architectural beauty and amenity for the property owners thereof."[26]

To fulfill that promise, Stein and Wright were working, as Mumford unfelicitously phrased it early in 1928, "like seven niggers" to complete their plans for "a new kind of city, in which automobiles and children can both exist without the children getting killed." Wright was far from happy with his work conditions. At the very beginning of the project, he reported friction between himself and "the office-men and lawyers" in the CHC, and in the summer of 1928 he came close to dissolving his partnership with Stein and ending all association with Radburn, an early sign of a discontent that eventually would end one of the most creative architectural partnerships in America. Wright, however, decided to stay with the project and by 1929, with the help of Ackerman and Kohn, he and Stein had completed most of the details of what was becoming known as "the Radburn Plan," a distinctively new version of the garden city.[27]

The key element of the plan was the asymmetrical "superblock," which Wright described as being "an immense block—fifteen times as large as an ordinary city block." The idea of more spacious blocks was nothing new, but the Radburn superblock was a special adaptation of the Sunnyside experiment with green open spaces that allowed for much longer and wider lawn and garden areas in its interior than was possible at Sunnyside. As a result, Radburn would be ribboned with winding parks varying from 150 to 250 feet wide onto which all houses faced, turning the old dream of a city in a garden into something of a reality. In making their design, Stein and Wright omitted the circular greenbelt by which Ebenezer Howard had walled in his garden city, but they compensated for this by creating more green open space at the very doorsteps of the inhabitants. "Every family in the whole community," boasted Wright in 1929, "is really living on the park. They live on their own private little share of it. But this is all a great connected park system all over town."[28]

The superblock was intimately related to another key component of the Radburn Plan, a two-part system of circulation suited to the Motor Age. One part was intended to serve and subordinate the automobile: each block was bordered by general service streets that were somewhat curved in rejection of the rigidly straight streets of the conventional grid, creating the asymmetry of the blocks and forming a general street system that allowed for but also slowed the movement of the automobile in the city itself. Branching off from these streets were a series of dead-end service streets, cul-de-sacs, whose sole function was to provide access to groups of houses. Here, auto traffic, having been slowed within the city, would come to a stop at the back doors of homes—to give way to another distinct and preferred system of circulation.

This second system consisted of paths threaded through the interior parks, allowing people to move by foot or bicycle throughout the city without need for the automobile. To protect especially children from the automobile, the paths were run through tunnels under the streets, making for two distinct systems of movement that would not conflict with each other—auto and foot traffic, each in its proper place. Overall, while setting aside some 15 percent of the total town area for parks, the plan reduced the amount devoted to streets to 21 percent, notably less not only than the 33 percent absorbed by streets in Manhattan but also less than the 25 percent that Wright and Stein had achieved in their first garden city plan.[29]

The Radburn Plan also involved less easily defined elements designed to make it conducive to a good life for the people. Along with trees, lawns, and gardens, the interior parks were to include a full range of recreational and athletic facilities, including swimming pools, tennis and handball courts, playing fields, gymnastics equipment, and playgrounds. To build a strong sense of community among the inhabitants, the planners organized their block groupings of homes into neighborhoods; each neighborhood of roughly 7,500 to 10,000 people would focus on its own elementary school, which would also serve for neighborhood social and cultural activities. As a focal point for the whole town, recalled Stein, the planners intended to locate the high school and the major community center on "a beautiful hill" overlooking a central recreation area. To highlight cultural life, they provided a place for a "regional theatre." Presiding over all would be the Radburn

Association, the principal public organization of townspeople, which would manage the parks, playgrounds, and other community facilities and eventually assume democratic control of the whole town from the CHC.

In his unpublished "Notes on the New Town Planned for the City Housing Corporation," Stein summed up the Radburn dream: "There will be a series of . . . small communities of five or six hundred families grouped around its own park and its own small educational and cultural center. These parkways [the interior park strips] will lead one into the other so that it will be possible to walk a couple of miles through parks without crossing more than two or three highways. Small store centers will be arranged at the junction of these small communities. Homes will have all the peace and quiet which existed in the old New England towns."[30]

Given the original hope of creating an economically autonomous regional city, Stein and the other planners gave surprisingly little attention to providing for manufacturing and other job-producing activity, something apparently to be left for future attention. They gave a little more attention to providing a main commercial center in the form of what Stein called a "regional market," which would have a parking lot for over a thousand cars, on the assumption that most of its patrons would come by automobile. Practically, the single most important selling point for Radburn was the promise of good, inexpensive housing in a green and quiet land, "planned and built by experts." The CHC hoped that good design and the economies of large-scale construction would enable it to sell six-room houses, free-standing or in rows, with garages, for about $7,500 each on easy credit terms, making it possible for workers as well as members of the middle class to acquire their own homes.

This did not please Mumford, who from his apartment in Sunnyside complained in late 1928 that Bing seemed intent on laying out Radburn "like a swell suburb, with single family houses and much vacant land; and that means waste." Mumford himself, however, was eventually to depart from Sunnyside to rural Amenia and to his own house and much vacant land. What was important for the CHC—which was intended to make a profit, albeit a limited one, for its investors—was ultimately not to meet the housing needs of the poor, as in England, but to satisfy the American dream of the working and middle classes. Chase rightly called it "the Americanized Garden City," the English version being built not "for the motor age but as a substitute for city slums."[31]

In the summer of 1928, the CHC began a $4 million construction program that included three hundred houses and one hundred apartments as well as the Plaza Building, the town's first retail and office center, located opposite the Erie Railroad station. By the end of 1929 most of this had been finished, along with Radburn's first gas station, designed by Stein, and the company was considering a construction program to build about 1,000 new houses annually. For a time, the houses sold well, especially to young middle-class people from northern New Jersey and New York City, so that by the spring of 1929 what had only shortly before been spinach fields had become the home of more than two hundred families with more soon to follow.[32]

The year ended, however, with the great stock-market crash, and by 1930 the nation was sliding into the worst depression in its history. For a time the collapse was hardly noticed at Radburn. As late as December 1930 *Survey* magazine could report that the CHC had been able to sell its houses and to prosper, providing "work for idle men and dollars." In early 1931 Wright and Stein still pursued their planning activities, going out to the site, where they "waded through swamp land and climbed hills and rearranged the public buildings." In their offices on West Forty-fifth Street, they continued to perfect their plan until Stein could proclaim it "a damned good one" that could allow them soon to retire "feeling that we have set the mold."[33]

Even before the onset of spring in 1931, however, it was becoming ever more apparent that the great experiment was unraveling, the victim in large part of the same large-scale effort that had promised such glorious results. By then, the efforts to introduce industry and skilled employment into the community had yielded little more than a couple of small warehouses, a reflection of the troubles experienced by business in the early depression. Contrary to the great hopes for regional cities that would decentralize economic activity, Radburn was on its way to becoming, as Stein later called it, "more of a country club without a golf course." Even as a suburb the new town was having increasing difficulty. With millions invested in land and in the development of an infrastructure of supporting roads and water lines, the CHC needed to sell large numbers of its houses—only to have bad times substantially reduce sales. In 1931 Bing expressed the hope that the soon-to-be opened George Washington Bridge across the Hudson would make Radburn more attractive to commuters into New York City, but the opening of the bridge brought no significant upsurge of sales.[34]

By early 1931 Stein was beginning reluctantly to recognize the extent of the crisis. In February he wrote that Bing was "having a hard time of it. He wonders how he could have made so many blunders," especially in buying so much land. The next month it seemed to him that Bing had become even more bewildered by the darkening situation: "I feel that the end is probably in sight—and now I do not care— The plan . . . is made up at last—the mould is there."[35] To some extent the mold was there, in the form of the two superblocks that the CHC was able to complete. The real question was whether the Depression was bringing a temporary interruption of construction and sales or a complete breakdown of the whole enterprise.

Unfortunately for the garden city in America, the CHC, the creator of Sunnyside and Radburn, was tottering toward complete collapse. Having invested many millions in real estate, which was rapidly depreciating in value, the CHC also had to deal with buyers and renters of its properties who were experiencing sharp reductions of income. In April 1933 a group claiming to represent 213 of 227 property owners at Radburn petitioned the CHC for reduction in interest they were paying on mortgages, from 6 to 4 percent, on the grounds that two-thirds of them could not afford to pay their mortgage installments and most of the rest were rapidly depleting their savings to make the payments. Something of the same situation confronted owners in Sunnyside, who went on mortgage strike to force a reduction in interest. This was during a time when the CHC was declaring net losses totaling more than $800,000 in 1932 and 1933, losses that pushed it into a financial reorganization in 1934.

The CHC struggled on, selling some of its Radburn lands and building a few more houses—only to confront a final and humiliating crisis two years later, when its tenants at Sunnyside organized a second strike to pressure it into accepting a new system of easier mortgage payments. Benefitting from the community spirit that the CHC had consciously tried to build, the strikers organized not only a general refusal to pay anything on their mortgages but a campaign of harrassment, which included legal action against CHC directors. Although she had not been a director since 1928, Eleanor Roosevelt, now the wife of the president, was served a summons to appear in court just before she was to address the National Public Housing Conference. As a result of such publicity, the once promising reform agency began to look like an oppressive landlord as it struggled unsuccessfully to avoid a final bankruptcy.[36]

All in all, the Depression made certain that the CHC approach, that of a limited-dividend private corporation, would not work either to resolve the housing problem or to guide the decentralization of metro-politan America—at least without substantial assistance from govern-ment. New and more perilous times had come, demanding new strate-gies and tactics. A new phase was opening that, with the advent of the New Deal in 1933, initially seemed to offer the RPAA an even greater chance to participate in the reshaping of America. It soon became evident, however, that these new times were as frustrating as they were promising.

XI

REGIONALISM: MUMFORD, MACKAYE, ET AL.

The members of the RPAA continued to pursue their own special destinies into the late 1920s, forming a loose weave of converging and diverging lives. For a time, Whitaker disappeared, having lost his roots both as editor of the *JAIA* and proprietor of the Twelve Opossum Farm. He believed that his departure from Mount Olive deeply saddened the country folk who lived nearby. "Only the simple plain people understand these things—and that not by reason but by the age old method of human emotion," he told Mumford. "City folks are too barren of simple feeling to know what it is about." He continued his Georgist disdain for cities as places ruined by calculation and speculation, places where, as he put it in 1927, "a standardized pecuniary reward is the only object." When Mumford criticized the Radburn project, Whitaker applauded, declaring that Bing's failure to rule out all elements of speculative profit threatened to introduce "the present game of land warfare" into the CHC paradise. Soon after, he left for Europe, to reappear early in 1929 on a farm outside of Foster, Ohio, well away from his old haunts.[1]

As Whitaker faded from the eastern scene, his sometime associate in the RPAA Chase established himself as a popular authority on the promises and perils of the second industrial revolution. By 1930 Chase had made enough money from his writing to buy the home of MacKaye's nephew, Keith MacKaye, in Pound Ridge, north of the city. Like some of his friends, he had grown tired of New York City, with its noise, dirt, congestion, and frenetic pace. "Why should we scamper like rats rather than walk like men?" he wondered. In 1928 Chase had been on of several prominent Americans asked by the *Nation* to write an article describing his ideal society. He responded in his "A Very Private Utopia" with a dream of a community "where beauty abounded; where cities were nobly planned, industrial areas segregated; where great stretches of forest, lake, and mountains were left wild and free and close at a hand; where houses and their furnishings were spare and fine and colorful, and there was not a single billboard on a day's march." It was a dream of which his brethren in the RPAA could approve.[2]

Although he disliked the metropolis, Chase was comfortable with the contemporary world of science and technology and had no sympathy for "the Frankenstein chorus" of antimodern romantics like Whitaker, who viewed the machine as a threat to true humanity. Unlike many of his peers, he saw the positive side of standardization and specialization. He believed the key to human progress was the more rational planning of the industrial system to promote efficiency and eliminate waste. On the other hand, he was not blind to some of the dangers of modern power. In his "The Two Hour War," published in the *New Republic* (1929), he warned that a great "holocaust" lay ahead, a great devastation caused by aerial bombs carrying deadly diseases, poison gas, and "radium atomite."[3]

Chase did not think that humankind would be obliterated, but he did believe that it would suffer profound horrors until it finally awoke to the need to abolish war. Chase and his friends were not confident that this awakening would come soon. In 1929, for instance, Mumford could find consolation in Chase's warnings only in the thought that the overcrowded cities would be prime targets of aerial attack, "and might be abruptly and ironically terminated by a few whiffs of deadly gas."[4]

While Chase and Mumford were establishing themselves as writers, other RPAA members were pursuing their profession as architects. Ackerman completed plans for a group of more than twenty faculty apartments at his alma mater, Cornell University, as well as designing various homes and business buildings, including Radburn's centerpiece office building and shopping center. Stein, along with his various works in New York City, Radburn, and elsewhere, published a major article in early 1930, "The Art Museum of Tomorrow," in which he dreamed of a massive sixteen-story museum with moveable partitions, relocatable windows, and other provisions for a flexibility that would allow it to exhibit all kinds of art.[5]

The same year saw the publication of an exceptionally long article by Stein's partner Wright, "The Place of the Apartment in Modern

Living." Taking the positive side of the RPAA's condemnation of the
single-family house as wasteful of materials and space, Wright argued
that the well-designed apartment house could be not only a cheap
shelter but a highly desirable place for living. Apartments figured
prominently in his concluding dream of a future "residential city" that
would house 250,000 people in the three-mile area surrounded by a
greenbelt of park lands. Five such cities could be aggregated along
with areas for industry, truck gardening, and recreation into a garden-
city urban complex with a population of one and a half million. "Even
this city requires a total spread of only nine miles. A somewhat
enlarged business center in the central unit would require merely an
increased height of apartments for the same population." Like most of
his friends, however, Wright chose his ideal place in the country,
acquiring by 1931 what he called the Mill Valley Farm at Mount
Olive, not far from Whitaker's former home.[6]

And so it went, as each member developed his own special talents
and interests. Fundamentally, they were all bound together by a common devotion not only to regional planning but to an underlying
philosophy of regionalism. All agreed that effective regional planning
and policy ultimately depended on popular values and culture, a supporting "regionalism" involving an appreciation of the significance of a
region deeper than reason or self-interest. Their version of popular
culture was the Romantic one popular among intellectuals of the time,
of a folk culture, one that was antithetical to the actual popular culture
of jazz, motion pictures, and spectator sports that dominated the common interests of the 1920s—for which they had an elitist disdain. Real
culture for them was rooted in the experiences of a rooted local people
intimately connected to their immediate locality for life. Mumford
insisted that "cultural regionalism, so far from being an embellishment
to technical plans, is an indispensible introduction to them," and Mac-
Kaye wrote that to "build up an indigenous setting we must first build
up an indigenous psychology."[7] Although they agreed on the importance of regionalism, most members of the RPAA were too busy with
their own pursuits to give much attention to it. Overall, the responsibility for developing the regionalist theory fell to Mumford and MacKaye.

Mumford had developed an interests in regionalism even before
World War I, when he had first encountered Geddes and the French
school of regionalist geographers. With the formation of the RPAA in
1923 this interest became a mission, not only to explain the philosophy
but to prove that regions and regionalism actually existed. In the world
at large he saw two complementary tendencies that he believed were

weakening metropolitanism and its chief instrument, the nation-state. One tendency, arising from the rapid development of modern communication and transportation, led eventually to one interconnected world; at the same time, the weakening of nationalism was opening the way for a resurgence of regional interests and loyalties. Eventually, the result would be a world of many regions where humans "can communicate widely in a universal language, and deeply in a local one." When the young poet and critic John Gould Fletcher criticized the thinness and weakness of regional cultures in the United States, Mumford took up the challenge. In October 1923 he published an article in the *Freeman,* "The Regional Note," which acknowledged the reality of Fletcher's charge only to advance the argument that the weakness of regional culture resulted from reversible historical circumstances rather than from some inherent disposition in American society.[8]

Most of Mumford's work in the 1920s was directed toward establishing this point, his basic contention being that during America's formative years regionalism flourished, a contention he soon proceeded to develop, especially in two major books of the mid-1920s, *Sticks and Stones* and *The Golden Day.* He gave special attention to the New England of Emerson and Thoreau as exemplifying regionalism at its creative best. In his view, this regionalism flourished only to be devastated by the Civil War, which he called a "white gash through the history of the country." On the far side of the gash lay the golden day of "a well-balanced adjustment of farm and factory in the East, of a thriving regional culture"; on the near side was the distorted world of Coketown and the Megalopolis. The post–Civil War period, Mumford declared in 1930, "reversed every value, giving insignificant poetasters precedence over Emerson and Melville, distributing stones instead of bread."[9]

All was net lost, however, since there remained in the ruins of the debacle a "buried renaissance" of regionalism and regionalist attitudes, especially in the form of the conservationist movement. There was, therefore, a potential on which to build a new regionalism suited to modern times, to restore the "broken rhythms" of the Golden Day. This, he emphasized, was not a matter of reviving the old forms of folk culture, which he said was ordinarily "just humbug and masquerade," but of recreating traditional culture in the light of modern conditions. It was the task of creative people like himself to activate the hidden potential into a cultural rebirth. "Regionalism must rely upon the artist, the poet, the philosopher." He saw various signs of a regional awakening—in public interest in his own works, in the fiction of writers like Carl Sandburg and Sherwood Anderson, in the architecture

of Frank Lloyd Wright ("our greatest regional architect"), and in regional theater and dancing. One special sign was the work of Mary
Austin, calling attention to the culture of the Southwest—not only to
the Indians and Mexicans, but "to still another regional individuality,
that of the dry lands, with a cooperative polity based upon the essential
needs of irrigation."[10]

Mumford's views regarding the real character of this awakening regionalism tended to be abstract. In 1926 he said that regionalism "means a
recognition of the diversity of soils, climate, industries, historical connections and social traditions in various parts of the country." He added that
it involved a local rootedness and commitment that ran counter to American habits. "It means the abandonment of the pioneer habits of nomadry
and exploitation; it means an encouragement of the process of settlement
and culture." At its most intimate, regionalism involved a vitalizing
identification with a locality to which a group of people instinctively
related as their home, a habitat for human beings, a natural place where
they were naturally happy, healthy, and creative. In perhaps his best
article on the subject, "Regionalism and Irregionalism," published in
three installments in the *American Sociological Review* (1927 and 1928), he
said that a region ideally had "a natural balance of population and resources and manufacturing as well as of vegetation and animal life."
Viewing each region as a special combination of geography and "social
heritage," he mentioned that there were ten such regions in eastern
North America alone, but, beyond referring to the conflict between the
Appalachian and corn-belt areas of Ohio (two regions in one political
unit), he said little about the particular characteristics of any of them.[11]

Mumford's works relating to regionalism were powerful influences
for a new appreciation of the American past and culture, but they had
two notable weaknesses. One was a superficiality in his understanding
of significant aspects of history, especially the Civil War. Following
the prevailing scholarship of his times, Mumford ignored the significance of the war in ending slavery and reformulating the race issue, a
reflection of what was probably the greatest weakness in his social
thinking: his failure to understand race and racism as essential elements of traditional society, especially in those areas where regionalism was strongest. The other weakness was his limited personal experience with the subject. City born and bred, he rarely traveled in the
United States and, with the partial exception of the area around the
Hudson Guild Farm, had little exposure to any region until in the
late 1920s he came to know Amenia and its surroundings in Dutchess
County, north of the city. Although he eventually settled there, what-

ever direct understanding he acquired from Amenia came after he had formed his views of regionalism.

In contrast, the outlook of his friend Mackaye was far more rooted in a region, in the special culture of Shirley Center and Appalachian New England. So poor that in 1928 he had to borrow money from Mumford, MacKaye rarely traveled far from his adopted home, but his mind and imagination ranged widely. When he tried to revitalize the local culture at Shirley Center against the metropolitan invasion, he could believe that he was engaged also in a worldwide battle to protect indigenous environments everywhere. "The Chinese environment is being attacked, and the Hindoo also," he wrote to Mumford, "and the original American environment as well." He took a direct interest in the forms of traditional regional culture, notably in "folk-play—the song and the dance and the various outdoor sports—signs of vital community life."[12]

Much of MacKaye's interest in popular culture was derived from his sister Hazel's popular pageants and, even more, from his older and better known brother, Percy. By the 1920s Percy MacKaye had published numerous collections of tales, poems, and plans inspired primarily by folk traditions. Before World War I he had concentrated on the mountain culture of New England, but in 1921—the same year in which Benton began to conceive the Appalachian Trail—he had gone hiking in the Kentucky mountains and encountered a people and culture with whom he claimed a strong identity. Out of this adventure came a new collection published in 1926 as *Kentucky Mountain Fantasies.* Although the book received a mixed reception—one critic denounced it as "synthetic stuff, not native moonshine"—it provided support for Benton MacKaye's hopeful conclusion in *The New Exploration* and elsewhere that a revival of popular interest in folk culture was adding significantly to the "psychic resources" of the nation.[13]

MacKaye balanced his interest in culture with a strong emphasis on "geotechnics," on the engineering of environmental forces. Although he did say that geotechnics should be subordinated to culture, since culture dealt with the ends of life, his enthusiasm for the practical tools and tangible forces of regional development were notably stronger than Mumford's. In 1928, some six months after his friend dealt with regionalism in the *Sociological Review,* MacKaye published an article, "Regional Planning," in the same journal, in which he claimed that no plan, however inspired, could succeed unless it were congruent with the forces and flows that shaped and reshaped man's environment. A year later, he expressed the hope that Herbert Hoover, the nation's "first engineer President," would be the man to control the chaotic forces of the expanding metropolitan order. Among other devices of control, MacKaye listed "the little city of Radburn" as a means to redirect the flow of population, but he placed his greatest hopes in Hoover's power to use federal transportation funding to promote a system of townless highways for America.[14]

Whatever the extent of their differences regarding regional engineering, MacKaye and Mumford agreed in their attitudes toward one form of attempted regional control, the RPNY. By 1929 this well-funded planning effort covering seven years was nearing completion. In a publicity pamphlet published that year the plan was described as providing for the efficient movement of the twenty-one million people and nearly seven million automobiles expected in New York City and its surrounding counties by 1965. "The essential feature of the Plan is the spreading out of population over a wider area, with industries, stores, living, transportation and recreational facilities so arranged that the existing congestion in the central part of the Region will diminish and traffic can move." Here and elsewhere, descriptions of the plan emphasized features favored by the RPAA, including planned decentralization and planned communities like Radburn.[15]

For MacKaye, Mumford, and others, however, the plan was dangerously flawed. In a short article he had circulated among members of the RPAA before its publication (in August 1930) in the *Saturday Review,* MacKaye praised the plan for its workmanship and boldness but only to make the point that its good qualities were devoted to a bad end, "trying to make it possible for twenty million to live where only ten million had lived before." Might it not be better, he asked, for the added ten million to be "spread around America rather than around Hackensack Meadows?"[16] MacKaye's attack continued a pattern of occasional sniping against the plan that the RPAA had begun seven years earlier. Less than two years later, it was followed by what was intended to be a major assault launched by Mumford.

Early in 1932 Mumford submitted a long critique of the plan to members of the RPAA for their review, and in June the critique was published in two installments in the *New Republic* as representing the position of the RPAA. Again there was preliminary praise of the plan—as a "tremendous work"—this time to support the claim that its strengths made it especially dangerous, since they served to sanctify a perverse idea of regional planning. While applauding many of the details of the plan, Mumford condemned its overall "drift," which was toward further metropolitan centralization, and especially its perversion of the very idea of a region. Whereas for the RPAA a region meant a natural area defined by geography and culture, for the RPNY planners the New York region was no more than "an arbitrarily chosen area" of metropolitan influence determined by the distance one could travel from New York City within two hours; by this definition, the area around the Hudson Guild Farm was at the outer limit of the region. What it all led up to was a plan whose real effect would be to make a congested area work a little better in the interests of congestion, throwing away the opportunity to carry out a real decentralization of population and industry that would significantly improve living conditions for all.[17]

After reading Mumford's article Stein declared that his friend had scored a first-round knockout in the battle of plans. Thomas Adams, the chief RPNY planner, however, replied with a sharp attack of his own, dismissing Mumford as "an esthete-sociologist, who has a religion that is based on high ideals but is unworkable." And in the battle for public support, Adams and his fellow planners won a strong advantage, because they did at least propose practical remedies for immediate problems; their regional plan would prevail.[18] By 1932, however, a force more powerful than either side had entered the picture, namely the Great Depression, which shattered the hopes of everyone and forced a rethinking of regional planning in general.

Like most Americans, the members of the RPAA were slow to recognize the extent of the economic crisis precipitated by the stock-market crash in October 1929. Even a year later they seemed unaware of the impending change when they gathered for what was intended to be one of their most important meetings. In the fall of 1930 Stein and other leaders decided to hold a "big weekend" at the Hudson Guild Farm, where they hoped to develop a more definite policy of regional planning, an aim keyed to a recent suggestion in the *New Republic* for a "Ten-Year Plan" to guide the development of New York State; the magazine referred to Stein's CHRP and to Wright's report. Stein, who organized the meeting, suggested that it discuss ways of incorporating controls over land usage, townless highways, community planning, industrial decentralization, and other elements of regional planning into one feasible program for real change. Among basic questions to be considered, he suggested, were "what political bodies, what institutions, what individuals are at present on the job of regional planning. How can they be made conscious of the needs and opportunities for co-ordinated regional development?"[19]

From the time that their train left Hoboken at 4:30 on Friday afternoon, some thirty conferees were kept busy. After dinner Stein spoke briefly about the aims of the conference. He was followed by Mumford, who presented a brief historical overview of the possibilities for decentralization. Then Wright concluded the evening session with a discussion of his state planning report, noting that at least it was being followed in a state program to convert inferior farm lands into forests and recreation areas. Saturday—which Stein intended to be the key time of discussion—began weakly with technical discussions by two new members of the RPAA, Russell Black and Louis Brownlow, regarding some of the problems involved in planning. This was followed by a hike around the farm and then, in the late afternoon, by MacKaye's exposition of his townless highway idea. That night they participated in a country dance with, in Stein's words, "the old farmer, Benton MacKaye, to call off the numbers," the meeting's involvement with regional culture. The last day began with a general discussion regarding the direction the RPAA should take in the future, followed by some talk regarding the problems of industrial decentralization, which ended rather abruptly as the conferees became concerned with catching the return train to New York.[20]

And that was it. Despite the planning and the activity, little was accomplished, a failure reflected in the almost total absence from the discussions of three critical ingredients of the immediate future. One was the Depression itself, which was totally ignored; at one point, Stein did refer to "the impending breakdown of metropolitan civilization" but this was a reference back to his predictions in "Dinosaur Cities" and had nothing to do with the economic crisis. The second involved the near total neglect of the subject of regionalism. Although Mumford in his historical overview touched briefly on the development of regional consciousness, the meeting was dominated by discussions relating to technical planning questions, especially to the means required to prepare and implement a regional plan.

This emphasis on means increased the significance of the third missing ingredient, any serious attention to the role of government, a continuation of the RPAA's unwillingness to deal with politics. There was one exception to this, in that the meeting did at least create a committee, of which MacKaye was a member, to lobby Congress in support of MacKaye's townless highways bill. On the whole, however, it disappointed hopes for a ten-year program or for anything else requiring political action. Its most significant decision involved the future character of the RPAA, the principal question being whether it should remain "a small, informal association devoted to research, or whether it should attempt propaganda and attempt to attract as many as five hundred members." The general feeling was in favor of remaining small and informal, a decision undoubtedly motivated in part by an aversion to politics.[21]

Within a few months, however, there came a dramatic change as some members launched a significant "propaganda" effort intended to influence public policy. In mid-January 1931 Stein, Mumford, and Wright dined together and talked about the Depression, treating it now as a force for radical change in a troubled world. "The world is again searching for understanding and new roads," wrote Stein. "Lewis queried if it were not time for us to formulate some definite suggestions as to planning—without too much worry as to whether they fitted the present system." Further meetings, involving Ackerman and MacKaye on occasion, led to the conclusion that the capitalistic system had "a few—very few—years to run." As a critical step in their propaganda campaign, on January 31 the planners decided to organize a round table of regionalism at the annual Institute for Public Affairs conference scheduled to meet at the University of Virginia in July.[22]

Aside from providing individual members with a podium to discuss their ideas, the round table offered the opportunity to invite influential people who might become new friends and allies. Of some special importance was a small group of southern "Agrarians," such as John Gould Fletcher and John Crowe Ransom, who only shortly before had challenged the industrial order from a southern regional perspective in *I'll Take My Stand*. In a notable understatement, Mumford called them "slightly reactionary, still dreaming of the past instead of shaping a more integrated future," but he believed that their traditionalism and their regionalism made them potential allies in the battle against the metropolitan invasion.[23]

Even more significant was a single person, the then governor of New York State, Franklin Delano Roosevelt. As a protégé of Alfred Smith, the previous governor, who had supported regional planning, Roosevelt was a likely ally and appeared even more so as a result of his support for policies favoring decentralization and the revitalization of rural society. In August 1930, in its call for a ten-year plan, the *New Republic* had challenged the governor to build on the work of Stein's regional planning commission, so it was not surprising that in late March 1931 Stein was able to lunch with Roosevelt in the governor's Albany office. There, Roosevelt did most of the talking, especially about his favorite subject of, as Stein described it, "reviving small industries in the farming sections so that the farmers would find something to do during the

long winter months," the great aim being to reverse the flow of population to the metropolitan centers. Roosevelt expressed enthusiasm for
regional planning, especially by the state, but then adopted a more
cautious position, explaining that "he must not tell the whole tale at
once—the public mind would not grasp it." Stein left with the suspicion that Roosevelt was telling him what he wanted to hear, but he also
concluded that the governor was deeply interested in regional planning
and would try to attend the Virginia conference.[24]

As it turned out, Roosevelt did attend the conference, speaking
before both the regional round table and the parent Institute for Public
Affairs and using the meeting to help build support for the Democratic
presidential nomination in 1932. Although he did endorse regional
planning, he subordinated it to his principal theme, the need to
strengthen state government, a position that enabled him to publicize
his achievements in New York and to identify with the states' rights
tradition of the South. The gains for regionalism were less clear. One of
the few articles on the conference began with the question "what is
regionalism?" only to conclude that there was no clear-cut answer, "in
that most of the speakers stated frankly that they did not know what
they were talking about."[25]

This glib generalization did not apply, at least, to Mumford, who
delivered a paper on what he called "the new regionalism," distinguish-
ing it from the metropolitan form exemplified by the RPNY. Again, he
tried to provide at least some definition of what he meant by a region,
emphasizing that it was no arbitrary construct but the unique result of
geographic and historical conditions. "The region provides a common
background; the air we breathe . . . the landscape we see, the accumulation of experience and custom peculiar to the setting tend to unify the
inhabitants and to differentiate them from the members of other regions." He was quite hopeful that geography and culture would eventually triumph over politics, creating new regional patterns, each of
which "will be a constellation of related cities, separated by parks and
permanent green areas, and united for common projects by a regional
authority."[26]

After two southern Agrarians had stated their positions MacKaye
spoke, looking and sounding like a Yankee. Most of the time he stayed
with the theme of regional culture, but he could not resist touting the
townless highway, displeasing Wright, the chief organizer of the round
table, who feared that anything related to planning might alienate the
southerners. This concern was deepened by an RPAA member who had
chosen not to attend the conference, Chase. He had his speech read for

him by Brownlow. In it Chase—who identified himself as a charter member of the RPAA—declared that the RPAA's call for planning had been vindicated by the Depression. Although he advocated national planning, he proposed that the best way to begin was to take a region such as New England, study it, and then prepare a plan for it. "From the psychological point of view, if not the pure engineering, the best unit is probably the economic unit . . . an area which embraces unity of soil, climate, general topography and racial mixture." Along with New England, he mentioned the corn and the cotton belts and the Northwest as subjects for planning, the aim in each case being "to make the home country fairer, happier, more to be loved."[27]

Although the conference enabled various people to publicize their ideas, it was basically a failure. It began without any clear-cut agreement as to what regionalism actually was, and it ended with none. Wright was unhappy with the identification of the RPAA with regional planning as it applied to urban development. "Anyone not fully familiar with our group went away with the impression that whatever R. is about," he complained, "it has principally to do with some fairly definite mechanistic process whether expressed in Bronx Parkways or By-pass Highways, and that very little is worth while which cannot be converted into 100% Kiwanis whoopie." What especially bothered Wright about this was that it antagonized the southern Agrarians, for whom rational planning and policy was a menace to the traditionalism they held dear.[28]

Whether the hoped for alliance between the RPAA and the Agrarians could have been achieved even without this connection is doubtful, if only because the two groups came from very different backgrounds. While Mumford was impressed by the architecture of the University of Virginia, he thought the southerners themselves were "lazy, slow-moving, torpid, imperturbable, snobbish, interbred, tolerant of dirt, incapable of making effective plans or organization." Oppressed by the heat and the dirt, he hurried back to New York before the conference ended. Stein toured eastern Virginia—"a country more foreign than England," he wrote—and concluded that there remained little of the agriculture and little of the traditions needed for an agrarian revival. "Virginia, and I presume most of the South, has got to build anew."[29] For their part, the Agrarians clung to their view that societies were formed by organic growth over time and that the old southern traditions were to be preserved against the new and the modern.[30] The meeting broke up without any agreement between the two groups of regionalists.

The hope of hooking the RPAA to Roosevelt's rising star also was disappointed. Although he endorsed regional planning, noting that his state had adopted it, he made no effort to relate to the RPAA. He was, however, too important to be ignored. In November 1931, at its annual meeting held at the Hotel Seymour on West Forty-fifth Street, the RPAA appointed Mumford and Stein to draft a memorandum to Roosevelt "suggesting a definite policy in regard to the formation of rural communities," the aim being to use Roosevelt's interest in reviving rural society to win him over to the RPAA strategy. By the opening of the new year, 1932, a nine-page draft "Outline for Memo to Governor Roosevelt on State Planning for New Communities" had been completed, urging the importance of developing a statewide master plan in general and more particularly of initiating a program of decentralization featuring the construction of planned communities, "large enough for the collective advantage of balanced industries and a degree of self-sufficiency—and small enough to evade the metropolitan disadvantages of inconvenience, expensive transportation equipment, congestion, and lack of social unity." The principal means of implementing this program was to be a new Housing and Regional Planning Authority, with power to assist private community development operations like the CHC.[31]

Whether Roosevelt ever saw such a memo is doubtful. In any case, he soon demonstrated how little he understood about the RPAA position by praising the RPNY as "laying the foundation for a better future." In this and other ways, he managed to reaffirm Stein's earlier skepticism. Roosevelt was "a fine fellow and an excellent talker," wrote Stein to MacKaye in July, "but I have not faith in his ability to make up his mind or to keep it made up. I am afraid he would make a pretty weak president." Both MacKaye and Mumford had their own doubts about the governor.[32]

Doubts or not, however, it was Roosevelt who was elected president in 1932, making him the best hope for significant change. Would the new leader initiate what in the summer of 1932 Chase had called "a New Deal for America"? In early 1933 the RPAA again tried to influence the new president, with some apparent success. Eventually, he would disappoint their hopes for a truly "new deal," but during the first year of his administration it seemed that the RPAA was becoming not simply a propaganda organization but a major influence for the growth of new policies that would change the face of America.

XII

WOMEN ON HOUSING:
EDITH ELMER WOOD AND
CATHERINE BAUER

In March 1928 Stein abandoned his long bachelorhood and married the rising young movie actress Aline MacMahon. The tough-talking but essentially sensitive Stein had found his one true love. During the times when Aline was away on the acting circuit he was desperately lonely, seeking solace in almost daily letters to her. He was the last of the members of the RPAA to be married. Except for MacKaye, a lifelong widower following his wife's suicide in 1921, by 1930 each of the members had a serious commitment to a woman, although in the case of Mumford it was, for a time, to more than one.

In general the RPAA was influenced by the changing views of gender relationships that characterized their times, accepting women as equals in the world as well as in the home, but there was not much conscious concern over the matter. Although men like MacKaye had backed women's right to vote, the attainment of this right by the 1920s had weakened interest in gender issues. "The literature of feminism," wrote Mumford in 1921, "is beginning to dribble off now that the pump of political action has ceased to work."[1] Quietly, despite the good intentions, the RPAA remained very much a man's world where women played a narrow role, at least until the 1930s, when the situation began to change.

Women sometimes attended the major association functions as the wives of members, but their participation was almost entirely social, at the occasional dinners and dances. The minutes of RPAA meetings related entirely to males until 1927, when they listed nine women among twenty-two attendees, mostly wives but also Stein's sister, Gertrude (not *the* Gertrude Stein). In the 1920s the group did have one respected female member, Edith Wood, but she proved the point. At only one meeting did the minutes acknowledge her, and this simply to note that "Mrs. Wood agreed" with a majority position. Typically, the only time she was asked to act in any way related to regional planning was to serve as a "hostess" at a tea planned by the CHC to promote its Sunnyside property.[2] If women were notably inactive within the RPAA, however, they at least had its moral support for their own distinct efforts to change the world.

Although some wives, such as Sophia Mumford, gave up careers for the home, Aline MacMahon successfully pursued a career in acting with the rather soulful approval of her husband. Of relevance to the RPAA cause was the work of Martha Binsley Bruere, the wife of occasional member Robert Bruere, who in numerous magazine articles championed women's rights, birth control, and various other causes. As coeditor of *Survey* magazine's Industry Department, she advanced the idea of a national service system to provide meaningful work for the unemployed and she urged that the effort of women to combine their traditional work in the home with meaningful outside employment be supported by better pay and working conditions. She was the only one in the group to take notice of the movement of southern blacks into northern cities, predicting that it would ease race relations in the South but create massive problems in the North. And she lent strong support to the efforts of her husband and other RPAA members to promote the cause of Giant Power, treating cheap electricity as the power that would so lessen the labors of women at home as to enable them to pursue outside careers. In 1930 she became the president of the Women's City Club of New York.[3]

Bruere's work, however, paled in comparison with that of Wood. Although generally passive in the RPAA, in the outside world Wood was a powerful influence on one issue central to the RPAA's concerns: housing. The oldest member, born in 1871, she came out of a reform world where traditional gender distinctions allowed for and encouraged the interest of women in health and housing questions, matters in which it was assumed they had special abilities. The daughter of one naval officer and the wife of another, she first became interested in the housing question in 1911, when, in investigating the plight of poor women, she discovered the slums of Washington, D.C. In 1914 the forty-three-year-old Wood, having raised four children, moved to New York, determined to study the housing problem at its worst.

By 1919 this Smith College graduate had gotten a Ph.D. from Columbia University and was making herself a leading authority on the issue of housing for the poor. Convinced that bad housing was a disaster for women and children, she came to demand public action to produce a constructive program, rejecting the old combination of regulatory laws and private enterprise as inadequate. During World War I she proposed the creation of a national housing fund of $500 million to be lent to states and municipalities both to clear slums and to provide good housing for the poor in rural as well as urban areas, the money to be spent under the control of planning commissions.[4] In response to concerns about the costs of such a program, she said in 1919 that if millions were being spent on public education then millions more should be invested in housing. "Are not health and morals more fundamental than formal education can ever be?"[5]

Wood was dedicated and aggressive in pursuing her constructive housing cause. In 1920 she agreed to debate with two men, J. J. Murphy and Ackerman, before the Press Debate Association in New York. The idea was that Murphy, former commissioner of tenements in New York City, would uphold the conventional regulatory approach while Ackerman would argue for a radical change in land use. In reviewing their arguments, which were sent to her in advance, Wood concluded that the two men were pulling their punches because she was a woman and issued a strong protest to the manager of the debate. Assured that the men now would "deliver blow for blow," she defended her demands for a constructive government policy. In late 1920 the three arguments were published by E. P. Dutton as *The Housing Famine*.[6]

Public interest in the housing issue declined in the 1920s, but Wood pressed on in her efforts to educate the public on the need for government action. In 1922 she published a book, *Housing Progress in Western Europe,* hoping that the example of successful foreign constructive programs might shame Americans into action. A year later she charged that, whereas Europe had substantially reduced its housing needs, one-third of the population in the United States occupied "sub-normal houses" and one-tenth were housed under conditions that produce acute physical, mental, and moral degeneration. Again she urged the need for a program of slum clearance and publicly funded housing, declaring that housing should be considered a public utility to be "carried out like the distribution of city water or gas, at a rate calculated to cover costs."[7]

Wood was not quite alone in her efforts. Between 1917 and 1929 she was head of the housing committee of the American Association of University Women (AAUW), a position that enabled her to organize other women into a force for change in housing. At one time there were, by her estimate, some fifty local housing committees at work on the problem. A scholar convinced of the importance of accurate statistics for good policy, she lobbied for the inclusion of questions regarding housing in both the state and national censuses—only to complain later that she was given promises that were not kept. Early in the 1920s she had attracted the attentions of both Stein and Whitaker, who induced her to join the RPAA soon after it was formed. Stein especially seemed interested in encouraging her membership, probably because he appreciated the importance of her support for his Commission of Housing and Regional Planning. In the late 1920s she served with RPAA members Ackerman, Bing, Kohn, Mumford, and Wright as advisors to the State Housing Board.[8]

Wood's participation in the RPAA was infrequent. Her residency in Cape May Court House in southern New Jersey limited her involvement in the organization, even though occasionally she spent some time in New York—as she did in mid-1925, when she gave a summer course at Columbia University Teachers College on "housing and town planning relative to family welfare." Moreover, although she paid her annual $5.00 membership fee to the RPAA, her loyalties on the regional planning issue were divided, since she was also a member of the Woman's Advisory Committee for the rival RPNY. She even applied for membership in its supporting association, although rather tellingly she refused to pay more than $1.00 of its $5.00 membership fee; her check was returned with the comment that her application could wait "until you feel that the Association is more deserving."[9]

More fundamentally, Wood's concentration on housing for low-income groups did not relate well to the RPAA emphasis on regionalism and regional planning. In the late 1920s, having purchased three shares of stock in the CHC, she did help to promote Sunnyside Gardens and Radburn, especially by lobbying members of the Columbia University faculty to buy homes in "the new town for the motor age."[10] In a letter to Thomas Adams of the RPNY, she declared, "I am fully in sympathy with the doctrine that industries and those who work in them should be moved to garden suburbs or satellite towns in un-built areas." On the other hand, she wanted nothing that would detract from her principal policies of constructive housing and slum clearance. "No comprehensive housing policy is possible without slum clearance to get rid of the unredeemable old houses, for as long as they are there . . . people will always be in them."[11] Basically, she remained a marginal figure in the RPAA, fearing—with some good reason—that the emphasis on garden cities would involve the sacrifice of the housing interests of the urban poor.

With the onset of the Great Depression, however, Wood's dedication to the housing question brought her renewed attention. In 1931 she published her major work, *Recent Trends in American Housing,* in which she declared that despite the prosperity of the 1920s workers in the United States as well as elsewhere had not been able to find decent housing for themselves. Nor would they ever, she charged, so long as the business of providing them with homes was left simply to supply and demand, since under that system builders tended to respond chiefly to the needs of the minority that could readily afford decent housing. "Supply and demand, unaided, have never, at any time or any place, furnished all classes of self-supporting families with a minimum health-and-decency grade of housing." Although she acknowledged that the increased wages enjoyed by American workers in the 1920s did enable them to afford better housing on their own, she contended that much of the new spending power was being diverted by advertising into nonhousing expenditures.[12]

By the end of 1931, with the deepening Depression and the collapse of wages and employment, she had begun to hope that desperation, if not idealism, would persuade Americans of the need for a government program. In this she received the support of Stein, who, in October 1931, proposed a meeting involving her, himself, and Mumford to develop a ten-year housing program. "It is of the utmost importance that we take stock and find out where we are," Stein told Wood. "Among other things, I have in mind the need of a wider understanding of the growing function of government." Encouraged by this new appreciation of her importance, Wood intensified her efforts to promote constructive housing and slum clearance, and for a time she had some influence over actual policy.[13]

In May 1933, when the RPAA met at Stein's home to consider a statement of policy regarding housing, Wood spoke out strongly in favor of immediate action to meet the needs of low-income groups on the grounds that unless "low rental demonstrations were made from the start, the real estate interests might successfully block any further development." The majority of members showed little enthusiasm for her position, ruling out slum clearance on the grounds that it was costly and time consuming. Mumford suggested a possible compromise in the form of a provision for low-income housing in the model communities favored by the majority. Finally, the RPAA agreed on a position statement, "A Housing Policy for the United States Government," published in the *Octagon* (the new journal of the AIA), which did urge attention to slum clearance and public housing, but it ranked these below the development of new communities in its ordering of policy recommendations and also declared that, in order to limit overall costs, "government-aided housing should be limited to low-priced land," a principle that favored outlying areas over more expensive inner-city slum sites.[14]

Wood made no protest to the RPAA against this, but elsewhere she continued to speak out for slum clearance, arguing that clearing slums would also eliminate an important cost to society. She admitted that she had no exact figures to show how much public money would be saved by clearance, but she insisted that "there is no myth about the economic high cost of slums," especially in the form of crime and sickness. Presumably these social savings would more than compensate for the higher cost of slum land. In support of this position Wood could draw on influences outside the RPAA. Although her housing committee had been abolished by the AAUW years before, she had made numerous contacts with people of influence, especially a group of women housing reformers in New York City. In 1931 she helped form the National Public Housing Conference headed by Helen Alford. The year before, Alford had advised Wood that "the present unemployment situation, though tragic in itself, offers an effective wedge for a program of city housing operations."[15]

And so it seemed in 1933, with the advent of the New Deal. Thanks to her reputation as an expert, Wood was given the opportunity to participate directly in the early stages of New Deal housing efforts. When Stein's partner and fellow RPAA member Robert Kohn became head of the Housing Division of the Public Works Administration (PWA) in the summer of 1933, he employed Wood as a consultant at $20 per day to evaluate a proposal for a housing project in Atlantic City. Soon she was sent to Detroit to examine another project, but it was the Atlantic City scheme that did most to introduce her to the practicalities of public housing. Initially she had been skeptical of the scheme, in part because its location would contribute little to slum clearance, but by October 1933 she endorsed it, having concluded that a clearance program could not succeed unless it had the support of a housing authority with money and power. Whatever its deficiencies, she advised, the project should be pursued, because it would create new housing in a city where it was desperately needed and provide private construction jobs for the great many unemployed: "The building trade workers are growing desperate at the prospect of another idle winter."[16]

Despite a debilitating heart attack in 1934, Wood continued to crusade for public housing. In 1935 she prepared a report for the PWA that was published in 1936 as *Slums and Blighted Areas in the United States,* in which she concluded that two-thirds of Americans lived in substandard housing, with a third of the population "living under conditions of a character to injure the health, endanger the public safety and morals and interfere with the normal life of their inhabitants." The decade before her proportions had been one-third and one-tenth. Although she included rural inhabitants in this, her special interest remained in the slum dwellers of the cities. "Class hatred, social unrest and revolutionary propaganda," she warned, "are the natural product of slums." Convinced by her study of the Atlantic City project that effective slum clearance could not be carried out by private enterprise, she lobbied for legislation in New Jersey that would create a public housing authority that would have the money and power needed to acquire slum properties for clearance.[17]

By 1936 she had also come out in favor of similar legislation on the national level, attacking the then popular idea of giving rent subsidies to the poor as a "major menace to the housing program," in that it likely would sidetrack a comprehensive government program. In that year she had cause to complain that the private building industry had selfishly blocked efforts to enact a constructive public housing program in Congress. A year later, though, she saw victory for her long effort when, in 1937, Congress passed the Wagner-Steagall Act creating the United States Housing Authority to manage a national program of slum clearance and of subsidized public housing for the poor. By then she had drifted away from the RPAA, impelled by the opposition of members like Stein and Mumford to slum clearance. In 1938 she wrote that the RPAA had not, in her view, gone far enough fast enough: "I never broke with my old associates of course. There was no occasion to. But my relations with them have never since been so close."[18]

During these years, Wood became something like the grand old lady of housing reform. Clad always in gray—in mourning for her husband who had died in 1933—she presented the image of a passing era, an earlier time of social action. In this respect Wood presented a significant contrast with another woman member of the RPAA in the 1930s, one who became involved in the housing question but in ways that reflected the concerns and attitudes of the postwar period—and more besides.

Whereas Wood came of age in the 1890s, Catherine Bauer achieved an early maturity in the 1920s. Born in Elizabeth, New Jersey, in 1905, she graduated from Vassar in 1926 after having spent part of the previous year studying architecture at Cornell. By the late 1920s she was striving to find a road to success in New York City without notable effect until, in 1930, she met Mumford. The two soon became involved in a passionate love affair, the handsome discontented intellectual and the young, bright, ambitious Teutonic goddess. Bauer would probably have eventually succeeded on her own; she impressed Stein as being a "keen young person," but undoubtedly her relationship with Mumford eased her way. Through him she met Stein and MacKaye; before long she was writing to MacKaye that "perhaps I shall yet get around to bicycling through Shirley Center." By the summer of 1931 she could say that "under the corrective eye of Mr. Stein and Mr. Mumford" she was writing a long article on regionalism for the *New Republic*.[19]

Before this, she had gone to Europe to study recent architecture there and had returned with some definite ideas that influenced her attitude toward planning and housing. In two short articles published by the *New Republic* in mid-1931 she presented herself as a rebel against the pretentious and stodgy in architecture, declaring in favor of the International (Bauhouse) style of architecture, whose houses were "frank, clean rectilinear units of concrete and glass," expressive of modern times. She noted that whereas wealthy Americans were still spending millions on traditional European designs, the Europeans were adopting what they considered to be in its functional simplicity an "American" house capable of being mass produced by American production methods. Through the right designs, they had discovered how to provide houses for the people. "Shining rows of concrete, glass, and gardens; freely planned groups centering around their own shops, schools, community centers . . . precast concrete units turned out in a local factory."[20]

Even before she published these articles, she had turned her European trip into an essay, "Art and Industry," which won a $1,000 prize from *Fortune Magazine*. It featured a new German suburb where Americanized design and construction had produced houses that rented for as little as $18 a month. She soon returned to Europe to do research for an article on housing that she was to write for *Fortune*. Her coauthor was to be Mumford, with whom she spent some time both abroad and in New

York. In August 1932, after they had returned, Stein wrote slyly to his wife, "Lewis and Catherine left early—They had work to do at her apartment—No, no—they are writing the article for Fortune—don't you know I never gossip." Sophia Mumford, with extraordinary discipline, bit her lip while her husband gloried in being able to love two women at the same time.[21]

By 1932 Bauer had made herself a significant figure in the RPAA, serving as its executive secretary and helping Mumford and Stein draft its manifestos. In varying ways she related to its leading members. In 1931, when she had first met Stein, she impressed him with her enthusiasm for the International style, making him, he said, "long to see the new world the Germans have created since the war." Before long, he was employing her to conduct a survey on community development, and in 1934 the two jointly authored an article in the *Architectural Record* advocating the replacement of an inefficient mass of ill-coordinated little stores in a community with one well-planned neighborhood shopping center. Although expressing preference for the kind of center to which one could walk rather than ride, they conceded that some centers would need to accommodate the automobile and provide adequate parking, as Stein had anticipated in his plan for a "regional market" at Radburn. From such thinking would come the modern suburban shopping mall.

In 1933 Bauer was living in a fifth-floor apartment—"served by the world's smallest elevator," said Stein—and working on a book on European housing supported by a $1,000 grant, which Mumford had been able to get for her from the Rockefeller Foundation; the book, *Modern Housing,* was published in 1934, a major step in what became a successful academic career as an authority on planning and housing.[22]

In her strivings to cultivate the leading members of the RPAA, Bauer did not ignore Wood. In March 1932, for instance, she urged Wood to attend the next RPAA meeting. "All this winter I have been the only female present." In the same year she tried to persuade a magazine with which she had connections to publish one of Wood's articles on housing, only to be told that the article was too "sociological." She praised Wood's two major books, declaring that, when she returned to Europe, Wood's "European book will be my bible." In 1934 she joined with her in applying to the Civil Work Administration for a $25,000 grant to fund a survey of workers' housing in New Jersey, and soon after she helped organize support for New Deal housing policies favored by Wood.[23]

The two women, however, differed fundamentally in their views of how to solve the housing problem. Whereas Wood preferred to work with existing powers, Bauer for a time moved in a more radical direction, leading one New Deal official to call her "a wild-eyed female." In 1933, for instance, she condemned Chase for rejecting the Marxist idea of class struggle in connection with public policy. "If anyone thinks that this can be accomplished without the active participation of a very large, well-disciplined and well-organized group of people who know exactly what they want and want it enough to be willing to die in the process of getting it . . . he is no worthy candidate even for literary leadership." In regard to the management of housing projects, writing from Philadelphia as the executive secretary of the Labor Housing Conference there, she advocated "representation of the people most vitally involved to insure that their needs are really met," a position that did not sit well with the RPAA stress on experts. [24]

Bauer also rejected Wood's tear-down-and-build antislum program in favor of "economy, imagination, large-scale planning, and mass production." In late 1933 she complained that the PWA had shifted the emphasis in its housing program from the construction of inexpensive housing on cheap land to slum clearance, which she said would be expensive, time consuming, and beneficial chiefly to the owners of slum properties. "Let the slums rot a while longer and build decent places for their tenants to live elsewhere." By then she had come to accept the need for a government program, but insisted that public money should be invested not in slum clearance but "in building complete communities, designed and administered as functional units and constructed by large-scale methods," communities like Radburn to be built with parks, playgrounds, and other amenities that required space not available in slum areas. [25]

Although Wood and Bauer remained friends, there had developed a deep difference in their approaches to the housing situation, which reflected some fundamental differences in their hopes and aims. Wood, out of her deep concern for improving the conditions of poor families, wanted especially to destroy slums, whereas Bauer, with her art and architecture training, wished to design good housing in good communities on a scale that required construction in the outlying areas of cities. Wood was to say of Bauer that "for all her radicalism, she has never been much interested in slum clearance or what became of people who lived in the slums. I don't think they have ever been *real* to her." [26] During the New Deal, both approaches received attention: Wood's in the public housing program created under the Wagner-Steagall Act and Bauer's in the plans for greenbelt communities. Unfortunately, in the end, the New Deal fell far short of satisfying either's hopes regarding housing. During the 1930s other members of the RPAA also experienced this dissatisfaction as desperate times raised hopes for radical change that were then disappointed by fundamental differences in ideas about how to reshape America.

XIII

HOUSING—FOR WHOM
AND WHERE?:
KOHN AND STEIN

During the early 1930s the RPAA made an effort to expand its membership with notably limited success. At the end of 1931 there were only nineteen members. Although it could claim to represent at least eight states, it remained basically a New York City organization, the New York area furnishing eight of the most influential members: Ackerman, Bing, Bruere, Chase, Kohn, Mumford, Stein, and Wright. Of the others, only MacKaye from Massachusetts, Wood from southern New Jersey, and Whitaker, then living in Ohio, had long-term significance, and each of them had connections with New York. By 1933 the association had reorganized its structure in anticipation of further growth. Stein had replaced Bing as president, MacKaye and Frederick Bigger of Pittsburgh were vice presidents, while, rather cozily, Mumford was secretary-treasurer and Bauer, the newest member, was executive secretary. Stein at least had rather big expectations regarding Bauer: "The idea is to have somebody who will pull together all the various materials we are interested in and try to keep the organization a bit alive when we get off on another track."[1]

Even in such a small group there was much diversity of thought, but by 1933 the RPAA had decided to concentrate on two issues, the Tennessee Valley and public housing policy, with a distinct inclination of the majority in favor of housing, the issue in which they were most involved. Five members (Bigger, Stein, Wright, Klaber, and Ackerman) belonged to the AIA's influential Committee on Site Planning and Housing, which in April 1932 had been able to persuade the AIA's national convention to condemn the prevailing individualistic and competitive system of home building in favor of large-scale construction of planned communities like Radburn. The priority given to planned communities had already been expressed in the RPAA's January 1932 "Memo to Governor Roosevelt on State Planning for New Communities."[2]

When Roosevelt became president in 1933 the RPAA continued its efforts to influence his thinking. In March Stein said that FDR was saying the right things regarding the need for a massive government mobilization as in a time of war, but asked, "Will he have the back bone to use that army to build homes and cities even if it decreases the 'value of existing property'?" A few days later Stein wrote of a dinner he spent dreaming with MacKaye: "Reforestation with little forest towns planned by B. MacKaye and remodeled towns by CSS—we could make it so simple for Czar Franklin." He was hardly disinterested in his dream, since he was then involved in designing and promoting Hillside Homes in the Bronx, a massive garden-apartment project for more than a thousand families for which he hoped to get government support. Moreover, he was busy writing his book, *New Towns for America,* advocating, as he put it in March 1933, "the rebuilding of all America as a background to building new communities": the Radburn approach to housing.[3]

After listening to an early radio address by the new president, Stein grew more confident that something would be done, but still he wondered whether Roosevelt could keep his word. To guide the new administration, he prepared an outline for "A Housing Policy for the United States," which he submitted to the May meeting of the RPAA. He emphasized the construction of planned communities located "as part of a plan for future social and economic development of [a] region so as to best distribute the population in relation to industry and leisure time." On May 17 eight members of the RPAA met with three others who had an interest in housing to rework the outline into a full report. The chief question was the familiar one of whether to emphasize programs to house the poor and eliminate their slum environment or efforts to provide well-planned full-fledged communities for all. Wood spoke for public housing and slum clearance, but the majority agreed with Mumford, who urged attention to developing communities, like Radburn, especially for the middle-incomed that would also include homes for the poor.[4]

Aside from concern over the costs of slum land adding to the cost of

housing, it became evident that there was much hesitation about building houses for only one class, even the neediest. In the final version of
"A Housing Policy for the United States," which was published in the
Octagon, American City, and other periodicals, the RPAA declared that
"the essential standards of modern housing are the same for all economic classes.
And the methods of planning, building, and community construction
are likewise the same. It is essential for the social health as well as the
economic value of the new housing that *any kind of class segregation be
avoided* in either the design or the layout of the new buildings. The
quarters of the well-to-do should be differentiated from those of lower
paid workers solely by having more than minimum dwelling space and
mechanical accessories." The context for the attainment of this rather
utopian ideal was not to be the inner-city slum, since in conclusion the
report declared that preference should be given to less crowded areas
where land could be found not only for parks and playgrounds but for
subsistence gardens—not unimportant during a time of growing concern about unemployment and hunger.[5] Overall, it seemed evident that
Stein and most of his colleagues hoped to establish their grand regional
strategy of decentralization as the dominant policy of the New Deal,
one that perhaps only coincidentally would also serve to benefit the
Radburn project, which, after three years of depression, had come to a
halt.

Whatever the specific hopes for working a radical change in America, the New Deal managed to bring both satisfactions and disappointments to all concerned. In 1933 anything seemed possible in housing
policy; in 1934 the possibilities had distinctly narrowed. Such was the
experience especially of the one member of the RPAA who had a real
chance to develop policy. This was not Wood nor was it Stein, but
rather it was Stein's architectural partner Kohn. By the early 1930s,
Kohn and Stein were part of a five-man partnership with offices at 56
West Forty-fifth Street, the other associates being Wright, Charles
Butler, and Frank E. Vitolo.

Although for the most part Kohn played only a quiet role in the
RPAA and in regional planning generally, he was a major force in the
business of architecture. In 1931, besides being head of the Ethical
Culture Society, he was president of both the New York Building
Congress and the AIA. As a spokesman for both builders and architects, he had two principal goals. One was to promote cooperation
between the two groups in order to improve efficiency in the building
industry, especially in the form of large-scale neighborhood projects.
For instance, in 1931 he urged architects to abandon their preoccupa-

tion with single buildings and to join with real estate men and contractors in "schemes of group housing on such a scale as would make it possible to offer the individual purchaser a completed house in a neighborhood that is settled." The other aim, demanded by the near collapse of the building industry during the depression, was to create jobs for professionals as well as workers. In 1931, when the AIA urged the establishment of a federal department of public works to stimulate construction, Kohn advocated using private architects rather than government bureaucrats to design the projects.[6]

Initially, he expressed a preference for letting a well-organized private construction industry take the lead in building housing, declaring in early 1932 that "the building industry is preparing to integrate its processes, but not to be managed and directed by government. We are suspicious of all political government." In the summer of 1932, however, he attacked President Hoover for his lack of vision and called for a massive program of public works, including housing projects. "The slums of tomorrow are still being built today, because we have left the field of low-cost housing to the rugged individualism of the speculator." In early 1933, with the coming of a new president, he called for a federal administrator of public works to put the unemployed to work on a "nation-wide program of modern housing" as well as on roads, bridges, and other projects, all under the direction of a ten-year national plan of recovery and reconstruction.[7]

When Roosevelt took office in March 1933, Kohn joined the great trek to Washington of those who hoped to shape the policies of the new administration. Before the end of the month Stein could write of his partner, "He is enthusiastically hopeful. The whole atmosphere has changed since Hoover left. Something is happening—is going to happen. Robert and his engineers were welcomed instead of turned away. . . . I think Robert is going to play an important role. And he is enjoying it." Soon Kohn was helping to shape the public works provisions of the Industrial Recovery Act. Not all went well. In June, following the passage of the Recovery Act, Kohn presented the president with a carefully thought-out list of appointees to direct a public works program, only to see Roosevelt go off on vacation and apparently forget about the list. "Dictators are fine—when they are on your side," wrote Stein of the matter.[8]

A month later it appeared that the "dictator" was on the side of the RPAA, since Kohn was interviewed by the administration for an important government position and, after giving his interviewers the RPAA position regarding planning and housing, was appointed to head the

Housing Division of the new PWA. By August he was at work creating
the new division with the help of Klaber, Wood, and Wright. Stein
thought that this was only the beginning of the group's involvement in
Washington, only half-facetiously predicting that the RPAA would
soon be moving its headquarters there.[9]

During the First World War, when he had headed the housing
program of the Shipping Board, Kohn had built planned towns. Why
not more of the same? Shortly before his appointment he had expressed
his conviction that planning would dominate the American future. "I
see the world bound to work towards a new order planned to use the
varied powers and uniqueness of men." The essential aim would be to
improve living conditions for the people, especially through the agency
of community housing programs. "We shall have, of necessity, a decade
of public works construction and the rebuilding of our cities, and the
building up of new and smaller industrial centers, all on a scale never
before realized." During his first weeks as head of the Housing Division, Kohn seemed driven by his vision and more. After completing the
preliminary organization of the division—which included employing
Wood and Wright as consultants—he embarked on an extensive tour of
American cities from Cleveland to San Francisco to determine, as he
put it, "what is being done by these cities to prepare comprehensive
slum rehabilitation and rebuilding schemes." He returned convinced
that there was much willingness among both public and private leaders
in a program to rebuild America.[10]

Perhaps, as it proved, there was too much willingness. Having spent
weeks away from his office promoting projects, on his return Kohn was
soon inundated by over five hundred proposals for housing and slum
clearance. Confronted by this deluge, Kohn seemed to fall into a state
of semiparalysis. Much of the problem involved determining the merits
of the proposals, at least some of which looked suspiciously like efforts
of slum-property owners to dump their declining properties on the
public. There were also questions about the availability of public and
private support for the projects. To these concerns the scrupulous Kohn
added anxieties over possible conflicts of interest, since among the
leading candidates for federal support were limited-dividend projects
like Radburn and Stein's new Hillside Homes apartment complex.
Could he support the projects of his friends? When he first took office,
his friends had hoped that he could be persuaded to support government aid for Radburn, which might have saved it, but this he refused
to do. "There is no talking to Robert.—He seems to be going so many
places he is going nowhere," Stein complained in December 1933. "He

seems constantly to wobble." Stein thought that the basic cause of this uncertainty was that Kohn had not developed a housing philosophy that would help him make firm choices.[11]

By early 1934 the previously much-respected Kohn was being subjected to mounting criticism, especially for his failure to initiate the kind of dynamic public works program that he himself had urged only shortly before. It was evident that, despite his previous experience, he had no talent for dealing with government bureaucracy. Moreover, his preference for limited-dividend housing directed by private corporations did not sit well with those interested in direct government action. Eventually, he forwarded eighteen projects for final approval, only to see them stalled by the PWA's Division of Investigations. For those who expected quick action in providing both housing and employment, Kohn's administration was a failure, and before the end of January 1934 his partner Stein was predicting his removal. To disassociate himself from the projects in which his partners were involved, Kohn had his name taken off their office door and their letterhead. He was determined to fight on, but Stein believed he could not win, in significant part because he had no plan of battle. "He is fighting in a fog."[12]

Not all went badly for Kohn. In March 1934 the AIA gave him its medal of honor for "inspired national leadership of the architectural profession; for initiating the unification of the building industry; for great vision, understanding and continued national effort for the betterment of humanity in housing and city planning." In his acceptance speech, he defended his administration, attributing much of the delay to the failure of private investors to provide capital for the limited-dividend projects he favored. By June, however, it was evident that he could not continue, and he offered to resign, only to find new difficulties when PWA head Harold Ickes fired Klaber and all his other chief assistants but refused to accept his resignation. In July, still anxious to promote the housing cause, Kohn prepared a letter to Ickes defending his administration,.but he was tired. "He showed me the letter," wrote Stein. "It hasn't any fire—like a bunch of firecrackers that don't explode." Finally, after several tormenting weeks, Ickes accepted Kohn's resignation and soon was blaming him for the failures of the PWA housing program.[13]

Kohn had his defenders. In response to Ickes's charge that the former housing head had pursued an "inept career," the architect and planner Henry S. Churchill in the *New Republic* declared that the Housing Division under Kohn had begun to initiate significant projects, and that the real reason for failure was that Ickes had not provided the necessary moral or financial support. Under the reorganization that followed Kohn's ouster, charged Churchill, there were about one hundred people in the division to deal with some fifty proposals, whereas earlier there had been only twenty-five to deal with more than four hundred schemes. [14]

In the reshuffling of the division a basic change of housing policy also took place. Although Kohn had come to accept the need for some public spending, he had clung to the old hope that the majority of the projects could be developed by private capital operating through limited-dividend corporations like the CHC. The problem was, however, not only that private capital was hard to find but that the prospect of providing housing affordable to the poor through such means was very dim. After Kohn's departure from the Housing Division, the majority of the proposed limited-dividend projects were canceled, and the emphasis shifted to government public housing and slum clearance efforts along the lines favored by Wood. Given the situation, there is some irony in the fact that among the few limited-dividend survivors was Stein's Hillside Homes, a project Stein had worked hard to promote.

In 1932 Stein had proposed that the government support a massive model-housing program, arguing that this would stimulate economic recovery as well as meet the pressing needs of the two-thirds of Americans who he said lacked decent housing. He developed this theme most fully in a speech prepared for delivery to the Brooklyn League of Women Voters in which he presented a dream to "rebuild Brooklyn." In the speech, he attacked the old enemies of the RPAA, individualism and speculation, as responsible for the slums and blighted districts that threatened the welfare of cities. He described the Depression as an opportunity to build "a new environment . . . creating new communities that will harmonize with the needs of life." The key was the construction of large-scale, well-designed projects like Radburn, where "land values are low enough to carry on housing on an economical basis," virtually ruling out slum clearance in favor of projects away from the centers of cities. Government on every level would be involved, but the actual work would be done by limited-dividend corporations like the CHC, which made housing "an investment rather than a speculation." [15]

Stein had his private dreams. In July 1933 he told his wife that he was working on a plan for a seaside housing development. He felt sure that "it would never be built. But it is such a pleasant dream—a Radburn with beaches and lagoons." His real project was far less romantic, but still it was a major achievement. Hillside Homes was originally conceived to be a limited-dividend enterprise designed, as Stein said later, to be "a self-contained, integrated residential neighborhood in New York," providing housing at rents of approximately $11 per room for 1,400 families. His aim, as he told his wife, was to create a residential environment that would not only be comfortable and healthy but that nearly everyone could afford. "Eliminate the useless ge-gaws—build and run a simple town for spacious living." The size and general character of this scheme demanded a large tract of land that could be procured for less than the cost of slum land, and eventually a large open site was found in the Bronx along the Boston Post Road. Stein took pride in the fact that the apartment buildings would cover less than a third of the land, the rest being set aside for lawns, playgrounds, tennis courts, and other community facilities along the lines of Sunnyside.[16]

The estimated cost of this project was over $6,000,000, a large sum that was difficult to raise even in times more favorable than the Depression. In 1932, during the waning days of the Hoover administration, Hillside received a loan from the Reconstruction Finance Agency, but final action was delayed by opposition of local real-estate interests to the special tax exemption given the project. The suspicion was that they did not want the project to compete with their rapidly depreciating slum properties, which they wanted to dump on the public for slum clearance. In 1933 the Hillside Corporation applied for a comparable loan from the PWA, only to encounter similar delays from the New York City Housing Board, which Stein angrily complained was "composed of little worms." Finally, in November, the project won the approval of the Housing Board, only to be stalled in the PWA's Housing Division by Kohn's hesitations and problems.[17]

Eventually, after Kohn's ouster, Hillside got the support it needed, and Stein could declare that it was "growing and taking shape like a great piece of sculpture." By the end of 1934 it was being proclaimed the largest government housing project in the East and had won the praise of, among others, Mayor LaGuardia. In June 1935 Stein could joyfully dedicate the project with the prediction that it would be "different from the rest of New York. It would be a quiet peaceful park surrounded by houses. Hillside will be a place of safety and repose, a place of sun light. From every room one will look out on broad vistas of gardens and restful lawns or gay play spaces." He went on to say that because the project was a self-contained environment that its managers controlled, it "will never be blighted" and would long function as a true community set apart from the urban wilderness.[18]

And so the RPAA had scored another victory, along with Radburn, over the crowded, bloated metropolis. Unfortunately, however, Hillside, like Radburn, did not meet the housing needs of the low incomed, its limited-dividend character requiring rents that for the most part only middle-class people could afford. If Kohn had been able to shape long-term housing policy, places like Hillside might have gotten the government subsidies needed to provide housing for the poor, but this was not to be. After exciting expectations for a truly grand program to rebuild America's cities, the Roosevelt administration produced the bits and pieces of a slum-clearance program involving expensive government subsidies for projects limited to the poor, thereby eventually exchanging old slums for new.

During its early years, the administration raised hopes within the RPAA for a true "new deal" in public policy that would reshape America. In 1933, when all things seemed possible, the Roosevelt administration had offered the prospect of a radically new policy, not only for metropolitan America through potential housing programs but for indigenous America and for regionalism through an actual program for Appalachia. Here again, the new times promised to make the RPAA and especially one of its members a leading force for changing the future, only to dash these hopes once more and to create another travesty of good ideas and good intentions.

XIV

PLANNING THE
TENNESSEE REGION:
MACKAYE

Stein was disposed to view President Roosevelt's attitude toward regional planning with a mixture of hope and skepticism. "He will say nice things," wrote Stein soon after FDR's election, "but what will he do in a practical way?"[1] The vagaries of New Deal housing policy soon confirmed the skepticism. Hope, however, remained alive in several other lines of policy, none more important and promising than one of primary interest to the RPAA, the planning of an entire region. Eventually, there too skepticism regarding a truly new deal for America would prevail, but only after enthusiasm for regional planning had received an unprecedented boost.

As governor of New York State in the late 1920s and early 1930s, Roosevelt compiled a notable record favorable to regional planning. He was a committed conservationist who advocated a program of reforestation, flood control, and recreation similar to that created by MacKaye, and his hopes of reviving rural and farm life led him at least to dream of a program to reverse the flow of population to the city. "I am a great believer in the larger aspects of regional planning," he told the state legislature in January 1932, "and in my judgment the time has come for this State to adopt a far-reaching policy of land utilization and of population distribution," a statement that the RPAA would remember after he became president. Although he muted his support for regional planning during his presidential campaign, he quickened the hopes of planners after his election by promising in a speech at Montgomery, Alabama (January 21, 1933), that he would devise a plan for the development of the Tennessee River Valley, "tying in industry, agriculture and forestry and flood prevention . . . into a unified whole."[2]

Much of this Roosevelt developed on his own, but throughout the early 1930s he was the focus of a sporadic lobbying campaign by the RPAA that likely influenced his thinking, although not always in the intended ways. In 1931 Stein went to Albany to persuade the governor to attend the Virginia conference on regionalism, in the process encouraging him to speak strongly but privately in support of planning; five years later, MacKaye was to declare with more enthusiasm than actual proof that here Stein had "planted" the seeds of the New Deal planning program. Soon after, as a follow-up, the RPAA requested that Roosevelt support the establishment of a state planning board like that proposed by Stein's Regional Planning Commission seven years earlier.[3]

With the Depression and the troubles of limited-dividend projects like Radburn, the RPAA turned even more to government despite its ingrained distaste for politics, trusting as usual to the power of good ideas to triumph over self-interest and short-sightedness. Early in January 1932 Stein, Ackerman, Wright, Kohn, Mumford, and Bauer met to discuss planning policy matters, but, wrote Stein, "we did not settle matters before the punch was served." The basis for discussion, apparently, was a draft of a lengthy memorandum to the governor on state planning for new communities that Bauer had prepared after consulting with Mumford and Stein. It not only proposed a state program of "rural and industrial re-centralization" through the construction of planned communities but, to guide the program, urged that the state housing board be reconstituted into a new version of Stein's Housing and Regional Planning Commission. What happened to this memorandum is unclear, although it seems evident that it was never finished in a form suitable for actual presentation to the governor.[4]

Soon after Roosevelt first proposed the Tennessee Valley development, the RPAA began a more definite campaign. In early February 1933 it released a public letter to the president-elect "heartily" supporting his plan as a "statesmanlike step toward creating the instruments for a balanced life within a balanced human environment" and urging the preparation of similar regional plans for every part of the nation. This call won quick support from the *New Republic*—a frequent ally— which presented Wright's 1926 state report as a model for the planning of the Tennessee Valley. In early March the RPAA prepared a letter to Roosevelt repeating its endorsement of the Tennessee proposal and declaring that "we believe it offers the opportunity of using the present emergency to build a better world." As an outline for the actual planning of the region, it proposed a three-part program consisting of planned new communities, townless highways, and "the conservation of the wilderness environment," plainly drawing on an article published by MacKaye in *Survey Graphic* five months earlier.[5]

Stein was a leading figure in the campaign, especially regarding housing policy, but on the subject of Tennessee he was overshadowed by MacKaye. The originator of the Appalachian Trail had a strong natural interest in anything relating to the Appalachian empire. Indeed, it may have been that interest that, years before, originated the term "new deal," the tag for the whole Roosevelt program. Two other RPAA members, Mumford and Chase, made significant use of that term before Roosevelt took office, but MacKaye was first. Probably thinking back to the days of Theodore Roosevelt's "Square Deal," when he had gotten his start, MacKaye wrote in his 1921 article on the Appalachian Trail that the regeneration of Appalachia depended "on some new deal in our agricultural system" and then added that there should also be a "new deal" in the treatment of the nation's forests.[6]

MacKaye's early employment in the National Forest Service inclined him to think of the first Roosevelt as a model President. After the election of Herbert Hoover, whom he called "our first engineer President," MacKaye expressed the hope that the new leader might introduce his own version of TR's activism, citing the Muscle Shoals on the Tennessee River—long a proposed site for a power dam—as an example of what could be done to harness nature in a way that could be converted "into leisure" for the people. Hoover failed this hope, but 1933 brought new expectations.

FDR's proposal in January excited MacKaye's enthusiasm as nothing had done for years. In February and March he was in New York City, where he frequently conferred with Stein at the latter's apartment on Sixty-fourth Street and Central Park West. "Last night," wrote Stein on March 10, "Benton and I home alone to a solid steak dinner and a talk that might have put the world to right." Both men were busy with big ideas. Stein wrote in mid-March that he was working on his book relating to new towns as a means of "reshaping America" as a whole, while MacKaye was in another room "surrounded by maps on which he was trying to chart a scheme for the development of our nation's

forests—reforestation—a plan of the United States!—Dreams, yes—
but some of the dreams or some part of them may be realized tomorrow
or the next day."[7]

In March, with Stein's encouragement, MacKaye began a series of
articles supporting the Tennessee Valley project, including one for the
New York Times. Late in the month MacKaye left for Washington to
lobby directly for his ideas. "It has been a great two months we had
together," wrote Stein—some of the most exciting in the whole history
of the RPAA. For a time, MacKaye was disappointed, since the *Times*
delayed publication of his article and Roosevelt failed to mention Tennessee in his first major policy message, but he kept himself busy on his
reforestation plan, a scheme for, as Stein put it, "keeping men busy
with axes in the national forests."[8]

Finally, in April, Congress began to consider a bill to create the
Tennessee Valley Authority, and soon the *Times* published MacKaye's
"The Tennessee River Project: First Step in a National Plan." In the
article MacKaye presented the plan as a necessary response to the clos-
ing of the frontier and the end of the era of free lands, a new response
that "would enable Uncle Sam again to open up the country." He
expressed strong support for reforestation and reclamation as much
needed ways to improve the agricultural situation of the Tennessee and
other river valleys as well as to promote forestry. He described as the
ultimate goal of the plan the decentralization of population "to give the
people of the great Eastern urban centers a chance for elbow room," this
to be achieved especially through a decentralization of industry facilitated by the availability of cheap hydroelectricity to be generated under
the plan. What could be done on the Tennessee could be done in
perhaps a dozen other regions of the country, areas covering as much as
a fifth of the country. "Here indeed is a new 'public domain'" to be
developed for future settlement.[9]

The *Times* article was quickly followed by one in the *Nation* in which
MacKaye, proclaiming himself an old "Forest Service man," applauded
FDR as a new version of Theodore Roosevelt who promised to revive
the "bully" days of conservation and to add a new program for the
decentralization of industry—which "means decentralized life—new
towns, new roads, new human settings"—ultimately to conserve not
simply the natural environment but the psychological and cultural
habitat needed for full human development.

Less than a month later *Survey Graphic* published his "Tennessee—
Seed of a National Plan," introducing him as one who "drew up the first
Tennessee Valley plan when he was a young research forester." Here,

MacKaye gave special attention to some of his traditional themes, supporting an extensive forestry program as a way to provide employment for the jobless and urging the need to protect indigenous areas "from the influx of the metropolitan slum." He gave particular emphasis to the Tennessee project as potentially part of a larger program to redeem all of Appalachia. If he were made dictator of public works in America, he said, he would build a system of "townless highways" and "highwayless towns" in the valleys from one end of the region to the other.[10]

By the time this article appeared, MacKaye had arrived in Washington to lobby both for his ideas and for a government job. He found the city an exciting place, a mixture of the days of the Hell-Raisers and of World War I. Again the technical experts were gathering, bursting with ideas as how to use government to reshape America. "One lives in this town," he told Stein, "at the modest rate of about a decade a week." As he attended meetings of one group after another, he believed he was sensing the awakening of a nation to planning, and he determined to make a special effort to influence the bill being considered by Congress for the establishment of the TVA.[11]

In late April, after observing that "Tennessee is my *piece de resistance,*" he said that he was rushing to compile all possible information on planning the Tennessee Valley. By mid-May he had outlined a plan for the valley embracing "forest areas, community areas, stream channels, highways" and was seeking support for it from, among others, Senator Norris, the originator of the Tennessee idea. Soon after, he met with a group of planners to discuss "how to reach the President with a scheme to organize the planning features (as against the waterpower features) of the Tennessee project." Notably, it was about this time that Norris and other congressmen amended the TVA act to make it what MacKaye later called "the American Magna Carta of regional planning." Of special importance was a provision authorizing the president to make plans covering the Tennessee Valley and contiguous areas "for the general purpose of fostering an orderly and proper physical, economic, and social development of said areas."[12]

Unfortunately, during a time when the nation was giving form to its greatest regional planning agency, MacKaye was not fully engaged in the process, spending much of his time seeking paid employment for himself and his ideas with his old agency, the Forest Service. When he first came to Washington in late March, he had tried to win support for his plan to employ the jobless in forestation projects and also for his old scheme of creating lumbering communities. Although Forest Service leaders were less than enthusiastic about his ideas, he was heartened by the enthusiasm of the foresters, some old friends, who had gathered in the capital. "They all agree that it's fun again to live; they are working like hell and love it."[13] It was as if the young Forest Service he had joined many years before was being reborn. Tired of his long semi-isolation at Shirley Center, MacKaye was anxious to return to government service, too anxious perhaps, because the first job he was offered he took.

On the surface the job had considerable promise, since it involved the development of a forestry program among the Indians. Typically, when he first learned of it, he outlined a program that he said would not only enable Indians to practice forestry but would "mould a real community" among them. This project brought him briefly into contact with Gutzon Borglum, who was engaged "in carving some kind of monument out in the Black Hills," and they spent some time discussing "Indian-Buffalo" culture. Although he was still in Washington at the end of May, he wrote that "it looks more than ever as if I'd join an Indian tribe," and less than two weeks later he was headed to South Dakota with a six-month appointment from the Department of the Interior. When he got to South Dakota, however, he was quickly reassigned to Gallup, New Mexico, to work with the Navajos, in whose tribal culture he began to take an interest—only to realize that he did not like the drylands environment.[14]

When he learned soon after that he had been appointed to a position in the Tennessee Valley Authority, therefore, he headed east as quickly as he could, in early September writing from Oklahoma City, "Thank God I'm headed for the Appalachians." Escaping from the desert, he was, spiritually at least, headed home, but shortly after he had reached Tennessee he was hospitalized for emergency surgery to remove a severe blockage of his intestines, an old problem exacerbated by the pressures under which he had been living for the previous months. By November he had returned north to recuperate, spending several weeks with Stein in the latter's apartment on Central Park West. By early December the gregarious Stein was growing restless, particularly since his wife was away. "Staying here with Ben has some how cut me off from the world—I must see people."[15]

Eventually, MacKaye was able to find another position with TVA, assisted by Stein, who had recommended him with the qualification that his friend's "outlook and interest is largely confined to the open country and the small towns" rather than to metropolitan areas. It was not until early April 1934, however, that MacKaye received a temporary appointment at a salary of $4,500 a year as a regional planner for the Authority. By the middle of the month he had moved to Knoxville, TVA's headquarters town, and finally was able to begin to establish himself as an influence on planning the Tennessee Valley.[16]

He found Knoxville to be "a little buzzing side-edition of Washington," which again reminded him of the exciting formative years of the Forest Service during the days of Teddy Roosevelt. Before long, he concluded that the place was even more stimulating than the capital, since he was "perpetually surrounded by experts and specialists on every subject under the sun and all talking at once," a possible harbinger of the long-hoped-for Veblenesque millennium when technicians would replace businessmen as the principal directive force. In anticipation of that millennium, MacKaye already had prepared a lengthy manuscript describing his plan for the valley, much of it a reformulation of his proposals in *The New Exploration*. He introduced it with the contention that regional planning was basically "government by vision, not dictation," intended to make the Earth a decent place for living by placing "culture ahead of industry, society ahead of mechanism, social development ahead of economics."[17]

Assigned to the Regional Planning section of the Division of Land Planning and Housing of the TVA, he was given what looked like an important role as coordinator of efforts to develop a comprehensive regional plan, which enabled him to say facetiously that he was "given the little chore of laying out a regional plan for the whole Tennessee Valley." Actually, his principal responsibility seems to have been to pull together the planning ideas of the various divisions of the TVA, from agriculture and forestry to dam construction and power generation. Initially, it was exciting work—"the best job of my life," he said— which took him back to "the honey moon of the U.S. Forest Service" during the days of the first Roosevelt. It brought him into contact with a rich variety of experts with visions of better worlds. In the first months he found in their diverse activities something like chaos but he thought he saw the beginnings in them of orderly plans and policies.[18]

Involvement in this exciting little world, however, did not translate into anything like effective influence, and he soon found that he was but a marginal figure in the decision-making process. In September 1934 he was able to show Wright and other visiting friends what he described as his "opus," a plan for the entire six hundred miles of the Tennessee Valley—which Wright concluded was generally in harmony with the position of the RPAA—but nothing seems to have resulted from his efforts.

In July 1935 MacKaye circulated among the leading members of the RPAA a long letter giving "a little boiled-down confidential low-down on the TVA." It was essentially a reply to a letter he had received three months earlier from Chase in which Chase had written, "Every time I think of the Tennessee Valley as the whole hope of the New Deal, I rejoice that you are in the middle of it." MacKaye acknowledged some truth in his friend's view, only then to make note of a deep problem. Part of his satisfaction with the job, he said, came from its freedom from responsibility. The head administrator, Arthur R. Morgan, "runs the locomotive while little me resides in the caboose."[19] From the rear of the train, he could see everything he wanted, but much of what he saw on the planning scene was not pleasing.

Although the power-generating side of the project was in the capable hands of David Lilienthal, MacKaye believed the planning side under Morgan suffered from fragmentation not only among six different departments but between two competing extremes of philosophy, neither of which satisfied him. While conceding that good planning involved a comprehensive concern for the physical needs of people, he stressed the importance—as he had done earlier—of "psychologic habitability," of planning a world in which people felt deeply at home. What he saw was a planning scene divided between "beautifiers," whose idea of improving conditions rarely rose much above the planting of pansies, and hard-boiled "engineers" indifferent to human sensibilities. "So to hell with aesthetes and to hell with he-men. What we need in tackling the matter of habitability (the urban, rural, and wilderness balance) is the ordinary gump with simple common sense."[20]

Significantly, he contrasted the planners of both extremes to the enthusiastic young people he had met in some of the Appalachian Trail clubs, particularly one in Atlanta, which he had attended only shortly before writing his letter. Here he found a group of dedicated "left-wingers" whom he concluded resembled his dream of a true fellowship, "a blend of intellect and gaity—a genuine discussion enlivened by square dancing—a setting of fireside, woods, mountains—one mighty chorus of *true* being."[21] Even in the Trail movement, however, he was finding bitterness and a reason for disillusionment.

Throughout his long championship of the Appalachian Trail he had held to the view that it was necessary to maintain the natural character along the Trail's crestline route, in the belief, as he said in 1932, that there had to be a counterpoint to industrial-urban reality. "Primeval influence is the opposite of machine influence. It is the antidote for over-rapid mechanization." In 1933, however, the National Park Service dropped a bomb into the movement by announcing plans to build a skyline drive for automobiles on the crest of the Blue Ridge Mountains, threatening to introduce the great agency of the metropolitan invasion into the heart of the mountains. "This clash of Trail vs. Highway on the mountain tops is something bigger than it seems," MacKaye wrote in the summer of 1935. "It is an early skirmish, perhaps the first significant skirmish in the retention of a humanly balanced world."[22]

MacKaye expected the trail clubs to support his view, but the Skyline Drive plan won the support of many members of the Appalachian Trail Conference, splitting the movement—"the celluloid outfit going one way and the real folks (the 'left-wingers') going the other." Disappointed by this sell-out to metropolitan interests, in 1934 MacKaye helped form the Wilderness Society to fight for the preservation of the wilderness side of the balance between society and nature, noting his belief that "the job of the regional planner is to *keep* the balance." In this he had the support of Mumford, Stein, and Wright, each of whom accepted his invitation to join the club.[23]

MacKaye's help in forming the Wilderness Society was a significant accomplishment, but it was accompanied by a failure to build a position for himself within the TVA, and in April 1936 he informed Mumford that he might soon be leaving that agency. "I am told," he wrote to Mumford, "that my philosophy of planning has been a 'real contribution' but that its further pursuit just won't fit the program for the next fiscal year." It was no surprise, then, when on June 22 he received a notice that his services as a regional planner "will no longer be required." He soon returned to Massachusetts, to Shirley Center, which in 1937 he proclaimed "America's most indigenous village." Among other things, he became involved with finding a refuge for his sister Hazel, who again began to suffer from mental depression.[24]

MacKaye did not totally abandon the TVA. In 1938, in response to a congressional investigation of the Authority, he laid down his ideal for the TVA program:

> First we dam a river and harness its energies. . . . Hereby we enslave a giant to our use, namely waterpower. This physical means we direct to economic and social ends. We make an industrial plan for the valley; acres and sites are allocated for the several kinds of factories— all efficiently related to one another. We make a Community plan for the valley; acres and sites are allocated for towns and cities of liveable

size and farms. Then we turn on the waterpower to bring these plans
about. This we do through proper management of the transmission
system, of the rate system, and of the two working together.[25]

In the same year MacKaye worked up an article applying the TVA
idea to all regions of the nation. Much of what he said there he had said
before, but there were two notable points that were at least partly new.
One involved a proposal to resist "chaotic community growth" not only
by his favorite method of natural barriers such as parks but also by
creating regional or "federated" cities, each "so designed that its several
component functions—of business, shopping, manufacture, education,
residence et al. would occupy special centers and be separated from one
another by ample rural areas." Such regional centers covering a county
or group of counties would ultimately replace the existing metropolitan
centers, providing a balance of "urban, rural, and primitive settings."[26]

MacKaye's second major point involved government and administration. Writing in 1938 under the deepening shadows of dictatorships,
he said that the most critical problem of the times was making democratic government both meaningful and effective. In particular, the
question was how to harmonize citizen control over policy making with
control by technicians over the technical aspects of good planning. The
answer, he said, might be found in the TVA, particularly in the making
of a river-valley system the major unit of democratic government, to be
subdivided into more local regional governments. By replacing artificially created states with governmental units rooted in regional life,
people would be enabled to take an active interest in the governing
process, responding to experts who would identify regional needs and
propose solutions for the people to accept—a system of governance
without politics and politicians.[27]

By the time he made these suggestions, however, a slowly recovering
economy and growing concern for world problems were steadily reducing what little opportunity there was to shape the TVA along the lines
favored by the RPAA. Over the years the great hope for regional
planning evolved into a source of electric power for the industrializing
and urbanizing South. Probably, this was inevitable. Within a year of
the formation of the TVA, Jacob Crane, a planner on the TVA staff (and
president of the American City Planning Institute) pointed out that,
whatever the dreams, the planning area had little cohesion, especially
in the political sense, because it included portions of several different
states. Since the Authority had no real association with state governments, said Crane, it could not command the force needed to reshape

the region, although he concluded by saying that it was probably a good type of agency for public power development.[28]

And so it proved. In the end, the failure of the New Deal to create a strong national presence in support of planning led naturally to an emphasis on power production. Although in one sense this was a triumph for the 1920s idea of Giant Power, it was a defeat of the larger RPAA hope for effectively planned regions where cheap power would be used to create what MacKaye in 1938 called "truly livable *living* for human beings to live in." Again, after raising hopes for radical change, the New Deal reverted back to the status quo, disappointing those who believed that the new class of experts should be allowed to have their way. One member of the RPAA, however, escaped much of this disappointment, chiefly because he surpassed even Stein in his skepticism of FDR and his policies. Having little faith in politics of any kind, Mumford looked to a very different influence to radically redirect the course of American development.

XV

NEW DEAL OR NEW ORDER?: MUMFORD

Writing long after the 1930s, Mumford identified the members of the RPAA with Aristotle's ideal of society: "a community of equals, aiming at the best life possible." He might have added, however, that they often differed in their hopes and dreams. Virtually from the beginning of the RPAA, Mumford in particular had distinguished himself from the others by a deep yearning for the truly radical. While his friends sought to reshape America from available materials, he dreamed of an entirely new social order embodying new values. He chose to view himself as a "eutopian" explorer of radical social possibilities as opposed to an impractical utopian thinker, devoting himself especially to promoting the ideals he believed could guide modern man's growing power over nature for human and humane ends. In 1921, for instance, he had praised Veblen's dream of a society managed efficiently by engineers, but he predicted that this would prove simply to be a more efficient version of a defective society unless its leaders learned what to produce for true human benefit as well as how to produce it.[1]

Mumford had much respect for technicians. In one of the most significant essays of his early career, "Toward a Humanist Synthesis," he addressed the familiar problem of bridging the gap between the physical sciences and the humanities by urging that humanists adopt the scientific method to produce a true social science. In establishing this point Mumford made an acute observation about his times and their relationship to technical expertise: "Through the world bureaucracy has grown at the expense of popular government because under the given conditions the bureaucracy is able to perform a large part of its work by the painstaking and accurate methods that are characteristic of scientific research."[2]

The way to the "New Jerusalem," Mumford believed, was by way of a fusion of scientific power and humanistic ends. For that to occur, however, a radical change in basic social values was required. Writing to his friend Van Wyck Brooks in 1925, he distinguished himself from "the old-fashioned revolutionists" who he said merely wanted to transfer power from one class to another whereas radicals like himself wanted "a revolutionary change which will displace a mean and inferior kind of life with a completely different kind." Here, he made an unintentional ironic reference to a future not yet realized by declaring that "an uprising merely means a *new deal;* a revolution means a different kind of game" (emphasis added).[3]

In November 1930, writing for a series on "Living Philosophies" in *Forum* magazine, he declared that "if I cannot call myself a revolutionist now, it is not because the current programs for change seem to go too far; the reason is rather because they are superficial and do not go far enough." Not even Russian Communism, with its ruthless drive to overwhelm the past, went far enough, since it was governed by the same utilitarian attitudes that dominated capitalistic America. "It is a new life I would aim at, not simply a new balance of power."[4]

By 1930 he had come to base this new life on a distinctly non-Soviet, "post-Marxian" form of communism. The Machine Age, he said, was preparing the way for a society that could meet all needs both by creating the productive machinery for material abundance and by conditioning people to cooperative habits. Where all basic needs of all people were satisfied, human ambitions could be shifted from a narrowing preoccupation with material comfort to living life to its fullest. "We must experience first hand manual toil and aesthetic ecstacy, periods of routine and periods of adventure, intellectual concentration and animal relaxation. We must know what it is to be a cook, tramp, a lover." Mumford denied that he hoped to abolish all evil in favor of perfection, since evil in the right proportions was part of life and perfection was death. His utopia was "to be alive, to act, to embody significance and value, to be fully human."[5]

In 1932, when *Forum* asked him to predict what the world would be like in fifty years, he presented his new order in a more concrete form. By 1982, he said, a world community with a common language would have replaced the warring world of nation states, allowing for the development of the region as the only significant entity most people would know. Plant breeding would make each region virtually self-sufficient in food and thereby reduce dependence on outside trade. Everywhere, communism would have replaced capitalism, allowing for a well-planned productive economy that would tend to make products as "free as air" to all. In some respects, this society would have the character of a "well-drilled beehive," but this would be countered by new forces in which freedom from want would allow for leisure and for "erotic and marital experiment, a whole series of initiatives in the culture of personality itself."[6]

By this time Mumford's affair with Bauer allowed for some erotic and marital experiment, but more generally he had not found the means that would take himself and the world to his promised land. In early 1929, responding to the self-congratulatory tendencies of a decade of progress before its collapse, he had sneered that "the most heartening sign of Renaissance in America is that there is a considerable body of intelligent people who realize that a new order and mode of being do not yet exist." In 1931 he rejected the hope that the new order could be found through democratic means, since the majority had been coopted by the existing order. "One does not make changes by converting the majority; one converts the majority by making changes." Such elitism left him profoundly skeptical of the political process. In 1932 at a meeting of student socialists at Barnard College, he called on socialists to devise some concrete goal they could use to awaken workers to the need for fundamental change, and he urged them "to live like Communists in preparation for the general upheaval, thereby to be enabled to step into the new order with the least confusion."[7]

By 1932 the Depression had excited Mumford's hopes for the collapse of the capitalist order. At this time, however, he saw little hope in Franklin Delano Roosevelt, and the first year of Roosevelt's New Deal simply reinforced his attitude. In September 1933 he told MacKaye that he expected the Roosevelt administration to do no more than produce "a half-baked revolution which would neither break with the past nor lead us into the future, but which would combine the worst features of both capitalism and socialism without deriving the benefits of either." In his view, Roosevelt was "a sort of political Mary Baker Eddy," a faith-healer who would never cure disease because he did not believe in radical operations.[8]

During these years in the early 1930s Mumford remained active in the RPAA both as its secretary and as a member. Thanks in part to Stein's persuasions, he took an interest in housing policy, supporting the Radburn line with its emphasis on large-scale construction of well-planned, well-sited dwellings but also by 1932 emphasizing the need for public subsidies to meet the needs of most Americans. In his most notable article on the subject, "Breaking the Housing Blockade" (1933), he advocated a massive national housing program featuring low-interest loans for the construction of "community units—villages, urban neighborhoods, whole towns." Rejecting Wood's housing strategy, he declared that slum clearance was a trap; it was better to build whole new communities where land was relatively cheap. A few months later he stated his aesthetic and social preferences regarding the design of new communities, condemning "the bourgeois suburb with its false scale of values and its pallid good taste" and calling for a new order of design in harmony with contemporary "industrial and recreational and domestic and sexual life."[9]

Even though he continued to take some interest in the RPAA, however, he had begun to drift away from it. His love affair with Bauer was distracting and her selection as corresponding secretary of the organization served to lessen his own responsibilities to it. Moreover, he had begun to drift away from New York, the city of his birth. In the mid-1920s he and his wife Sophia had discovered the rural delights of the area around Amenia in Dutchess County, and by the 1930s they had acquired a house and some land there. Although they continued to have their principal residence in New York City, first in Sunnyside Gardens and then elsewhere in the Borough of Queens, their hearts and minds relocated to their garden and apple orchard at Amenia. "My notion of heaven," Mumford wrote in 1932, "is an apple-orchard on a warm mid-afternoon in September." Finally, in 1936, he completed his move away from the city to rural America.[10]

He continued to commute to the city partly in connection with his extensive writings for the *New Yorker*, but in 1937 he could write, typically, that given his other work "the alternative is to quit the *New Yorker* or to quit Amenia next winter; and that leaves only one answer: chuck the *New Yorker!*" Although he continued to hold the ideal city in high esteem, his contempt for the real overcrowded city deepened. In 1940, for instance, he wrote to MacKaye that he had reached the conclusion "that the bulk of our planning and living in the future, will have to be in terms of a mainly rural environment. In other words, megalopolis is not merely on the downgrade; but its death, or rather suicide, instead of being a lingering matter . . . will probably take place in a decisive way within the next generation." In his darkly pessimistic view, rural places like Amenia were places of refuge in a new "Dark Ages" descending on the world."[11]

Years before he reached this lugubrious rejection of the metropolis, he had chosen a path that inevitably weakened his connections with the RPAA. Unlike the architecturally oriented majority of the members and unlike the forestry oriented MacKaye, Mumford had placed theory above practice, consecrating himself to the radical intellectual's task of conceiving a system of thought that could ultimately revolutionize the fundamental assumptions that guided both thought and behavior. Without the transformation of those assumptions, he believed, efforts to improve modern life would remain little better than half-baked new deals unproductive of significant change. Regional planning would rarely transcend the limits of an RPNY unless society were educated to a fundamental appreciation of regionalism—an object toward which he had striven in his first three books.

By the end of the 1920s Mumford had produced an impressive set of ambitious and influential works on various significant aspects of culture, and in the 1930s he elevated his ambitions even more. In 1931 he wrote that a pattern of adolescent illness had left him for many years with the conviction that he would die before he reached the age of forty, a fear that he believed led him to limit the scope of each of his works in order to be sure of completing it. Now, however, at age thirty-six he was beginning to contemplate a life beyond forty and to devise larger works. The next year brought him the opportunity when he was one of forty-two scholars and artists chosen for a Guggenheim Award, in his case to write a book on "form."[12]

What that meant had already been determined. In 1930, inspired perhaps by Chase's popular *Men and Machines* (1929), he had written a theoretical article, "The Drama of the Machines," for *Scribner's,* and this had led to an invitation from Columbia University to teach an extension course on the Machine Age. Now the Guggenheim Award made it possible for him to carry out an exhaustive study of technology in European museums and libraries. In March 1933, just before he was to begin writing the book, he had a "shattering quarrel" with Bauer that seriously weakened their relationship but strengthened his need to work. In June 1933 Stein visited the Mumfords at Amenia and reported that "Lewis is working with tireless energy." The result was the publication in 1934 of his massive and trail-breaking *Technics and Civilization,* a historical and philosophical study of the interaction between technology and culture in Western society.[13]

Mumford intended in the book to "out-Marx the Marxists" and to out-do everyone else, radical or conservative, as an authority on the significance of technology to modern society; he especially set out to overturn the Marxist belief in technological determinism by demonstrating that human culture had created the machine rather than the reverse. Most of the work is a history of technology over the previous seven centuries, beginning with a preindustrial Golden Age in medieval times, when machinery had served the purposes of life. Like his previous books, however, it is fundamentally history devoted to an exposition of his social ideals. Broadly, he viewed the machine in highly positive terms as an expression of human rationality and as "an instrument of life," but he argued that this force for happiness and freedom had been perverted under the influence of capitalism into a source of human misery.[14]

Fortunately, new forces were appearing to challenge this perversion, beginning with Romanticism, which had reasserted the preeminence of organic life over lifeless mechanism. From the Romantic response to industrialism had come regionalism, often in Mumford's view a sentimental reactionary rejection of all things modern but also a broad potentially popular movement that could restore the machine as an instrument for life. What was needed was to absorb into the Romantic respect for life the lessons of reason, scientific objectivity, and rational order that machine production provided. Regional plans conceived by rational experts could then harness the machine to concrete human ends determined by the special character of a particular region.

As against the modern trend toward regional specialization, Mumford urged that each region produce, with the aid of plant breeding, its food and other basic necessities, thereby reducing its involvement with the outside world and giving it greater freedom to determine its own destiny. At the same time he hoped that through a program of economic regionalism it would be possible to work out a rational reallocation of industries related to the special resources of particular regions and to effect "the re-settlement of the world's population into the areas marked as favorable for human beings." Eventually, the planet would become a federation of balanced regions, miniature worlds of small farms and small industries, each of which would find its own way of harnessing the power of the machine to the needs of life. "When automation becomes general and the benefits of mechanization are socialized, men will be back once more in the Edenlike state in which they have existed in regions of natural increment like the South Seas; the ritual of leisure will replace the ritual of work, and work itself will become a kind of game."[15]

If Mumford's new order resembled in basic ways a romanticized premodern order, the means he chose for his return were not too different from those used by Thomas More and the other great utopians of the past. In his view the world would not radically improve and the machine would not be subordinated to life until capitalism was eliminated and replaced by a non-Marxist form of "basic communism." On one level he advanced the distinctly unutopian view that this might require some kind of upheaval, possibly a violent one. At one point he proposed that government take charge of all banking functions as a first step in the process, declaring that "if such control cannot be instituted with the cooperation and intelligent aid of the existing administrators of industry, it must be achieved by overthrowing them." In their place would come "the geographer and the regional planner, the psychologist, the educator, the sociologist," and other experts capable of managing the rational order created by the machine, all presumably operating under humanistic goals established by philosophers like Mumford. Essentially, however, both the nature and the timing of the new political order remained obscure, as it had been in the 1920s when Veblen had popularized the idea of rule by technicians.

Lacking faith in either politics or the working class, Mumford preferred to devote himself to changing the ideals and consciousness that governed social decisions, continuing the work first attempted in *The Story of Utopias* a decade before. Even more than then, he believed he could help actualize a new movement in modern civilization, which he continued to call "eutopianism, the belief in the possibility of renovating society through the application of reason and social invention to political and economic institutions." Through his writings he could help to effect a eutopian revolution by reeducating readers to the radical ideals and attitudes required for a true transformation of society. [16]

Before completing *Technics and Civilization* Mumford had concluded that he needed more than the one book to achieve his objectives and had begun to conceive of his The Renewal of Life series. Seven years later he recalled that in 1931 he had submitted a draft of the book to his then lover Bauer, whose criticism had helped turn the book "from a compact restatement of past views into what I trust proved a more penetrating and wide-ranging study." In his first work he had chosen to deal with one essential dimension of modern civilization, the machine and technical culture; in his second, he chose another dimension, the city and urbanization, and produced perhaps his greatest and most influential book, *The Culture of Cities,* published in 1938. Among those who most influenced this study, he listed Patrick Geddes first and then his colleagues in the RPAA, specifically Whitaker, Stein, MacKaye, and Wright, as well as Bauer. [17]

In his brief preface to the book Mumford announced its essential purpose: "to establish, for the purpose of communal action the basic principles upon which our human environment—buildings, neighborhoods, cities, and regions—may be renovated." Roughly half of its nearly five hundred pages is the urban equivalent of the technological history he presented in *Technics and Civilization,* beginning with a positive view of medieval towns and ending with a lurid account of that paleotechnic hell, Megalopolis. The concluding pages of this part feature such words as "shapeless gigantism," "congestion," "blighted," "depletion," "defacement," "sick," "poison," and "decay." Basically, it is history designed to tell an apocalyptic tale of decline and death in preparation for Mumford's version of redemption and rebirth.[18]

Redemption is the tale told in the second half of the book, which deals far more extensively with regionalism and regional planning than was possible in *Technics.* Here, Mumford presents one of the most comprehensive accounts of the subject ever written, discussing many of the ideas promoted by the RPAA, but this is an account shaped to his eutopian purposes. "If there are favorable habitats," he asks, "for animals and plants, as ecology demonstrates, why not for men?" In answer he says that humankind had finally achieved the ability "to create a new biological and social environment, in which the highest possibilities of human existence will be realized, not for the strong and lucky alone, but for all co-operating and understanding groups, associations, and communities."[19]

This emphasis on groups is linked to his belief that the region was a natural unit of human existence and activity. Ideally, each region would have its own special combination of human diversity, where everyone would be at home in friendly territory, free to develop his or her full potential. Each region would be a little world scaled to human beings, a world predominately of small farms, factories, and villages without the inhuman gigantism of Megalopolis. Although the degree of dependence would be significantly lessened, no region would be totally independent from the others, providing a place for moderate-size cities as mediums for the exchange of both ideas and goods among the regions.[20]

The way to this ideal world was to be plotted by regional planners on the basis of careful surveys of the natural and cultural resources of the earth's ecological regions. Here Mumford refers to most of the basic elements of planning advocated by the RPAA: townless highways, garden cities, Giant Power, the TVA, and cultivation of the landscape. He commends Wright's 1926 report as a "masterly outline regional plan," which he subsequently said "showed the latent possibilities for a new order." Except for garden cities, however, he says little about these elements; the Appalachian Trail, which did so much to inspire the formation of the RPAA, he mentions only as an example of the effects of regional surveys. Essentially, what emergences is a rather vague promise that planning by the right experts will produce a beneficial resettlement of people and industries into environments expertly designed to meet human needs, a promise grounded in a system of control guaranteed to offend many Americans. "The standards set for production," he writes of planning, "must not only include private consumption but public works—houses and highways, parks and gardens, cities and civic institutes, and all the interconnecting tissue that finally comprises an organic region. Only when the whole has been plotted out can the individual function be directed with efficiency."[21]

To achieve that degree of control required a fundamental change in power relationships, which Mumford barely discusses other than in the form of the substitution of communal ownership of land for private ownership. This core element in his basic communism would "put the division and supervision of the land in the hands of the appropriate local and regional authorities, who would map out areas of cultivation, areas of mining, areas of urban settlement, as they now map out areas of public parks." More generally, he concludes that his new world could be attained "only when our political and economic institutions are directed toward regional rehabilitation." Although he includes an extensive chapter entitled "The Politics of Regional Development," however, he fails to explain the steps by which regional control could be established, leaving the reader with the strong impression that he is a parlor radical, a dreamer of new orders, who has had little direct experience with the real world of planning or human activity.[22]

In this respect *The Culture of Cities,* for all of its brilliance, may well have done a profound disservice to regional planning. By downplaying the practical mechanics of planning elements like the townless highway, Mumford created a picture that manages to be both naive and menacing, utopian and totalitarian, a picture of a world where ultimate good is placed under the control of an elite, which he barely acknowledges but that must exist. Published in 1938, just before Americans began to turn their thoughts to war, the book became something like the last word for the time on the subject of regional planning, a misfortune given its failure to deal adequately with the significant practical ideas of the RPAA. This might have been avoided if it had not been for the flagging energies and influence of most of his friends and for the demise of the association itself.

XVI

THREE WISE MEN: CHASE, ACKERMAN, AND WHITAKER

When in his acknowledgements at the end of *The Culture of Cities* Mumford listed some members of the RPAA, he omitted the names of several others in the association whom he might have mentioned, none more notable than Chase. In basic ways Chase and Mumford were the chief rivals within the group, competing for the same goals but with distinctive if not opposing styles. They both aspired to and succeeded at making a living by writing for large audiences on a wide variety of general subjects. Each gave special attention to educating the public in the implications of technology, Mumford in his *Technics* and Chase in his somewhat earlier *Men and Machines*. And, although Chase was some seven years older than Mumford, they were the bright young men of the regional planning movement, each an enthusiastic advocate of planning as the way to solve social problems.

If there were similarities between the two men, though, there were also fundamental differences. In the summer of 1936 MacKaye visited them and their wives. "It was a fascinating experience," MacKaye wrote to Mumford, "to study the inner workings of your two minds." He had already seen the difference between them reflected in the most recent books of the two. Chase's book, on conservation, "is of the Brain Trust," while Mumford's, on technics, "is of the Soul trust." Years earlier the difference was evident in their attitudes toward the big city. In the 1930s both men abandoned New York City as a hopeless place to live, but, whereas Mumford saw the metropolis as basically hostile to life, Chase proclaimed himself "no city hater" and saw significant potentialities in it. "One can nominate a dozen engineers and architects," he wrote in 1930, "who, given a free hand, could make even New York genuinely inhabitable—at a cost not much greater than that of a new subway program." He shared Mumford's penchant for utopian thinking, but, while his rival dreamed of a basic communism founded on humane values, he wanted a technocratic utopia of rational order and efficiency.[1]

Chase's inclinations were evident in his appraisal of the economic collapse after 1929. Regarding the prosperous 1920s he saw both sides. It had been an age of great material progress and of great energy, complete with such ambitions as sending a rocketship to Mars, but it had also been a time of much poverty and unemployment. Initially, like most observers, he failed to appreciate the extent of the crisis, predicting in November 1929 that the stock-market crash would not disrupt the general economy and, indeed, would serve the public welfare by diverting money from stock speculation into building construction and other useful work. Less than a year later, however, he concluded that the "main spring" of prosperity had been broken. The task confronting a depressed America, then, in his view, was not simply reviving prosperity but developing an entirely new economic mechanism.[2]

Chase's basic technocratic bent grew stronger. Engineers, he said in 1931, had been the primary builders of the modern world, but their work was under the direction of selfish monetary interests that had perverted the machine and technical skill for short-sighted benefits. What was needed was a great national version of the situation that he believed existed at Radburn, where the "engineering mind" had been given a free hand to construct a human environment on a rational basis. He was careful to distinguish between what he called the engineering mind and the mentality of the average engineer, who he believed was subservient to money, whereas the true technocrat was a thoroughgoing professional "dedicated to building and not to profit-making."[3]

Although he dreamed of control by pure-minded technicians, Chase realized that any effectively planned economy would have to include a diversity of economic powers, including business. Looking back to the First World War he advocated the creation by the national government of a supreme economic council to bring together all the major economic interests and to coordinate their efforts under a ten-year plan. One special element of this plan was to substitute "a vast slum razing and home building program for the declining motor car industry." Another was a massive forestation program designed to employ hundreds of thousands of the unemployed.[4]

Chase emphasized the need to give national control a strongly regionalized form, arguing that "the only kind of master planning that will ultimately take root and come to be cherished by the underlying population is regional planning." One of the first tasks of what he called the national Peace Industries Board would be to create regional boards to do the real work of economic planning and management. Speculating in the *Nation* on what he would do "If I Were Dictator," he proposed that the United States be mapped into its natural regions, within each of which programs would be developed to promote partial economic self-sufficiency and to stimulate local traditions and the arts. He also promised to deal with the special problem of New York City by tearing down some twenty square miles of it and making spaces to grow grass and flowers. Once he had things running smoothly, he promised to retire from his hypothetical dictatorship in favor of a permanent board of technicians, preferably engineers, which would direct the economy.[5]

In a series of articles published in the *New Republic* during the summer of 1932 he expanded his ideas into what he called "A New Deal for America," giving a positive and central importance to Mumford's mere new deal; the publication of the first of the articles on June 29 introduced this term for future use to designate the policies of the yet to be elected Roosevelt administration. Again, Chase advocated economic planning supported by effective controls—including controls over the rate of technological innovation in order to limit the disruptive effects of new inventions. In his conclusion, as a solution to economic collapse, he proposed a "Third Road" between Soviet-style Communism and the emerging Fascism of Italy and Germany, in which control of the economy would be shifted from business, with its short-sighted, inefficient concern with profits, to an elite of skilled scientific managers, the "perhaps one hundred thousand technicians, engineers and operating managers" who were already working the system for business.[6]

Under Chase's New Deal, production to meet human needs would replace production to make profits and cooperation would replace competition, eliminating most of the wastefulness of the existing system. As an example of what could be eliminated, he made note of "the rusting skeletons of motor cars, befouling untold miles of country roads," a particularly obnoxious expression of practices that had turned half of the natural resources used in production into "junk and litter and waste." As an example of what might be done, he proposed a massive program to rehouse the American population in planned communities like Radburn, employing hundreds of thousands in construction—and not coincidentally creating opportunities for architects like his friends Stein and Wright.[7]

Chase, who had a steady position as a research economist with the Labor Bureau in New York City as well as a considerable income from his writings, held no government office under Roosevelt's New Deal except as a consultant for the National Resources Committee in 1934 and the Resettlement Administration in 1935, but he did generally identify with its policies. In 1934 he defended the administration's spending for public works against the critics of deficit spending, arguing that it was needed to help restore prosperity and in any case added significantly to the nation's stock of useful wealth in such forms as highways and new housing. The next year he told the National Education Convention in Atlantic City that the Depression had made government action a necessity. "We must be prepared to see an increasing amount of collectivism, government interference, centralization of economic control, [and] social planning."[8]

He showed a special enthusiasm for the TVA, which he described as "putting water to work in the first comprehensive program of planning with nature ever attempted." He recalled that in the 1920s regional planning had been strictly an academic matter when he, Mumford, MacKaye, Stein, and other members of the RPAA had met in cafés on Forty-fifth Street in New York to dream aloud of a well-planned America, but now the Depression had created radically new conditions that promised to transform dreams into practical realities. In July 1931, at the conference on regionalism in Charlottesville, he had suggested that the time had come to take a specific region, study it in detail, and develop a program for it that would make "the home country fairer, happier, more to be loved." Indeed, the time seemed to have come. In 1934, on a visit to the TVA, he had, with his friend MacKaye, climbed up into the Great Smoky Mountains, where he had observed the government forestry program at work, and at Knoxville he had seen some of the assemblage of technicians who he hoped would lead America: "engineers, foresters, architects, statisticians, economists, sociologists, and educational experts."[9]

In listing the basic missions of the TVA, Chase noted that the most general—the improvement of the well-being of the people living in the area—was also the weakest in political acceptance when compared with such things as flood control and hydroelectric power. "It may yet prove the undoing of the whole experiment," he said. "It is bad form to consider the social well-being of two million people scattered over seven states." More optimistically, however, he looked on the TVA as a possible prototype for similar programs in all of the major river valleys of America. In 1937 he said that sooner or later the nation would have to create a system of regional authorities to work with nature. The head of an authority in each region would be instructed "to hold the soil, water, wild life, cover crops, at par, turn over the land to the oncoming generation in at least as good a condition as you find it. It is your job to make your section of America a healthy, vital, attractive homeland which your children can earn a living from and enjoy."[10]

Chase developed a special interest in conservation, especially in what he called "a new ecology which respects nature and still permits technological progress." Nearly a decade before, he had been attracted to MacKaye's geotechnics, praising *The New Exploration* as "the first large-scale attempt that I have seen to plan an environment where genuine culture and recreation and culture can flourish." In his *Rich Land, Poor Land* (1936), in which he applied his talent for popularizing technics to the management of nature, he proposed a distinctly non-Thoreauvean formula for the new ecology: "The first step is to understand what nature demands as a minimum; the next step is to calculate the highest possible living standard considered therewith; the third step is to arouse the American people to bring the two together." He was especially concerned with arousing Americans to the dangers of soil erosion, the result of the mismanagement of the land, which would progressively impoverish the nation unless the waste of this most basic resource was reversed through such agencies as the TVA.[11]

Throughout the 1930s Chase was a strong defender of the New Deal, arguing that government intervention and planning—a general centralization of control—was needed both to resolve such basic problems as conservation and to revive a faltering economy. In 1935 he spoke strongly in support of a $4 billion plan to improve the Mississippi River. "You poor damned fools; do you think that a great river system is only a mechanism to turn an honest penny?" After years of abuse, the great river was presenting its bill, which had to be paid to avoid more floods, more mud, and more obstructions to navigation. He defended public spending in part with the argument that public works added to the overall wealth of the nation, and he went beyond that to defend deficit spending as necessary to compensate for the decline of business spending as a way of stimulating economic growth.[12]

In his enthusiasm for government, Chase found less than united support from his colleagues in the RPAA, not only Mumford but most

of the others. Of them, only MacKaye could be said to be close to Chase
in intellectual style and general outlook. Before the 1930s Chase had
been something of an outsider in respect to the New York core group
headed by Mumford and Stein, even though he lived in the same city.
They appeared to mistrust his enthusiasm and his interest in current
trends, the qualities that made him a successful popularizer. Probably
most agreed with Mumford when he told MacKaye that, in *Men and
Machines,* Chase was too accepting of mechanization. "I don't think
Stuart has tussled with some of the hard problems hard enough."[13] In
the 1930s Chase's enthusiasms for government planning and action did
nothing to change his position among men who found it difficult to rise
above their suspicions of politics.

Those suspicious of politics included not only Mumford and Stein
but also Ackerman, who responded to the Depression in his own eccentric way. During the twenties, Ackerman had concentrated on his
architectural career—with some success, since several of his designs
received notice in the *Architectural Record.* As an architect and consultant for the CHC he had done extensive design work on both Sunnyside
and Radburn. Although the least published of the RPAA members, he
occasionally spoke out in significant ways.

In 1930, for instance, Ackerman called for extensive research to
replace what he considered obsolete housing designs with those more in
tune with man's basic instincts, the aim being to reconcile "our modern
means and the instinctive traits of character with which we are en-
dowed." Two years later he supported Kohn's proposal that the federal
government use private architects rather than its own designers in the
planning of public buildings, arguing in part that private architects
were more likely to provide for regional variations in design: while
government bureaucrats naturally favored standardization, private architects with local roots would provide designs reflecting the "distinct
historical backgrounds, traditions, and cultural characteristics" of the
various regions.[14]

In his thinking if not in his practice, Ackerman was one of the most
radical of architects, his attitude strongly colored by a distaste for the
profit system he had inherited from both Henry George and Thorstein
Veblen. During the conservative twenties he had said little, but with
the great collapse he was awakened by the potential for radical change.
In 1932 and 1933 he and Stein were particularly close, the two men
and their wives living in the same apartment house across from Central
Park. They met frequently, often with one or more other members of
the RPAA, for dinner in Stein's apartment, where they had, as Stein

put it in March 1933, "so much to say to each other—a real closeness." At a time when all seemed possible, these events sparkled with ideas as the group tried to work out their routes to new times—and Ackerman was one of the most enthusiastic in his involvement.[15] It soon became apparent, however, that he was disposed to follow a route that left him even further from the New Deal than the others.

Given his concern for regional architecture Ackerman might have been expected to favor the TVA when the RPAA began to rally behind that proposal, but he soon concluded that government schemes like the TVA would be a waste of time without a fundamental reordering of the economy, that meaning, for him, the total elimination of the price system in favor of an economic order run by technicians. In 1932, calling himself a "technologist," he declared that "Bolshevism, Communism, Capitalism, and its offspring, Fascism, are utterly impotent to deal with the advanced technological situation in which we, of the North American Continent find ourselves placed." The only answer was to create a centralized economic system in which scientific reason replaced profit as the basis for decisions, the object being to produce an unlimited abundance for all rather than wealth for the few. Stein noted ironically that his friend was dreaming of a world "where there was no want and no profit, where street cleaners and movie stars would receive the same return—all they needed."[16]

Ackerman's technocratic fantasies did not bring him into alignment with Chase or many others in the broad technocratic movement. In fact, with the advent of the New Deal, he broke with the movement at least in part over the issue of deficit spending. He was basically hostile to a government debt, not only because it was part of the price system but because it would allow those who owned it to escape the obligation to work. In an article distributed by the Continental Committee on Technology in 1933, in which he urged central control by technicians over "the great social mechanism," he said that where there was "no debt, there could be no leisure class. All those physically capable must work for a given period of their lives, within those function divisions for which they were best fitted."[17]

During the depths of the Depression Ackerman received some public attention, but his efforts to publicize the need for a radical new America were doomed by a clumsy writing style that often left his readers baffled as to what he was attempting to say. In 1932, for instance, he wrote that "any scheme of social organization designed to utilize our resources and our ability under conditions of security offered by technology in the name of science will involve the disallowance of the price

system." After encountering such statements, Stein said that it was
unlikely that many people would ever understand Ackerman. "It is a
shame that the greatest mind in the architectural profession should
have so little ability at expression."[18]

Even if Ackerman had been a more gifted writer, however, he would
still have been handicapped by a cranky intellect that puzzled most
other thinkers, including his friends. His most distinctive strength
among his colleagues was an analytical ability to work with numbers,
especially to calculate costs, but that strength also seems to have left
him with a feeling of isolation from the often illogical world of human
diversity. Stein, who probably knew him best, saw a cleavage in his
thinking between "the unreality of the practical world of to-day—and
the real functioning world of the future which exists only to him and a
few others."[19]

Despite his suspicions of the New Deal, Ackerman was persuaded by
Kohn to come to Washington, where he served as a consultant for Kohn's
Housing Division. Confronted with a whirl of bureaucratic politics he
could not understand, Ackerman soon concluded that most of those who
served the early New Deal had little contact with what he believed was
reality. "Here," he complained to Mumford, "action has the quality of
having been reflected in a mirror with a highly distorted surface." He
soon wanted to leave, but he was induced to stay by Kohn, who considered him "the only really analytic mind" that he had in regards to
housing matters. By March 1934, however, Ackerman concluded that
the position of the embattled Kohn was hopeless and accepted a posting,
offered through Stein, as the technical advisor for the New York Municipal Housing Authority. Moving back to New York, he became involved
with slum clearance and public housing over the next several years. For a
time both he and Stein were special lecturers in the New York School of
Architecture. After 1934 little was heard from him regarding technoc-
racy and the overthrow of capitalism.[20]

Ackerman was not the only RPAA member to be awakened to radical
fantasies by the Depression. After years of a sometimes sullen isolation
Whitaker reappeared in the movement he had instigated years before.
Over the years his hostility to industrial society had grown stronger,
especially to the automobile, Henry Ford's "infernal machine," which
he said in 1931 was incapable of producing anything significant among
its disciples "except a belief that with more speed they will get somewhere." In December 1932 he showed up at Stein's apartment where,
according to Stein, "he and Ackerman compared notes with much
pleasure and laughter—on the downfall of capitalistic society."[21]

While Whitaker was dreaming his Georgist dreams, he was also much involved in finishing his magnum opus, *From Rameses to Rockefeller: The Story of Architecture* (1934), in which he intended to present "a complete new point of view on the whole business of architecture." Along with considerable scholarship, the book displayed a strong animus in favor of modern architecture and against his old enemies, land speculators and developers. In part it was a tribute to Louis Sullivan— "sage, prophet, and craftsman"—to whom he devoted a five-page dedication that read like a love letter to his long-dead hero, beginning with "here I sit, Louis, thinking what I am to say about you and your ideas."[22]

Even more, the book was a story of good and evil, much of it the tale of the generally unsuccessful struggle of a minority of dedicated architects and builders against both public bad taste and the greed of land speculators. Where there should have been good housing amid beautiful surroundings there was an urban world of haphazardly crowded cities radically at odds with human nature. After darkness, however, perhaps the dawn. Near the end of the book, Whitaker said that the Depression had opened the way for the entire rebuilding of America along the lines of planned communities like Radburn. Leading the way would be what he called the "spirit of modern architecture," an honest craftsmanship guided by Sullivan's dictum that "form follows function" to create graceful, inexpensive buildings suited to human instincts, as opposed to the pompous, overblown styles favored by professional architects corrupted by the interests of land speculators. In his dream all of the craftsmen of the nation would join together to construct a new civilization of happiness and harmony. "Build us a fine and pleasant world," he urged in bringing his book to a close. "Make a plan—and let the beginning of your plan be this—a fine and spacious room for every man, woman, and child."[23]

Whitaker's book was far less an analysis of contemporary circumstances than a final statement of faith, combining the essentially Georgist economics of his youth with his longtime criticism of public architecture, especially that in Washington, D.C., which he denounced in the book as "a Roman architecture for an arrogant bloated government." As in the past, he saw there a powerful example of perverted taste that had led Americans throughout the land to waste billions of dollars on the "blind worship of style," money that might have been used to provide tasteful, comforting housing for all people.[24]

Whatever his feelings about Washington, however, he would temporarily reestablish his connections with that city. In April 1933 he was

there to help MacKaye promote his ideas for the TVA. For a time soon
after, he became involved with an attempted socialistic "colony" in
southwestern New Mexico, but he soon concluded that efforts to establish such cooperative societies in a capitalistic world were doomed to
failure. By the summer of 1933 he had decided to use his Washington
contacts to get employment with the newly established TVA, his ratio-
nale being that his presence was required to deal with "real estate
sharks" who he had heard were taking up land options in the valley in
order to benefit from the Tennessee project. His application for a job,
however, only evoked a reply that there were already some 30,000
applicants listed for such jobs. "So you can see," he wrote ironically to
MacKaye, "that the regional planners are more numerous than we
suspected."[25]

It was probably just as well that Whitaker did not find a place with
the New Deal. His personality had not mellowed with age. Stein
observed that the bad as well as the good in his character had grown
stronger, especially a stubborn disposition to do things his way. In his
book he made it plain that he was no friend of the emerging public-
housing program, condemning it as creating new public debt that
worked chiefly to drive up the price of land for the benefit of speculators. Like his friend Ackerman, he rejected deficit spending, in his case
because he believed that it only added to the burdens imposed by a
radically defective capitalism on society. For him as for his friend, only
radical change would save the world. In 1936 he wrote to Mumford
that the depression had forced on mankind the choice of either property
or life as the basis for human relations: "We are caught, all of us, in that
act of the drama. If it puts an end to liberalism, it may be worth the
price, for in liberalism there is no hope. What hope lies beyond communism, who can say? A world of new people has to come into being. A
world of traditionalism and hoary emotionalism has to go."[26]

A few months later, in a public letter in the *New York Times,* he
urged Americans to forgo their concerns with individual rights and
property and to accept the need for public control and perhaps ownership of the land. Only through the scientific, well-planned management of its land could America eventually eliminate its slums and
begin to restore its ravaged landscape. It had been the absence of such
power in the past, he said, that left architects and planners like himself
"powerless to guide the building of decent, comfortable and pleasurable
communities, as they were likewise powerless to avert the spread of
slums." It had been that same absence that had prevented the

conservation-minded from averting the droughts, dust storms, floods, and soil erosion that were afflicting a careless, wasteful nation.[27]

Even with the public concern raised by the dust bowl and similar environmental disasters, Whitaker saw little hope that Americans could be persuaded to accept radical change. Although Whitaker never completely abandoned his dream, in his last letter to Mumford he declared "I don't see any light on the horizon" that could offer hope for fundamental improvement. What he did see was a great battle between "wit," which he identified with the private ownership and the pursuit of short-sighted profits, and "intelligence," the basis for true progress—a battle that wit seemed to be winning with the support of the mass media and their influence over popular thought. "My guess is that in printing-press, movie, and radio the witty ones now hold the fort."[28]

In 1936, his letterhead read "House at Drovers' Rest Four Miles Beyond Langley on the Road to Great Falls, Va." Undoubtedly from this last refuge in Virginia he thought back to the 1920s, to his home at Mount Olive, and to those brighter days when he could believe it was possible to begin the world over again. Although he had the comfort of his longtime wife, Gene, as well as the support of friends like Stein and MacKaye, he seems to have concluded that there was little reason for clinging to life, and in August 1938 at age sixty-six he departed for a better world with presumably better architecture. His obituary summed up his life's story: "He was often involved in controversy. One of his pet hatreds was the architectural jumble of Washington which he said could not be considered beautiful because the government buildings militated against the hordes of government employees who worked in them. He frequently . . . praised the arrowlike Washington monument as the only beautiful memorial in the capital."[29]

By the time of Whitaker's death, the RPAA too had disappeared amid the deepening clouds of a troubled world. Before this, the association had lost another of its members, whose life epitomized the hopes raised in it by the New Deal and the Great Depression and whose death was an omen of its demise.

XVII

THE WRIGHT WAY

By all accounts, among the members of the RPAA Henry Wright was the most sensitive to the land as the site for buildings. "He had an almost sensuous feeling for the land and contour," said an associate, Albert Mayer. "He was an artist in land." Wright's longtime partner Stein described him as having an almost supernatural ability to relate "buildings and living to the facts of nature—to the sun, the winds, the views, but, above all, to the form of the land." Although he was, in the words of another associate, "a nice man to know," a man without ego and always willing to listen to others, he could be stubborn in his insistence on the commitment to good site planning. There was one defect common to home construction in America, he said in 1931, "whether our houses are erected brick by brick to resemble medieval castles or are electro-welded to look like escaped sections of the county jail, namely our total and utter lack of appreciation of the fact that the quality of the house plan is definitely and irrevocably related to its site and setting." Site planning was far more than laying out lots; it involved a commitment to developing the full potential of the site for human living.[1]

He did much of his best work in partnership with others, especially Stein, who balanced his idealism with a strong sense of political realism. The two had worked well together in the planning of both Sunnyside and Radburn as well as in the preparation of the New York State Plan of 1926. For a time in 1928 Wright grew dissatisfied with the situation at Radburn and dreamed of going to Russia, "our best and first hope," where he believed his planning ideas might best be accepted. In the end, however, he continued his creative partnership with

Stein into the early 1930s, when they were employed by the Buhl
Foundation of Pittsburgh to make the preliminary plans for a model
community in that city.

Although they did not do the final design work for what became
Chatham Village, Wright and Stein had a critical influence in persuading the sponsors to shift their emphasis from freestanding single-family
houses to row houses, the key being their convincing estimate that only
row houses could be constructed cheaply enough to make the project
successful. Before they were finished the two men had also provided the
basic site plan for the community, using a modified version of the
superblock design established in Radburn. When it was completed in
1936, Chatham Village was a model community of close to two hundred dwelling units, which occupied only 30 percent of the forty-five
acre site, the rest devoted to playgrounds and green space, including a
twenty-five acre forest and some two miles of pedestrian trails.[2]

Stein called Chatham Village an "outstanding American example of
housing and site planning," declaring that he was not being boastful,
because the principal work had been done by others, especially by
Wright, whose genius he believed had created the basic context for the
community. In October 1931 the two men published a short article in
the *Architectural Record* declaring that the Depression had created both
an opportunity and a need to break away from the old "illogical" forms
of land subdivision and to "exercise a higher type of imagination" in the
creation of community designs such as that for Chatham Village. Years
before, Wright had complained that society spent less time and imagination on its housing designs than on the design of its automobiles.[3]

Wright had long crusaded against "illogical" land management. In
1927, as chairman of the AIA's Committee on Community Planning,
he warned that suburban subdivisions were wasting large expanses of
metropolitan space, for instance that Chicago developers had platted
enough land to house eighty million people; the result was not only
much spoiled land but increased costs of housing to pay for the expenses
of haphazard development. At the same time he condemned small
developers for blotching large areas of Queens and Brooklyn in New
York City with ugly rows of small look-alike houses with tiny yards
that were sure to become slums in the future. Wright also disliked
conventional apartment-house development; in 1932 he created a stir
by condemning the buildings then being erected for the well-to-do
along New York's Riverside Drive as "slums or potential slums," their
chief defect being that they covered at least two-thirds of their land
areas, when "everybody knows that a one-third coverage is now consid-

ered the maximum permissible for decent multi-family dwellings."[4] Wright had yet to experience the combination of high-rise projects, open spaces, and poverty that in the future would be considered breeders of crime.

By the time he had finished with Chatham Village, Wright had evolved a planning strategy that he believed he could implement with a variety of techniques he had developed over the years. Basic to all was a rejection of the traditional grid system of streets and land division in favor of some version of the superblock, which allowed for a more sophisticated use of the land. Much of that use was determined by Wright's belief that the most efficient utilization of the land was obtained by limiting the coverage of buildings to approximately a third of the whole area, reserving the rest for playgrounds, gardens, lawns, parks, and woodlands. This coverage, he was certain, could be obtained by a careful planning of the buildings, the great majority of residential structures being neither single-family houses nor tall apartment houses but three-story row houses; these would avoid the wastes of free-standing houses and allow for the efficient deployment of land while avoiding the inconveniences and costs of tall buildings, where elevators and lobbies would be required. With the right kind of group housing, he believed, it would be easy to provide such "community features" as day nurseries for working mothers.

Wright was not simply a dreamer. Along with his artistry in land, he gave careful thought to analyzing the costs of development. Although he complained about the failure of society to produce imaginative housing designs, he also believed that innovative plans were not enough. In 1932 he wrote (in his all-too-characteristically long-winded fashion) that what especially was needed was "more business common-sense effort in the selecting and developing from the welter of excellent plan ideas, a sensible and well-balanced and economic program which will conserve the best resources of each given area for the essential, most efficient, and well-coordinated operation of a comfortable existence for all its population."[5]

By 1932 Wright was becoming acutely aware of the Depression, although less as a problem than as an exciting new opportunity. The economic collapse, he believed, challenged the customary practices that had left the nation with "miles of unused vacant lots on sparsely populated wastes of cement sidewalks and rusting utility pipes," and it was up to enlightened advocates of better design to seize the moment. He declared that the time had come for businessmen to be replaced as directors of development by skilled technicians. Only knowledgeable and dispassionate technicians, he said, could develop the moderate-cost urban dwellings needed by most cityites; only they could guide "the evolution of new dwelling forms adjusted to the new age."[6]

The advent of the New Deal turned his thoughts toward publicly funded housing projects. In the summer of 1933 he urged a program to take advantage of collapsing land values in slum areas by rebuilding those areas along the lines of Sunnyside. "We can provide through good planning and community organization all the pleasures of ample green and attractive shrubs and flowers" (never, apparently, did he consider the skeptic's scoff that many of the poor would never appreciate shrubs and flowers). Six months later, having recognized that at least in Manhattan slum land values remained much too high, he proposed that slum clearance be downgraded as a goal and that cheaper lands in the outlying boroughs be used to build communities for as many as fifty thousand inhabitants on well-planned sites. By providing for tens of thousands of people previously confined to the slums, he predicted, this scheme would soon reduce slum land values to the point that clearance projects could be initiated. Thus, "a chain of soundly built housing communities might be established from Hell Gate to South Brooklyn which would redeem the existing mass of blighted areas and slums."[7]

Wright was generally cautious in his enthusiasms and he held to his view that vision had to be mated with careful analysis. "The need for scientific procedure was never more urgent than at the present." For a time, though, he genuinely believed that the New Deal could make possible a massive program of "urban reconstruction and community planning and building." In July 1933 he was in Cleveland attending a conference on public housing—which he called a "real conference" that he believed would have a significant effect on housing developments—when he learned that Kohn had been appointed head of the PWA's Housing Division.

That appointment was one sign of a hopeful future. The Cleveland conference was soon followed by the launching of three housing projects in that city, the first housing and slum clearance projects to be initiated under the PWA, and Wright was involved in their preliminary planning. This work had its complications. Expecting to receive an offer to join the Housing Division from Kohn, Wright told Mumford that he was having trouble deciding whether to accept a federal job at a meager salary or continue to be "an advisor to various projects at fairly fat fees." Finally, he accepted a role as a sort of roving consultant for the PWA Housing Division so that he could continue with the Cleveland projects. "When better slum clearance is done, Cleveland will do it." In

September he could write to his friend Mumford, "I'm doing tremendous things and making momentous decisions almost every day," making it worth the time that he was "sleeping on trains, or not sleeping,
even making and breaking friendships."[8]

It was a thrilling time—but like such things it was not to last.
Before long he began to complain of incompetence and indecision in
government and of "land greed" and corruption in the city slum-
clearance programs. Far from seeing the continuation of "fat" consulting fees, he found delays in funding the new projects that left his fellow
"technicians" to eke out a slim living. As late as February 1934 Stein
wrote that his friend had yet to receive "a cent for all the work he did"
on the Cleveland projects. Even Kohn proved a problem. In September
1933 Wright called his chief a "brick" who could be depended upon to
support his efforts, but the brick soon began to crumble. In November
Wright complained that in Cleveland, where he believed a housing
program had the best chance of succeeding, he had labored long and
hard to transform "a truck load of individual projects, architects, lawyers, land accumulators, engineers, landscape architects, soothsayers
and trombone players into one intimate family of brotherly love," only
to have the director of housing come along one day and upset the whole
arrangement.[9]

On the other hand, he appreciated the work that level-headed Kohn
was doing in navigating through the "rocks and shoals of land greed
and political patronage" in order to accomplish anything. And in April
1934 he could report some progress on the housing front. Although he
was tempted at one point to change the name of Cleveland Housing
Incorporated to the "As if and when society," three projects were eventually begun, to be completed by 1937, while another in which he had a
lesser role was launched in Indianapolis. In Atlanta he became involved
in two housing schemes dictated by Southern segregationalism. In one,
intended for black people, backyards had been virtually eliminated
because it was believed that the inhabitants likely would not keep them
up. It was, he told Mumford, to be a "sort of little heaven, all front
yard, all beautifully kept up by Govt . . . or somebody for the dear
frail colored brothers to look on and enjoy." He apparently did nothing
to change that project, but he was able to report that he had reorganized the project for whites, saving $245,000 in site development
costs.[10]

Whatever the gains, however, Wright's days with the PWA ended
soon after Kohn was ousted as division head. Fortunately, Wright had
already become involved with two other endeavors more in harmony

with his basically apolitical attitudes. From the beginning he had urged a go-slow approach to slum clearance until housing authorities had acquired the technical experts and expertise needed to assure success, the clue to the bad housing of the past being ignorance and ineptitude. In Cleveland he had fought unsuccessfully against the disposition toward large-scale clearance projects, proposing that the program begin with "a small project on vacant land to cut our eye teeth on, to learn the problems we now won't learn until we must spend millions." Soon after Kohn became head of the Housing Division, Wright was able to persuade him to set up an advisory group headed by Albert Mayer, which soon evolved into a more formal planning body, the Housing Study Guild, which included Wright and Mumford among its selected body of housing experts. [11]

In early 1934 Wright, Mumford, and Mayer published their ideas for a housing program in the *New Republic* under the general heading "New Homes for a New Deal." Wright published an essay, "Abolishing Slums Forever," in which he stated the fundamentals of his planning philosophy, especially that real housing was not simply a matter of erecting buildings but "a matter of community building," made available to all through "low costs that derive from good technical planning on one hand and the steady use of imagination and intelligence on the other." In March he joined with Mumford and Mayer in urging the need for an extensive investment in research and education to assure "competent technical direction" in housing. [12]

The three men also sketched a national policy of planned development featuring a new housing administration equal to the PWA with powers sufficient to develop and manage a long-ranged "community housing" effort supported by at least $5 billion a year. Convinced that land speculation had been a leading cause of bad housing in the past, they insisted on the need for public ownership and control of all land used not simply for housing but for related commercial, industrial, recreational, and agricultural purposes. The authors declared that their proposal was radical only in the sense that it would get at the root causes of the housing problem. Through this program, they promised in conclusion, "we will transform the entire face of our country and lay a foundation for a stable and healthful community life." [13]

Although it had some effect on such New Deal creations as the Federal Housing Authority (FHA) and the Works Projects Administration (WPA), the influence of the Housing Study Guild fell far short of its ambitions; but for Wright the guild was only part of a larger effort to promote technical skill and understanding. In the late 1920s he had

taken over an old mill in the vicinity of Mount Olive, Whitaker's old
New Jersey neighborhood, and had converted it into a summer residence and studio. In 1932 he decided to use it as a summer school to
train young architects, telling Mumford that his teaching was "about
the most important job" he had had for some time. In the same year he
may have inspired the Hudson Guild to use its nearby farm as a place
for a work-study program for unemployed draftsmen; the members of
this Hudson Guild Architectural Work Shop later elected Stein as their
"patron."[14]

Wright, having a strong ability as well as need to teach, attracted a
half dozen graduate students in architecture, who at one point made an
extensive study of site planning, producing a series of plans for housing
on hillsides, a reflection of his work at Chatham Village in Pittsburgh.
Later he said that this work had "led to the discovery of a special
technique for hillside housing, particularly for steep hillsides, which
should in time open a new field for attractive small dwellings." He
argued that the absence of such designs had prevented the development
of much hillside land conveniently related to the centers of cities,
thereby denying space that might have been used to relieve overcrowding. Subsequent summer schools in 1933 and 1934 seem to have been
less successful, but Wright continued, as Stein put it, to "get a push
from his little gang of students around him," and he could boast in
1934 that two of them had found places in Kohn's Housing Division,
one in a key position.[15]

In any case, Wright was actively engaged not only in planning
public housing but in preparing a major work on the subject, his
Rehousing Urban America, published in 1935 by Columbia University
Press. He intended this book to be, in part, a "comprehensive digest of
the elements of good community planning and housing technique."
Although he defended the need for community planning to eliminate
the wasteful suburban sprawl of the previous decades, he said that his
chief aim was to provide "a manual of good housing practice" that
would help rehabilitate cities, not simply to build new towns.[16]

In stressing city rehabilitation over suburban development, however,
he made it plain that he continued to oppose the preoccupation with
slum clearance of Wood and others, his reason being that slum land
remained too expensive to develop for housing without creating some of
the same crowding and other conditions that had made for slums in the
first place. He favored a comprehensive strategy that, while including
some clearance of slums, would concentrate on more outlying residential areas that had become victims of urban blight, places where land

was cheaper and the problems of redevelopment less formidable. In such areas, Wright contended, it would be possible to eliminate the gridiron pattern of streets and the accompanying system of narrow lots that had doomed the areas to deterioration and to rebuild on the model of Sunnyside, with low-rise apartment houses and superblocks with open green interiors.

Housing projects of this sort would be cheaper as well as better than slum-clearance projects. If enough housing were provided this way, then competition would drive down the price of slum property to the point that clearance could take place. Since only some of the slum land would have to be used to meet the diminished housing needs of the poor, the rest could be used to provide "a generous belt of open space surrounding the central business district—in which the usual public buildings for amusement and cultural purposes would naturally center."[17]

Rehousing Urban America strengthened Wright's reputation as an authority on moderate-cost housing and urban rehabilitation. It received generally favorable reviews, although the one provided by Wood in *Survey* magazine was notable for its lack of enthusiasm, especially when she observed that the main thesis of the book was "that intermediate blighted areas should be replanned and rebuilt with government assistance before slums are attacked." In 1935 Columbia University appointed Wright to head a program in town planning and housing that had been set up in its School of Architecture with the support of a four-year grant from the Carnegie Foundation; it was to be, he wrote to Mumford, "a school within a school of architecture in which the entire course will be directed primarily to training in site planning."[18]

In the same year he was also appointed to help plan the new government greenbelt town, Greenbrook, to be located near New Brunswick, New Jersey. The head of the planning division of the Resettlement Administration, which was responsible for the program, was Frederick W. Bigger of Pittsburgh, a long-time member of the RPAA. As designed by Wright and his associates on the project, Mayer and Henry C. Churchill (colleagues in the Housing Study Guild), Greenbrook was to be a large town of nearly 4,000 families on 1,400 acres, exclusive of more than 2,000 acres of surrounding greenbelt. Although he consciously tried to make it an improvement over both Radburn and Chatham Village, it embraced their essential features, including four superblocks, each with an interior park, and a preponderance of row houses to cut costs and assure adequate open space. It would have been a major addition to the greenbelt town program, but it was blocked by legal controversies and in 1936 was dropped.[19]

This disappointment meant nothing to Wright, since on July 9, 1936, at the very beginning of what looked like a promising new phase in his career, he died at age fifty-eight in Dover, New Jersey, after a short illness; he left a widow and four children. "It is cruel," wrote his old friend and partner Stein, "that it should happen just now—when Henry was feeling that he was on solid ground—and that he could devote himself to passing on to the young men that flame of his." In an obituary essay he wrote for the *American Architect,* Stein took note of Wright's principal weakness, his impatience with all the details involved in transforming plans into realities—the better to note Wright's greatest strengths, his inquisitive analytical intellect and his dedicated search for "a simpler and finer way of living in modern communities."[20]

Among those who eulogized Wright was his colleague on the Housing Study Guild Mayer, who concluded that Wright had, like Veblen, directed those whom he had influenced "along the path of revolt of the technical man" against incompetence. Most of the eulogizers noted his technical knowledge and his willingness to share his expertise. Henry Saylor, a colleague in the Resettlement Administration, said that Wright not only had advanced knowledge about housing matters but had succeeded in making "a vast accumulation of technique . . . available for his many students, disciples, and followers." In 1937 some of his friends organized the Henry Wright Library under the sponsorship of the Federation of Architects, Engineers, Chemists, and Technicians to provide what they hoped would be a permanent working memorial to their friend that would perpetuate his expertise.[21]

Writing to MacKaye, Stein declared that this library would be an important means of carrying on the work of the RPAA. Unfortunately, by this time—September 1937—it came close to being the only means, since the RPAA itself had ceased to function, and its members no longer maintained anything like a common front in their associations with regional planning. In a real sense, the death of Wright in 1936 signaled the end of the kind of regional planning he and his friends had hoped would radically reshape America, a dream that faded out both because of its internal weaknesses and because of changing circumstances during the last half of the 1930s.

XVIII

FADE OUT

The Great Depression, although it defeated the work being attempted at Radburn, initially stimulated the RPAA to new heights of significant activity. In March 1931 the association urged Governor Franklin Roosevelt to create a regional planning board for New York State and by the end of the year it recommended a state program for the creation of planned communities. Although the presidential election year of 1932 saw no similar action, early 1933 brought first an RPAA memorandum in March favoring a national regional planning program and then a lengthy statement in May describing a national housing program. These early months of the New Deal also saw the creation of the TVA and the initiation of a national public housing program, each of which came to involve RPAA members. The RPAA seemed to be moving forward to a new and momentous phase. In fact, however, this was a last flurry of activity for the association. After May 1933 it did not meet again as a group and by 1936 it was definitely fading away.

Why? More than a decade later Mumford said that the RPAA had broken up because some of its members had gone off into government service and it had failed to recruit new members—with the exception of Bauer—to replace them. Still later he essentially repeated this explanation, but he added the claim that "after 1932 a serious breach took place between Wright and Stein." Mumford was not sure of the reasons for the break in this important partnership, but he was definite about its results, the formation of the Housing Study Guild (involving Wright) as a distinct effort apart from the RPAA and the loss to the association of both Stein's "ample means" (including a place to meet) and his able leadership.[1]

Mumford's explanations have some validity, but there is no real evidence that differences over public housing had a significant effect on the RPAA nor that a breach between Stein and Wright was as deep and significant as Mumford remembered, if it had occurred at all; as late as December 1934—after the formation of the Housing Study Guild— Wright made friendly visits to Stein. Such ideas were at best partial and also likely self-serving in that they distracted from his own contributions to the RPAA's demise. The truth was simpler, in that this loosely organized group was pulled apart by the individual concerns of its principal members; and it was more complex because this process involved the personal as well as professional preoccupations of these members, particularly of the three men who had been the mainstays of the RPAA since its founding in 1923.

Mumford, the wordsmith and intellectual of the group, for instance, became distracted by his love affair with Bauer and then by its breakup in 1934. Whatever her talents, Bauer proved to be a disturbing presence for all concerned. In 1932 she had a serious quarrel with Mumford and by the next year was supplementing him with a new lover. By 1934 she had not only broken with Mumford emotionally but had repudiated the housing policy preferred both by him and the RPAA. During this same period Mumford also was occupied both with finishing *Technics and Civilization* and with the Housing Study Guild. Moreover, these years also saw the shift of much of his personal life from the city to Amenia upstate, lessening his contacts with Stein and the others. In 1935 he was also a contributing editor to the *New Republic*, a lecturer on sociology at Columbia University, and visiting professor of art at Dartmouth College—diverse roles that won him independence as an intellectual while diminishing his involvement with the RPAA. Little wonder that he gave little real attention to the association.[2]

Special circumstances also served to distract MacKaye, the chief inspirational influence in the RPAA. MacKaye was also bothered by personal problems, in this case by the prolonged and deep mental depression of his sister, Hazel, who required special care. His professional situation provided another set of distractions. After his involuntary separation from the TVA in 1936 he retained a friendly interest in it, and he had other involvements, especially efforts to promote both the Wilderness Society and his townless highway idea.[3]

The latter interest led him into a prolonged effort to persuade the state of Massachusetts to accept his scheme for the "Bay Circuit," which he had termed in 1930 "a super by-pass for Boston," designed to prevent the growth of what he called "wayside fungus." It was to be a broad highway loop featuring the separation of its north and south traffic lanes by a wide median of parkland dedicated to hiking and other forms of outdoor recreation. Along with a highway designed to speed the flow of its traffic, Boston would have a surrounding greenbelt capable of satisfying the needs of the "outdoor culture" that MacKaye predicted would steadily grow in importance, not only in that city but throughout the world. It would be an important exercise of geotechnics in that it would control the "wanderings" of Boston's population and lessen the pressures of the metropolis on the countryside. Despite his call for a highway governed by the aim "to let the folks outdoors . . . and not commerce nor economics nor ballyhoo," however, his plan was ignored in favor of one for the famous Route 128, eventually a heavily industrialized bypass highway.[4]

While MacKaye was preoccupied by highways and forest trails away from New York, Stein was retreating from some of his previous concerns. In the early 1930s, he had settled into a contented life with his new wife, Aline, his chief complaint being that her acting career took her frequently away from their home—an apartment high above Central Park. In a deeply personal way he loved his life in New York City, his access to its cultural life and its excitements, its vitality and mystery, as seen from his apartment window. "Spring came all of a sudden," he wrote to Aline in 1931. "The park is green—the trees budding—and the baseball field is crowded with players and spectators." On the other hand, he retained the professional loathing of the bloated, congested metropolis that he had revealed in "Dinosaur Cities" years before.[5]

Stein spent most of the early 1930s completing his Hillside Homes apartment complex and thinking about housing policy. As he had done in the past, he took a special interest in efforts to provide affordable housing for the low incomed. Although he supported the slum clearance program favored by Wood and others as better than nothing, he continued to hope that Americans would eventually recognize that their cities had to be entirely rebuilt on new forms and new principles similar to those exemplified by Radburn. During the early days of the New Deal, he became actively involved in a scheme to build four new towns, traveling out to California to investigate sites for two of them. With the help of his architectural associates, Charles Butler and Frank Vitolo, he developed a plan for one intended to house 18,000 people on a Long Island location at Valley Stream just outside of New York City;

the plan involved a Radburn pattern of superblocks, separation of pedestrian and autoways, and interior parks with the addition of a surrounding greenbelt.[6]

As the principal manager of RPAA affairs, Stein was sensitive to the growing divergence among its members over policy as they responded to the Depression's apparent opportunities to transform dreams of basic change into actualities. "I am finding a growing difference among those to whom I am close," he wrote to his wife shortly before the New Deal had begun. "Frederick . . . Lewis, Robert—all the same objective—a saner world—but off on different roads." A few months later, in part to reverse this trend, he convened a meeting of the RPAA at his apartment to discuss housing policy; attending were Stein, Bauer, Kohn, Mumford, Wood, and Wright, plus two out-of-town members, John T. Bright and Russell Black, and three nonmembers who were experts on the housing question. This 1933 gathering proved to be the last meeting. Although Stein recognized the need for more joint discussions, he was for a time too busy working on Hillside Homes and other projects to organize them. In September 1933 he wrote to Mumford from a train between Chicago and Baltimore that he was relieved to learn that his friends favored a postponement of the fall meeting.[7]

Proposals for some kind of gathering were occasionally raised in the future, but nothing came of them, in no small part because of Stein's inability to provide effective leadership. From the beginning of the New Deal he was virtually shut out of any position of influence on New Deal policy, except for a limited advisory role in the government's later Greenbelt town program. With the completion of his Hillside project, he was left with little to do, an unaccustomed idleness that helped induce a nervous breakdown sometime in 1935. As late as February 1936, although he was recovering from what his wife called "those old devils 'nerves,'" he had not yet returned to work, thereby depriving regional planning of one of its ablest leaders.[8]

There was some activity that indicated the RPAA was not completely dead. In October 1935 Mumford referred to a "pow-wow" held at Stein's home to discuss the formation of a teaching institute in community planning. Less than a year later MacKaye proposed a revival of the association. In August 1936, while reading through the page proofs of Chase's *Rich Land, Poor Land*, MacKaye wrote to Mumford that it complemented the latter's own work and then said in reference to his recent firing from the TVA that "if our old R.P. Assn. gang would only resurrect & Assemble itself we'd plant the pompous pansy planters in their pretty proper places!! *Think this over.*" Within a few days, he was in New York, where he spent some time with both Chase and Stein, writing to Mumford that this experience had deepened his feelings of association with "the fellers named on the R.P. letterhead."[9] This seems to have been the first proposal for the resurrection of the RPAA—indeed, it may have the first expression of an awareness that the association needed resurrection.

Nothing immediate came of MacKaye's suggestion, but Stein took an interest in the idea. In November 1937 he wrote to Mumford that he had become convinced of the need for "a clear expression of the Regional City idea. We must reawaken the Regional Planning Association." A month later, after visiting Stein in New York, MacKaye made the same suggestion to Mumford. In late January 1938 Stein actually sent out meeting notices to the old members, but nothing seems to have occurred. A year later, Stein—who had moved to a suburban retreat north of New York City—was in California and then in Washington on business, perhaps too preoccupied with renewing his career to give much attention to the RPAA.[10]

Although in the late 1930s something of a rally of the membership did take place, it was focused on one temporary objective and it owed its beginnings to Kohn rather than to Stein and MacKaye.

In 1936, Kohn—a former president of the AIA—was appointed to an eight-man committee responsible for the design of the upcoming New York World's Fair. He accepted this position with the expectation that he would be able to use it to influence the popular designs of the future. In 1937 he announced that the art and architecture of the fair would emphasize the contribution of the machine in making beauty available to the people, in the form not of standard museum art but of objects of popular use.[11]

Kohn also hoped to use the fair to promote improvements in housing, and apparently it was that aim that led him to conceive of a movie on regional planning to be shown to fair audiences. With the help of grants from the Carnegie and Rockefeller Foundations, this led to the making of the notable documentary film *The City,* which featured a narration spoken by Morris Carnovski and music by Aaron Copeland. Stein, Kohn, and Ackerman were involved in its production as directors of a nonprofit entity, Civic Films Inc., and Mumford wrote most of the narration.[12]

The film is basically a triptych constructed along regional planning lines. The first part features a romanticized view of a traditional New England town (filmed in MacKaye's Shirley Center)—a "prologue," said Stein, intended "to show that towns did exist, and if you will still exist, with all the essential characteristics of the garden city." The second part presents a contrasting picture of the congested, frenetic metropolis at its worst (the makers waited until Labor Day to film congested traffic and chose smoke-saturated Pittsburgh to illustrate the industrial scene). Having moved from Eden lost to modern hell, the film ends in a regional planning heaven of townless highways and parklike superblocks, using images drawn chiefly from the government Greenbelt towns.

The film was rejected for commercial distribution. Ackerman grumbled that prospective distributors feared that "the audiences would laugh and walk out because it did not conform to the pattern of thought which was conceived as characteristic of moronic audiences." However, an uncut version was shown to an interested audience at the American Institute of City Planning meeting in Boston in May 1939, and it became a regular feature at the World Fair, receiving critical praise comparing it favorably to *The River,* a documentary on flood control and the TVA made in 1937 and already an established classic. Later it was cut by about a third, with results that won the praise of the normally hypercritical Ackerman, who said he was "happily surprised" by the sympathetic interest that evidently had guided the editing.[13]

Unfortunately, *The City* did nothing to revive the RPAA. Whitaker died in August 1938 during the early stages of the film's production, his death inducing memories of better days at the Hudson Guild Farm in the 1920s but doing nothing to reverse the forces that were pulling his protégés apart. Typically, when the filmmakers came to Shirley Center to photograph traditional bliss (after hunting through New England for their ideal place), MacKaye had left it in search of government employment, soon finding a new job with the Forest Service. In 1939 he advised his friends that he had become a "sexagenarian" laboring in the Forest Service "midst merry company and on the lusty job for flood control." Three years later, he had moved on to St. Louis to take on a new job with the Rural Electrification Administration.[14]

Earlier, in 1938, Mumford had sailed for the Hawaiian Islands, where he prepared a planning report for the Honolulu Parks Board, and the next year he prepared a similar report for the Northwest Regional Council, which had selected him chiefly for his earlier criticism of the RPNY. After a "two weeks tour" of the coastal portions of Washington and Oregon, Mumford predicted that the Northwest would experience a decline in population and advocated a policy to promote a selected immigration into that area. During this period he lapsed into periods of gloom over the prospects of remaking the world. In 1940 he told Mac-

Kaye that, where he had once thought that Megalopolis would decline gradually, he now believed it would "probably take place in a decisive way within the next generation," a change he associated with the coming of a new "Dark Age" that might overwhelm human civilization.[15]

By 1939 Mumford's attentions were turning away from planning to world events, his principal work being *Men Must Act,* in which he called for a moral and economic campaign to resist the spread of Fascism; in 1940 he lumped Stalin together with Hitler and Mussolini as the heads of a "fascist barbarism" threatening civilized life. Other members also were directing their attentions to the darkening larger world, although not in the same way. As usual Chase managed to agree and disagree with Mumford: in his own book, *The New Western Front,* he condemned Fascism but called on the United States to pursue a policy of neutrality and isolation. MacKaye had already caught this drift of the times, noting that "perhaps the one 'realistic' problem of immediate concern is how to dodge stratospheric bombs; perhaps we all should be thinking nought else but cyclone shelters and anti-aircraft gunnery." At age sixty he determined not to be realistic and urged again that the RPAA be revived to provide the world with a plan to guide it after the whirlwind had passed.[16]

The whirlwind, however, had to pass before any new attempt at revival was made. Finally, in 1948, three years after the end of World War II, Stein launched a new regional planning effort, in significant part to resist a new version of that old rival, the RPNY, with its centralizing tendencies, and he soon had the support of MacKaye and several others. Mumford, who confessed that he had wanted to bury the RPAA "under the sod, on the theory that a dead organization should not lie around and moulder publicly," changed his mind and by the end of 1948 had become an active member of the newly named Regional Planning Council of America. Over the next several years, the RPCA carried on a campaign against the RPNY and for an extensive government program of new town development, beginning with efforts to save the greenbelt towns of New Deal days from being sold off to private owners.[17]

By 1951, however, it was evident that despite frequent meetings the new organization was not taking hold. "People are willing to follow our lead but not to develop leads of their own," complained Mumford. "Like Ulysses, Stein, MacKaye and Mumford are 'not now that strength which in old days moved heaven and earth,' and the people who should be taking over our posts and functions have not yet appeared." Nor was there much chance of new recruits in the years that lay ahead in the

1950s, when cold war and Red scares extinguished virtually all dreams of radically reshaping America. During this period, the TVA would become largely a power-generating complex and the government-built greenbelt towns would be sold off to private enterprises. The RPNY would continue to be the greatest planning influence on the great metropolis of America.

Over the next decades Mumford continued the crusade for regional planning in his numerous writings, and the Appalachian Trail, garden city, the townless highways, and other planning elements advocated by the RPAA found a permanent place in subsequent developmental strategies. In 1963 Mumford thought he could see a revival of the "New Town standard," and the next year, when New York State adopted a report he thought was based on Wright's earlier report, he said hopefully that "after forty years, our ideas have sprouted again."[18]

There was, indeed, some basis for hope. In the 1960s and later, new enthusiasm and new strategies for reshaping America appeared, the work of a new generation that was often indifferent to the inspirations of the past but that entertained some of the same essential dreams, of a world of planned communities and intimate contact with nature. And beyond that, it is possible that humankind is slowly and awkwardly realizing the essential and animating vision of the RPAA, a vision of a world organized into intimate regions where humankind can feel truly at home with itself, its environment, and its history. With the rapid development of global communications, the advance of technology, the spread of environmentalism, and the weakening of nationalism in our increasingly modern world, Mumford's eutopian vision of a globe organized into millions of local regional communities may be on its way to becoming a reality. Although that way has been marred by bloody conflicts—often between nationalism and regionalism over territory—the final result at some future time may be the fulfillment of the RPAA dream. Why not?

NOTES

The following abbreviations are used in the Notes and Bibliography.

AR   *Architectural Record*
BM   Benton MacKaye
CHW   Charles Harris Whitaker
CS   Clarence Stein
EEW   Edith Elmer Wood
EWP   Edith Elmer Wood Papers, Columbia University
FLA   Frederick L. Ackerman
HW   Henry Wright
JAIA   *Journal of the American Institute of Architects*
LM   Lewis Mumford
MFP   MacKaye Family Papers, Dartmouth College
MP   Lewis Mumford Papers, University of Pennsylvania
NYT   *New York Times*
RDK   Robert D. Kohn
SG   *Survey Graphic*
SP   Clarence Stein Papers, Cornell University

CHAPTER I: THE VIEW FROM THE OCTAGON

1. "The Famous Octagon House," *House Beautiful* 44 (Oct. 1918), 244–45; "The Octagon," *JAIA* 4 (1916), 522; Federal Writers Project, *WPA Guide to Washington, D.C.,* 282–83.

2. "Journal of the American Institute of Architects," *JAIA* 2 (1914), 586–87.

3. "Charles Harris Whitaker," *Who's Who in America* (1932–33), 2427; obituary, *NYT* (Aug. 13, 1938), 13.

4. CHW to Louis Sullivan, July 13 and Sept. 26, 1923, Whitaker-Sullivan Correspondence, Art Institute of Chicago.

5. CHW, *From Rameses to Rockefeller: The Story of Architecture,* 323–27.

6. CHW, "On the Relation of Art to Life," 13–16, and *From Rameses,* 216–18, 199, 323–25.

7. CHW, editorial, *JAIA* 6 (1918), 422, and "What Is the Function of Architecture in a Democracy?" 465–68; LM, *Sketches from Life,* 423. Alan I Marcus, "Back to the Present: Historians' Treatment of the City as a Social System," in Howard Gillette Jr. and Zane L. Miller, *American Urbanism,* 15–16.

8. CHW, "The Forests of Soignes," 244–45.

9. "Report of the Board," 517; CHW, "Our Stupid and Blundering National Policy of Providing Public Buildings," 56; *NYT* (Mar. 4, 1916), 10, and ibid. (Dec. 3, 1916), sec. 7, 12.

10. CHW, "The Smokestack Menace to Washington," *NYT* (Mar. 4, 1916), 10, and "The Proposed Disfigurement of Washington," 489.

11. CHW, "Our Stupid and Blundering National Policy," 56, and Shadows and Straws, *JAIA* 5 (1917), 209.

12. "Our Stupid and Blundering National Policy—Post Offices," *JAIA* 4 (1916), 100.

13. CHW, letter to *NYT* (Dec. 27, 1916), 8, and "The Fight on the Public Buildings Bill," ibid. (Dec. 31, 1916), sec. 7, 2.

14. CHW, "Our Stupid and Blundering National Policy," 99–102, "An Open Letter to the Members of the Sixty-fourth Congress," *JAIA* 4 (1916), 239–41, Shadows and Straws, *JAIA* 5 (1917), 6–9, and ibid. 7 (1919), 4–6, and "The Federal Building Situation," 270–72.

15. Theodore Tiller, "Washington in War Time," 629–32; William De Wagstaffe, "How's Washington Now?" 733–40; Harrison Rhodes, "War-Time Washington," 466–68.

16. CHW, Shadows and Straws, *JAIA* 5 (1917), 209, 421–22.

17. CHW, Shadows and Straws, *JAIA* 5 (1917), 421, 479, and ibid. 6 (1918), 107, 159, "What Is a House?" 481–85, and "Land and the Housing Question," 113–14.

18. CHW, editorials, *JAIA* 6 (1918), 422, and ibid. 8 (1920), 52–53, "What Is the Function of Architecture?" 465–68, "Will the Kitchen Be Outside the House?" 66, and *The Housing Problem in War and in Peace,* 116.

19. CHW, Shadows and Straws, *JAIA* 4 (1916), 481–82.

20. CHW, "England's Housing Ventures," 611, and "Wanted—Ten Million Houses," 112.

21. Ellen Maury Slayden, *Washington Wife,* 283; CHW, "The Housing Issue in the United States," 155–57.

22. CHW, "Housing Issue," 156–57, "Land and the Housing Question," 113–14, "The Impasse in Housing," 202–3, and "Architecture and the Public," 447–48.

23. CHW, editorials, *JAIA* 6 (1918), 422, 468, and 532, "What Is the Function of Architecture?" 465–68, and "Post-War Committee on Architectural Practice," 6–8, 25–28, and 390–95.

24. CHW, "Post-War Committee," 28, 390–95, and Shadows and Straws, *JAIA* 7 (1919), 143–45, and ibid. 8 (1920), 51–53.

25. CHW, "The Interrelation of the Professions," 12–13, CHW to LM, Mar. 5, 1920, MP, CHW to Louis Sullivan, June 15, 1923, Whitaker-Sullivan Correspondence, Art Institute of Chicago.

26. *NYT* (Jan. 15, 1921), 3.

27. LM, introduction to CS, *Toward New Towns for America,* 12, and *Sketches,* 333.

CHAPTER II: IDEALISM IN PEACE AND WAR

1. *Who's Who,* (1922–23), 161; *NYT* (June 8, 1915), 8.

2. FLA, "The Architect's Part in the World's Work," 149–58.

3. FLA, "Architect's Part," 154–56, "Report of the Committee on Public Information," *JAIA* 2 (1914), 587–88, and "The Battle with Chaos," 446.

4. FLA, "Battle with Chaos," 445–56, and "The Relation of Art to Education," 192–93, 234–37.

5. FLA, letter to the editor, *NYT* (Dec. 26, 1913), 10, "Progress of Building Regulations in New York City," 351, and "Shall We Save New York?" 160–61.

6. FLA, "The Influence on Architecture of the Condition of the Worker," 353–54, "War-Time Housing," 97–100, and "What Is a House?"; EEW, *Recent Trends in American Housing,* 66–67.

7. *NYT* (Jan. 11, 1918), 14; ibid. (Jan. 14, 1918), 12; and ibid. (Jan. 29, 1918), 14.

8. FLA, "War-Time Housing," 98–100; *NYT* (Jan. 29, 1918), 14.

9. Wood, *Recent Trends,* 68–69; Lawrence Veiller, "Industrial Housing Developments in America," 344–45; FLA, "Houses and Ships," 85–86.

10. *Who's Who* (1922–23), 1819; RDK, "History of the Committee on City Development of the New York Chapter," 124–26; *NYT* (Jan. 16, 1916), sec. 7, 5.

11. FLA, "Houses and Ships," 85–86; United States Shipping Board, *Third Annual Report of the President of the United States Shipping Board,* 29; William G. Tucker, "The Plumbing Standards for the Housing Projects of the Emergency Fleet Corporation," *AR* 46 (1919), 47–52; FLA, "Cottage or

Tenement?" 112; Roy Lubove, "Homes and 'A Few Well Placed Fruit Trees': An Object Lesson in Federal Housing," 469–86; Richard S. Childs, "The Government's Model Villages," 584–92.

12. Richard S. Childs, "Building a War Town," 469–70.

13. Veiller, "Industrial Housing Developments," 141–51; Sylvester Baxter, "The Government's Housing Activities," 563; John Taylor Boyd Jr., "Industrial Housing Projects," 92.

14. Lubove, "Homes," 485; EWW, *Recent Trends,* 76–80; United States Shipping Board, *Third Annual Report,* 79, *Fourth Annual Report* (1920), 107–8, *Fifth Annual Report* (1921), 213–14, and *Sixth Annual Report* (1922), 203–6. Congressman George W. Edmonds, a supporter of the program, said before the program was enacted that, when possible, houses "are going to be built in an attractive style, so that they will attract workmen. They believe that when they build these houses they eventually will be able to sell them all, because their venture stops with the war, of course." *Congressional Record,* 65th Cong., 2nd sess., 1918, 12, pt. 10:1963.

15. RDK, "Housing in a Reconstruction Program," 341, "The Significance of the Professional Ideal," 1–5, "Comment on Mr. Thomas's Paper," *AR* 48 (1920), 425–26, "Industrial Relations," 346–47, 75, and "Post-War Committee on Architectural Practice," 118.

16. FLA, "Houses and Ships," 86, and "The Hearing," 804.

17. FLA, "National Planning," 15–23.

18. FLA, "The Economy of Zoning," 732.

19. FLA, "National Planning," 20–25, and "Our Stake in Congestion," 141–42.

20. CHW, "A Disease and Its Symptoms," 310; FLA, "Where Goes the City Planning Movement?" 518–20, and "Preliminary to City Planning," 18.

21. John P. Diggins, *The Bard of Savagery: Thorstein Veblen and Modern Social Theory,* 38–39, 71; LM, "Thorstein Veblen," 314; FLA to EEW, Sept. 29, 1919, EWP.

22. FLA to EEW, Sept. 29, 1919, EWP; FLA, "Economy of Zoning," 732.

23. FLA, "The Hearing," 804, and "More Plans for More Chaos," 133.

CHAPTER III: GREEN DIMENSIONS

1. BM to Percy MacKaye, July 26, 1914, in Percy MacKaye, *Epoch: The Life of Steele MacKaye,* 2:468.

2. Steele MacKaye's life is summarized in the introduction to his son's biography of him, Percy MacKaye, *Epoch,* 1:ix–xx. Also see Gamaliel Bradford, "An American Genius," *New Republic* 52 (1927), 294–95.

3. See the appendix to Percy MacKaye's *Epoch,* 2:xiii–xv, as well as pp. 472–73. Also see the obituaries of Harold Steele MacKaye, *NYT* (June 23, 1928), 15, and ibid. (June 26, 1928), 24, and of James MacKaye, ibid. (Jan. 23, 1935), 17.

4. Percy MacKaye, *Epoch,* 2:143; Paul T. Bryant, *The Quality of the Day: The Achievement of Benton MacKaye,* 15–35; BM, *The New Exploration: A Philosophy of Regional Planning,* 48–49.

5. BM, *New Exploration,* 69.

6. Bryant, *Quality of the Day,* 42–60; BM, "Growth of a New Science," in *From Geography to Geotechnics,* ed. Paul T. Bryant, 21; Percy MacKaye, *Epoch,* 2:475.

7. Bryant, *Quality of the Day,* 80–84; BM, "Growth of a New Science," 26–28.

8. Bryant, *Quality of the Day,* 83–85.

9. Ibid., 88–89; Hugh B. Johnson, "In Memory of Benton MacKaye," 68; BM, "Growth of a New Science," 31.

10. Karen J. Blair, "Pageantry for Women's Rights: The Career of Hazel MacKaye, 1913–1923," 23–39.

11. *NYT* (Apr. 19, 1921), 2; Ellen Maury Slayden, *Washington Wife,* 328, 339.

12. Bryant, *Quality of the Day,* 90–92; BM, "Growth of a New Science," 30.

13. Bryant, *Quality of the Day,* 94, 102–4.

14. Ibid., 95–97; BM to Louis E. Post, Dec. 27, 1915, and to Vincent Was, Jan. 10, 1916, MFP.

15. BM, "From Homesteads to Valley Authorities," in *From Geography,* 33–35, and *Employment and Natural Resources.* Also, BM, "Powell as Unsung Lawgiver."

16. Bryant, *Quality of the Day,* 107–11; BM, "The Soldier, the Worker, and the Land's Resources," 52–53, and *Employment and Natural Resources,* 9–14, 66–84.

17. BM, "Making New Opportunities for Employment," 125, and *Employment and Natural Resources,* 29–30.

18. "Common Sense and the I.W.W.," *New Republic* 14 (1918), 375–76; Alvin Johnson, "Land for the Returned Soldier," 218–20; Bryant, *Quality of the Day,* 108–11.

19. Bryant, *Quality of the Day,* 111–19; John L. Thomas, "Lewis Mumford, Benton MacKaye, and the Regional Vision," 72; BM, "From Homesteads," 35, "The First Soldier Colony," 1065–68, and "The Lesson of Alaska," 930–32; BM to Ralph Zon, Dec. 21, 1917; Zon to BM, Dec. 31, 1917. Also see Post Office Department Order No. 3560, Oct. 8, 1919, MFP.

20. BM, "A Plan for Cooperation between Farmer and Consumer," 1–21.

21. BM et al. to Ludwig C. A. K. Martens, Mar. 23, 1920; BM, personal vita (1920), MFP.

22. BM to Ethelberta [Hardy?], Apr. 23, 1921, to Miss Brunnacker, May 7, 1921, and to Mary L. Clayton, May 7, 1921; *NYT* (Apr. 19, 1921), 2, and ibid. (Apr. 21, 1921), 13.

23. BM to Mary L. Clayton, May 7, 1921, and to Clarence Stein, Oct. 30, 1934, MFP.

24. BM, "An Appalachian Trail: A Project in Regional Planning," 325–30, and "The Great Appalachian Trail from New Hampshire to the Carolinas," *NYT* (Feb. 18, 1923), sec. 7, 15; Bryant, *Quality of the Day,* 123–31. Gifford Pinchot sent a copy of the regional forest proposal to every member of the Society of America Foresters, noting that it had been described in the May 1921 issue of the *Journal of Forestry.* Pinchot to BM, July 16, 1921, MFP.

25. Bryant, *Quality of the Day,* 125–27; BM, "An Appalachian Trail," 325–26.

26. BM to Mrs. Louis Post, May 16, 1918, MFP; BM, "An Appalachian Trail," 327–28, and "Great Appalachian Trail," 15.

27. BM, "An Appalachian Trail," 330, and "Great Appalachian Trail," 15; Percy MacKaye, "Untamed American," *SG* (Jan. 1924), 327. For important background on this subject see Henry D. Shapiro, *Appalachia on Our Mind: The Southern Mountains and Mountaineers in the American Consciousness, 1890–1920,* 217–61.

28. BM, "Great Appalachian Trail," 15, and "A Trail through the Appalachians," 210. MacKaye quotes part of his speech in a letter to CS, Jan. 19, 1923, to Albert Bushnell Hart, Mar. 3, 1922, and to CS, Feb. 22, 1922, MFP.

29. Bryant, *Quality of the Day,* 137–38; BM, "A Trail through the Appalachians," 210.

30. BM to CS, Feb. 10, 1922; CS to BM, Mar. 2, 5, Apr. 14, Dec. 2, 1922, MFP.

CHAPTER IV: CREATION

1. CS to C. L. Richey, Oct. 7, 1933, MP; BM to CS, Mar. 7, Nov. 15, 1922, Sept. 14, 1927, MFP.

2. BM, *The New Exploration,* 27, 110–18; BM to CS, Aug. 31, Nov. 15, 1922, MFP.

3. CHW to BM, May 11, 1921, MFP; LM, *Sketches,* 384.

4. CHW, "Alloy," 198–99.

5. EEW, "What Is a House?" 69–70; CHW, "What Is a House?" 3–8, and "Ten Million Houses," 23, 109–12.

6. CHW, "The Vanishing Sanctuary," 251–53, and "The Impasse in Housing," 201–3.

7. CHW, "New Tale of Two Cities," 611, "Ten Million Houses," 112, and "Vanishing Sanctuary," 353.

8. CHW, Straws and Shadows, *JAIA* 7 (1919), 505–6, "Locality and Humility," 417, "Vanishing Sanctuary," 253, and "The Interrelation of the Professions," 12–13.

9. Stuart Chase to BM, Oct. 16, 1922; CS to BM, Sept. 27, Oct. 24, Nov. 19, 1922, MFP; CHW to LM, Nov. 25, 1922, "Sat. A.M." 1923, Aug. 1, 1924, MP; CS to Catherine Bauer, Sept. 27, 1961, SP.

10. LM, "A Modest Man's Contribution to Urban and Regional Planning," 19–28; Marjie Baughman, "A Prophet Honored Abroad Even More than at Home," 30–33; obituary of Stein, *JAIA* 63 (Apr. 1975), 94; Roy Lubove, *Community Planning in the 1920s: The Contributions of the Regional Planning Association of America*, 32–33.

11. Bertram G. Goodhue to "whom it may concern," Feb. 7, 1918; W. W. Black to CS, Nov. 29, 1918, SP.

12. CS, mss. diary, Jan. 2, 4, 11, 30, Feb. 7, 11, 15, 1919, SP.

13. New York State, *Report of the Housing Committee of the Reconstruction Commission.* 41–55.

14. CS to EEW, Mar. 13, Nov. 19, 1920, EWP; CS, "The Housing Crisis in New York," 659–62.

15. EEW, *Recent Trends,* 102; Lubove, *Community Planning,* 35; CS, "Legal Obstacles to City Planning," 335. Also *NYT* (Nov. 5, 1922), sec. 10, 1.

16. LM, *Sketches,* 337, and "A Modest Man's Contribution," 20–22.

17. LM, "A Modest Man's Contribution," 19. Some of the history and work of the Hudson Guild is discussed in *NYT* (Sept. 5, 1920), sec. 2, 4, ibid. (Aug. 30, 1925), sec. 7, 8, ibid. (Sept. 5, 1926), sec. 7, 4, ibid. (June 26, 1927), sec. 2, 1, and ibid. (Mar. 10, 1936), sec. 2, 6. Also, John Lovejoy Elliott, "The Warm Doorstep," *Survey* 43 (1920), 769–71.

18. *JAIA* 9 (1921), 254, 10 (1922), 391, and 63 (Apr. 1975), 94; CS, "Congestion of Population," 349, and "The Future of Our Big Cities," 24.

19. CS, "Community Planning and Housing," 399–400, and "Congestion of Population," 349.

20. LM, "A Modest Man's Contribution," 20; CS, "Community Planning and Housing," 126–27, and "The Regional Planning Association of America," 292–93.

21. "Architects to Aid in City Planning," *NYT* (Mar. 12, 1923), 15; CHW to LM, Sept. 23, 1922, MP.

22. CHW to LM, Nov. 25, 1922, MP; CS to BM, Mar. 7, Aug. 31, Dec. 2, 1922, MFP.

23. CS to BM, Mar. 20, 1923, MFP; "Minutes of the Organization Meeting . . . Apr. 18, 1923," MP.

24. LM, *Sketches,* 341–42; Program Committee, "Report on the Ways and Means of the Regional Planning Association, June 12, 1923," MP.

25. LM, *Sketches,* 342–43. For Geddes and the RPNY, see CHW to LM, Sept. 23, 1922, MP, and Charles Downing Long, letter to the editor, *NYT* (July 6, 1923).

26. "Minutes of the Meeting of the Regional Planning Association, June 7, 1923," and preamble to "Constitution of the Regional Planning Association, June 8, 1923," MP.

27. Program Committee, "Report on the Ways and Means," and "Minutes of Meeting . . . June 7," MP.

28. "Constitution . . . June 8," MP.

29. Program Committee, "Report . . . June 12, 1923," and "Minutes of a Meeting . . . July 13, 1923," MP; BM to CS, May 6, July 28, 1923, MFP.

CHAPTER V: TOWARD A GOLDEN DAY

1. Lubove, *Community Planning,* 41.

2. CS, *Toward New Towns for America,* 15; Carl Sussman, introduction to *Planning the Fourth Migration: The Neglected Vision of the Regional Planning Association of America,* 22, 43. For confirmation of these generalizations, see the minutes of the RPAA meetings in MP.

3. LM, *Sketches,* 3–7, 13–37, 74–81; Donald Miller, *Lewis Mumford: A Life,* 26–29.

4. LM, *Sketches,* 100–44, 184; Miller, *Lewis Mumford,* 34–88.

5. LM, *Sketches,* 144–218, 327, and *Findings and Keepings,* 79, 160, 203–4; Van Wyck Brooks, *Days of the Phoenix,* 52–67, 120, 154–55; Miller, *Mumford,* 52–73, 81–85.

6. LM, *Sketches,* 147–55, 409, *Findings,* 100–101, and "Who Is Patrick Geddes?" 523–24; Lubove, *Community Planning,* 83–87.

7. LM, "The State of the State," 59–61, "The Place of the Community in the School," 245–46, and "Attacking the Housing Problem on Three Fronts," 332–33.

8. LM, *Sketches*, 334–35; LM to CHW, Nov. 19, Dec. 28, 1919; CHW to LM, Feb. 3, Apr. 19, 1920, Feb. 25, 1921, MP; LM, "England's American Summer," 296.

9. Miller, *Mumford*, 156–57; LM, *Sketches*, 185, 303–4; Marshall Stalley, ed., *Patrick Geddes: Spokesman for Man and the Environment*, 38, 147–48, 284; Robert Spiller, ed., *The Van Wyck Brooks–Lewis Mumford Letters*, 18–19.

10. LM, *Sketches*, 303–4, *Findings*, 74–75, 352–53, and *The Story of Utopias*, 4–8, 24–26, and 147.

11. LM, *Story*, 11–13, 23.

12. Ibid., 191–212, and *Findings*, 74–75.

13. LM, *Story*, 212–34.

14. Ibid., 15–23, 275–91, and 301–8.

15. LM, *Findings*, 74–75, *Sketches*, 329, *Story*, 301, and "The Adolescence of Reform," 272–73.

16. Spiller, *Brooks-Mumford Letters*, 14–15; Miller, *Mumford*, 163; Bruno Lasker, "The New-Never Land," *SG* (Nov. 1, 1922), 193, 199–200; A. Emerson Parker, "Utopias That Make the World Tolerable," *NYT* (Dec. 24, 1922), sec. 2, 11.

17. CHW to LM, Dec. 5, 1922, MP.

18. LM, "New Trails for Old," 396–97.

19. LM, "Devastated Regions," 217–20.

20. Brooks, *Days of the Phoenix*, 154–55; LM, *My Works and Days*, 243, and "American Architecture," 344–46.

21. CHW to LM, Nov. 22, 1923, and Jan. 4, 1924, MP; LM, *Sticks and Stones: A Study of American Architecture*, 9, 208.

22. LM, *Sticks and Stones*, 9, 29–30.

23. Ibid., 133–47.

24. Ibid., 56–60, 175–82; LM, "Americanized Europe," 253–54, and "The Autobiography of an Idea," 132–33.

25. LM, *Sticks and Stones*, 195, 206–9.

26. Ibid., 209–22.

27. Ibid., 208, 235.

CHAPTER VI: PLANNING NEW YORK STATE

1. *American City Magazine* 29 (1923), 191–93, 578–80. In the next two years this magazine published at least fifteen more articles relating to regional planning. *NYT* (May 25, 1924), sec. 10, 1, and ibid. (Oct. 12, 1924), sec. 11, 15.

2. *NYT* (July 6, 1923), 12, ibid. (July 9, 1923), and ibid. (Dec. 11, 1923), 21.

3. State of New York, *Reconstruction Commission,* 39–43, 52–55.

4. *JAIA* 10 (1922), 1, 52, and 82–83; *NYT* (Aug. 16, 1923), 17, ibid. (Aug. 22, 1923), 9, and ibid. (Aug. 26, 1923), sec. 8, 1.

5. *NYT* (Aug. 26, 1923), sec. 7, 1.

6. *American City Magazine,* 31 (1924), 31–32; State of New York, *Report of the Commission of Housing and Regional Planning,* 63–66.

7. *NYT* (Sept. 28, 1924), sec. 1, 2, sec. 9, 8; G. Smith, "Buffalo Is Buffalo," 92–94. Also see the annual reports of the Niagara Frontier Planning Board, 1925–28.

8. *NYT* (Feb. 8, 1925), sec. 10, 10; State of New York, *Housing and Regional Planning,* 4, 66–68; *American City Magazine* 32 (1923), 575.

9. *NYT* (June 10, 1924), 8; Alfred E. Smith, "Seeing a State Whole," 158–60.

10. State of New York, *Housing and Regional Planning,* 63–68; Evan Clark, "Guiding New York State," 3, 13.

11. BM to CS, May 26, 1924, and to R. Bruere, July 31, 1932, MFP; BM to LM, Nov. 11, 1924, MP; BM, "Regional Planning Studies for the RPA of America . . . May 12, 1925," ms., MP; *NYT* (May 16, 1926), sec. 8, 16. MacKaye declined an invitation from Norman Thomas to help draft the city planning plank of the Socialist Party platform on the grounds that his interests involved "all cities at once . . . a plan for the city of New York should be based on a plan for the state." BM to Thomas, Mar. 21, 1925, MFP.

12. CS, "Henry Wright," 25–26; Henry Churchill, "Henry Wright, 1878–1936," 293–99; obituary of HW, *NYT* (July 10, 1936), 19.

13. Albert Mayer, "Henry Wright," 530; Alwyn T. Covell, "Co-operative Group Planning: Henry Wright, Architect and Landscape Architect," 467–75.

14. CS, *Wright,* 25–26; Churchill, *Wright,* 293–94; LM, "Community Planning and Housing," 492–93; HW, "The Road to Good Houses," 165–68, 189, and "Shall We Community Plan?" 320–24.

15. [HW], *Report of the New York State Commission of Housing and Regional Planning,* in Carl Sussman, ed., *Planning the Fourth Migration,* 145–46. Also see Sussman's introduction, 143–44.

16. [HW], *Report,* 147–69, 175.

17. Ibid., 179.

18. Ibid., 171–79, 194.

19. Ibid., 181–94; "The City That Jack Built," *New Republic* 42 (1925), 254–55.

20. *NYT* (Feb. 24, 1926), 2. Also see, in particular, two special issues of *SG Giant Power* (Mar. 1924) and *Regional Planning* (May 1925).

CHAPTER VII: GIANT POWER

1. Robert B. Westbrook, "Tribune of the Technostructure: The Popular Economics of Stuart Chase," 387–408; Stuart Chase, *The Tragedy of Waste*, 275, and "The Concept of Planning" 212.

2. Chase, "Portrait of a Radical," 295, and "On the Threshold," 711–15.

3. Westbrook, "Tribune," 319–20; Chase, "Portrait," 296–300, and "A War Budget for the Household," 169–70.

4. Chase, ms. vita (1920), MFP.

5. Westbrook, "Tribune," 390–91; Chase, *Portrait*, 301, and *The Nemesis of American Business*, 27; *NYT* (Oct. 21, 1919), 19.

6. Westbrook, "Tribune," 391–93; Chase to BM, Oct. 16, 1922; BM to CS, Nov. 15, 1922, MFP.

7. Chase, "Are You Alive?" 68–70; RPAA meeting minutes, June–July 1923, MP; Chase, *Tragedy*, 179, 190, 197–202, and *Portrait*, 308.

8. Chase, "My Great-Great Grandfather and I," 190–92, "What Shall We Do to Be Saved?" 13–14, and "The Tragedy of Waste," 40.

9. Chase, *Tragedy*, 256–57.

10. R. Bruere, "Our Chained Prometheus," 610–14, and "The Anthracite Paradox," 613; Chase, "Gasless America," 586.

11. Chase, *Tragedy*, 234–35.

12. *Who's Who* (1932–33), 413; R. Bruere, "Antioch," 259–61, 295, and "A Bit of Mellifluous Phraseology," 371–72.

13. *Survey* (Oct. 29, 1921), 131, 184–85, ibid. (Nov. 15, 1922), 273–80, and ibid. (Nov. 15, 1926), 248–50.

14. R. Bruere, "The Coal Disgrace," 261–62, "Our Chained Prometheus," 606–16, "Two Governors Prod the Elephant," 69–72, and "The Non-Partisan Third Party," 446.

15. R. Bruere, "Pandora's Box," 557–60, 646–47.

16. M. Bruere, "Nothing to Lose but the Home," 629–32, "Following the Hydro," 591–94, and "What Has She Done with It?" 275–76.

17. BM to CS, Sept 23, [1923], Oct. 18, 1923; Paul Kellogg to BM, Feb. 29, 1924, MFP.

18. BM, "Appalachian Power: Servant or Master?" 618–19.

19. R. Bruere, "Giant Power—Region Builder," 161–64, 188, "West

Lynn," 27, "The Great Obsession," 473–78, announcement, *SG* (Feb. 1927), 547, and "The Mind in the Machine," 581.

CHAPTER VIII: UPS AND DOWNS, 1925–1926

1. BM to LM, Sept. 17, 1924, MP.

2. CS to BM, Sept. 16, 1924, MFP; LM, *My Works,* 106.

3. LM to BM, Dec. 18, 1924, MFP (copy in MP); LM, *Sketches,* 344–45.

4. "The Regional Community," *SG* (May 1925), 129.

5. Introduction, *SG* (May 1925), 177; LM, "The Fourth Migration," 130–32.

6. LM, "Regions—To Live In," 151–52.

7. Ibid., 151; BM, "The New Exploration: Charting the Industrial Wilderness," 153–55.

8. BM, *The New Exploration,* 156–57, 192–94.

9. CS, "Dinosaur Cities," 134–38; Chase, "Coals to Newcastle," 143–46; R. Bruere, "Giant Power—Region Builder," 161–64, 188.

10. James K. Hart, "Two Generation Communities," *SG* (May 1925), 174–76.

11. Editorial comment, *SG* (May 1925), 178.

12. *NYT* (July 13, 1924), sec. 10, 2, ibid. (Apr. 5, 1925), sec. 2, 1, ibid. (Apr. 19, 1925), sec. 12, 1, and ibid. (Apr. 26, 1925), 16.

13. *NYT* (Apr. 21, 1925), and ibid. (Apr. 26, 1925), 26.

14. "International Congress on City and Regional Planning," *Housing and Regional Planning Bulletin* 8 (Apr.–May 1925), 1–3; *NYT* (Apr. 22, 1925), 16; LM, "Realities vs. Dreams," 198–99.

15. CS to EEW, Apr. 3, 22, 1925, EEW; BM, "Toward Global Law," in *From Geography,* 103.

16. LM, "Realities vs. Dreams," 199; Letters, *SG* (June 1925), 268.

17. Bryant, *Quality of the Day,* 171–96; CS to BM, Aug. 3, 1927; BM to CS, Nov. 5, 1927; HW to BM, Nov. 6, 1928, MFP.

18. LM to BM, Dec. 22, 1926, MP; Chase, "A Very Private Utopia," 539.

19. LM, *Sketches,* 388–407, to BM, Dec. 22, 1926, MP; Betinna L. Knapp, ed. *The Lewis Mumford/David Liebovitz Letters, 1923–1961,* 22.

20. *NYT* (Mar. 7, 1926), sec. 2, 1, and ibid. (June 7, 1925), sec. 11, 1; CS to BM, July 16, 1925, MFP; Herbert W. Smith, "A Teacher Forges New Tools," *SG* (June 1927), 258.

21. CS to BM, July 16, 1925, MFP; RPAA, "Minutes of the Meeting of the RPAA, June 17, 1926," MP.

22. LM to BM, Dec. 22, 1926, MFP (copy in MP); RPAA, "Minutes of the Meeting . . . April 13, 1927," MP.

23. *NYT* (Jan. 8, 1925), 21, and ibid. (Nov. 12, 1925), 1–2; CS, "The New York Puzzle," 84; G. Smith, "Problem: Find Four Walls," 338.

24. State of New York, *Report of the Commission of Housing and Regional Planning for Permanent Housing Relief*, 17, 29–33, and 51–52; *NYT* (Apr. 12, 1925), sec. 11, 1.

25. *NYT* (Mar. 17, 1925), 1, ibid. (May 11, 1926), 1, and ibid. (July 1, 1926), 2; EEW, *Recent Trends in American Housing*, 112, 261.

26. CS to BM, July 16, 1925, MFP; CS to LM, Sept. 13, 1925, SP; *NYT* (Nov. 12, 1925), 2.

27. CHW to LM, Nov. 6, 1924, MP, "Five Architects and One Truth," 401–5; CHW to Louis Sullivan, June 15, 1923, Whitaker-Sullivan Correspondence, Art Institute of Chicago.

28. Robert Twombly, *Louis Sullivan*, 436–37. The correspondence in the Art Institute of Chicago between Sullivan and Whitaker regarding Sullivan's *Autobiography* has been published in George E. Pettingill, "The Biography of a Book," 42–45, and "A System of Architectural Ornamentation: Further Sullivan-Journal Correspondence," 25–30.

29. Max Dunning to Sidney Adler, Apr. 28, 1924, Art Institute of Chicago; CHW to LM, Oct. 19, 1925, MP.

30. CHW, "Cities Old and New," part 3, 406–7, and part 4, 510.

31. "The Sixteenth Convention," *JAIA* 15 (1927), 226, and "One Hundred and Twenty-Five Years of History," *JAIA* (Apr. 1982), 72–73; CHW to BM, Aug. 12, Oct. 15, 1927, MFP.

32. CS to LM, Sept. 13, 1925, SP.

CHAPTER IX: THE SAGE AND THE SIEGE OF SHIRLEY CENTER

1. BM, *New Exploration*, 19; Bryant, *Quality of the Day*, 171; RPAA, "Report . . . since the Meeting of June 17, 1926," MP; BM to HW, Nov. 11, 1928, to CS, Nov. 5, 1927; CS to BM, Aug. 3, 1927, MFP.

2. LM, introduction to BM, *New Exploration*, xvi; BM to CS, Sept. 14, 1924, Aug. 31, 1927, Dec. 16, 1928, to LM, Dec. 3, 1926, to Agnus Gould, [1928], and to HW, Nov. 11, 1928, MFP; LM, *Sketches*, 341.

3. BM to LM, July 9, 1925, MP; BM to LM, Dec. 3, 1926, to CS, Dec. 3, 1926, Aug. 14, 1927, and to HW, Nov. 11, 1928, MFP.

4. BM, *New Exploration*, 22; BM to Chase, Dec. 3, 1926; Raphael Zon to BM, May 26, 1925, MFP; BM to Sophia Mumford, Aug. 1, 1925, and to LM, May 23, 1927, MP.

5. BM, *New Exploration,* xxiii; *NYT* (May 16, 1926), sec. 8, 16; BM to R. Bruere, Dec. 17, 1926, MFP; BM to Edward W. Hartman, July 17, 1927, MP.

6. BM, "Outdoor Culture," in *From Geography,* 176–77; *NYT* (June 3, 1927), 20.

7. BM to LM, Mar. 9, 1927, and RPAA, "Regional Studies for the RPA of America . . . May 12, 1925, MP; BM to CS, May 26, 1924, Nov. 11, 1927, and to William R. Greeley, Nov. 16, 1927, MFP.

8. BM to CS, Nov. 15, 1922, MFP.

9. BM to CS, Mar. 10, 1923, MFP.

10. BM, *New Exploration,* xxiv–xxv; Bryant, *Quality of the Day,* 193–203; LM, *Sketches,* 340; BM to CS, Mar. 10, 1923, and to Louis F. Post, Jan. 20, 1927, MFP.

11. BM to LM, Dec. 3, 1926, MFP; BM to LM, April 4, 1927, MP. For Spengler, see BM, *New Exploration,* 22–23, and LM, "A Philosophy of History," 140–41.

12. BM to Mrs. Floyd, Aug. 25, 1925, MFP; BM, *New Exploration,* 110–11, 113, and 118, "The New Northwest Passage," 603, and "Industrial Exploration," 70–73, 92–93, and 119–21.

13. BM, *New Exploration,* 29–30, 51–52, 55, 61–64, and 134–40; BM to R. M. MacIver, Nov. 8, 1930, MFP.

14. BM, *New Exploration,* 71–72, 141–50; BM to CS, Mar. 8, 1925, MFP.

15. BM, *New Exploration,* 154–56, 170–71; BM to Raphael Zon, Dec. 9, 1928, MFP.

16. BM, *New Exploration,* 153–54.

17. Ibid., 159–66, 175–90, 206–7.

18. Ibid., 30–44, 214; LM, *Sketches,* 342–43.

19. BM, *New Exploration,* 14–15, 126–28; BM to LM, May 23, 1927, MP.

20. T. H. Reed, review of *The New Exploration, American Political Science Review* 23 (1929), 1050; Chase, *Nation* 127 (1928), 634; *NYT* (Dec. 23, 1928), 17; W. P. Eaton, *Saturday Review* 5 (1928–29), 620; BM to Chase, Dec. 9, 1928; Raphael Zon to BM, Dec. 3, 1928; BM to Zon, Dec. 9, 1928, MFP.

21. BM, *New Exploration,* 191–97.

22. BM to the RPAA, Dec. 22, 1928, and to Harry B. Dow, Dec. 22, 1928, MFP; BM, "Our Iron Civilization," 342–43.

23. BM to LM, May 23, 1927, and to Edward T. Hartman, July 11, 1927, MP; BM To Geoffrey Bolton, Mar. 9, 1928, and to HW, Nov. 11, 20, 1928, MFP; BM, *From Geography,* 47.

24. Chase, *Nemesis of American Business,* 153, 155–56; BM to Chase, July 20, 1935, MFP.

25. BM, *New Exploration,* 182–90; CHW to LM, Apr. 9, 1929, MP; BM to Geoffrey Bolton, Mar. 9, 1928, and to HW, Nov. 11, 1928, MFP.

26. BM, "The Townless Highway," 93–95.

27. BM to Waldemar Kaempffert, Mar. 26, Apr. 12, 1930, MFP; BM, "The Town That Took the Wrong Road," 112–14.

28. BM to CS, Oct. 10, 1929, and to LM, Aug. 16, Sept. 19, 1930, MP.

29. BM to CS, July 2, Dec. 5, 1930, and BM, ms. article, "Highway Approaches (Boston)," MFP.

30. BM to LM, Sept. 19, 1930, MFP; LM to BM, July 22, Oct. 22, 1929, MP; LM, "From a Country Notebook," 313–14; BM and LM, "Townless Highway for the Motorist," 347–56.

31. Charles Davis to BM, May 30, 1930; BM to Hon. Robert Crossner, [Jan. 1931]; Frederick Kirby to BM, Jan. 31, Feb. 2, 21, 1931, MFP.

32. BM to LM, Aug. 16, 1930, MP; BM, "Cement Railroads," 541–42.

33. BM, "Region Building in River Valleys," in *From Geography,* 156, and "A New England Recreation Plan," in ibid., 161–68.

CHAPTER X: SUNNYSIDE AND RADBURN

1. List of Stein's works, SP; *NYT* (Mar. 7, 1926), sec. 2, 1.

2. Bruce Bliven, "Houses of Tomorrow," *New Republic* 42 (1925), 34; CS, "Housing New York's Two-Thirds," 509–10; editorial, *New Republic* 50 (1927), 127; *NYT* (Jan. 22, 1926), 21.

3. For a discussion of this matter see Edward K. Spann, *Brotherly Tomorrows: Movements for a Cooperative Society in America, 1820–1920* (N.Y.: Columbia University Press, 1989), 227.

4. Eugenie Ladner Birch, *Edith Elmer Wood and the Genesis of Liberal Housing Thought, 1910–1942,* 102–10; *NYT* (Aug. 2, 1923), 16, ibid. (Dec. 8, 1928), 20, and ibid. (Jan. 29, 1929), 3; EEW, "How to Get Better Housing," 4–9, 69–70; EEW to Elizabeth Coit, Mar. 10, 1939, EWP.

5. "Competition for the Remodeling of a Block of Old Tenements in New York City," *JAIA* 8 (1920), 135–37; John Taylor Boyd Jr., "Garden Apartments in Cities," 69–73.

6. CS, "The New York Puzzle," 85; statements in *NYT* (Mar. 16, 1924), 16, ibid. (Apr. 12, 1925), sec. 11, 1, and ibid. (Nov. 9, 1924), sec. 11, 2; CS, "Co-operative Housing," 168–69, and "Cooperative Homes for Brain Workers," 1.

7. Editorial, *SG* (Apr. 1924), 48; Bing, "Can We Have Garden Cities In America?" 190; CS to EEW, Oct. 25, 1924, EWP.

8. CS, *Toward New Towns for America,* 19–20, and "Henry Wright," 26.

9. Ordway Tead, "Labour in War-Time," *Freeman* (May 11, 1921), 212; Bing, "The Wreck of the British Guild," *SG* (Jan. 1924), 348, 355; *NYT* (Mar. 21, 1922), 26.

10. Editorial, *SG* (June 1924), 311; *NYT* (May 6, 1924), 36, ibid. (May 28, 1924), sec. 2, 2, ibid. (May 23, 1925), 14, ibid. (Oct. 23, 1925), 12; City Housing Corporation, *Circular* (1926), 1–3; Bing, "Can We Have Garden Cities?" 190.

11. Lubove, *Community Planning,* 58; CS, *Toward New Towns,* 22–24.

12. CS, *Toward New Towns,* 24–28; HW, "Shall We Community Plan?" 320–24, and "The Road to Good Houses," 165–68, 189; "Housing for Wage Earners," *NYT* (Nov. 16, 1924), sec. 10, 7.

13. "Sunnyside—An Experiment in City Housing," *SG* (Nov. 15, 1924), 189; "Model Community Buyers Moving In," *NYT* (Sept. 7, 1924), sec. 10, 1; CHC advertisement, *NYT* (Oct. 10, 1926), sec. 11, 5; CS, "Wanted: A Place to Play," 452, 458.

14. James G. Young, "Home Building Put on Low Profit Basis," *NYT* (Jan. 31, 1926), 8; LM, *Sketches,* 410–20, and *Green Memories,* 26–31; BM to CS, Nov. 18, 1924, MFP.

15. *NYT* (May 23, 1925), 14, ibid. (Nov. 6, 1926), 16, and ibid. (May 5, 1927), 25; City Housing Corporation, *Circular* (1926), 1–2.

16. *NYT* (Apr. 15, 1926), 18, ibid. (Nov. 28, 1926), sec. 9, 13, and ibid. (Sept. 15, 1929), sec. 12, 21; CS to EEW, Oct. 25, 1924, EWP; Bing, "Can We Have Garden Cities?" 172–73, 190.

17. City Housing Corporation, *Circular;* RPAA, "Minutes of the Meeting . . . June 17, 1926," and "Report of the Secretary and Treasurer . . . since the Meeting of June 17, 1926," (Apr. 13, 1927), MP; CS to EEW, Oct. 25, 1924, EWP.

18. CS to EEW, Sept. 14, Oct. 4, 1927, EWP; RPAA, "Summary of Discussion of Problems Connected with a Garden City . . . October 8 and 9, 1927," 1–3, MP.

19. RPAA, "Discussion . . . 1927," 2–3.

20. Ibid., 6–7; CS to Aline Stein, Feb. 1, 1933, SP.

21. RPAA, "Discussion . . . 1927," 2–5.

22. Ibid., 5–6.

23. By far the best study of Radburn, and one that also sheds much light on both the RPAA and the CHC, is Daniel Schaffer, *Garden Cities for America: The Radburn Experience.* I have chosen not to use this work extensively here because I wish to present a view evolved from my own research and thought. "Flivver Town," *Survey* (Nov. 15, 1927), 203–4; G. Smith, "A Town for the Motor Age," *SG* (Mar. 1928), 6, 94–98; *NYT* (Jan. 25, 1928), 1, 13, ibid. (Jan. 26, 1928), 22, and ibid. (Feb. 12, 1928), sec. 11, 9.

24. LM, "The Fate of Garden Cities," 37–39; LM to BM, Nov. 5, Dec. 20, 1928, MFP; LM, *Sketches,* 346.

25. LM to BM, Jan. 20, 1928, MFP; Chase, "A Suburban City for the Motor Age," 4; *NYT* (Jan. 26, 1928), 22, and ibid. (Feb. 9, 1928), 45.

26. *NYT* (Feb. 19, 1929), 53; Henry M. Propper to EEW, Nov. 30, 1928, and Mary G. Schenburg to EEW, Mar. 18, 1929, EWP; by-laws of the Radburn Association, quoted in Robert B. Hudson, *Radburn: A Plan for Living,* 111.

27. LM to BM, Jan. 20, 1928, MFP; HW to LM, June 21, 1928, MP.

28. CS, *Toward New Towns,* 37–44, and "Notes on the New Town Planned for the City Housing Corporation," typescript in SP; HW, "Planning a Town for Wholesome Living," 682–84.

29. CS, *Toward New Towns,* 41–47; G. Smith, "Town for the Motor Age," 696.

30. CS, *Toward New Towns,* 48–51, and "Notes on the New Town," 4, SP; Hudson, *Radburn,* 53–60; Propper, "When Radburn Opens," 645–50; G. Smith, "Town for the Motor Age," 696; "Community Life in Radburn," *SG* (Apr. 15, 1931), 99–100.

31. CS, *Toward New Towns,* 51; City Housing Corporation, *Radburn: Garden Homes,* 1–14; Chase, "Suburban City," 4; LM to BM, Dec. 20, 1928, MFP.

32. Propper, "Construction Work Now under Way," no. 31, 81–82, and no. 41, 98–99, 143–44; *SG* (Jan. 1928), 444; *NYT* (Apr. 27, 1930), 12, ibid. (May 26, 1930), 20, ibid. (Oct. 12, 1930), sec. 11, 2, ibid. (Dec. 14, 1930), sec. 12, 2, and ibid. (Apr. 19, 1931), sec. 11, 1. Also see Louis Brownlow, *A Passion for Anonymity,* 211–24.

33. *Survey* (Dec. 15, 1930), 308; CS to Aline Stein, Feb. 15, 16, and 29, 1931, SP.

34. Stein, *Toward New Towns,* 68–69; CS, interview (1965) in "Radburn," *The New Jersey Builder* (Nov. 1965), 3–4; Bing to CHC stockholders, Dec. 31, 1931; CHS, *Eighth Annual Report* (1932), EWP.

35. CS to Aline Stein, Feb. 18, Mar. 1, and Mar. 6, 1931, SP.

36. Loula D. Lasker, "Sunnyside Up and Down," 419–23, 439–41; *NYT* (June 4, 1933), sec. 2, 13, ibid. (May 20, 1934), 14, ibid. (Aug. 2, 1934), 29, ibid. (Apr. 8, 1934), sec. 11, 1, and ibid. (Dec. 4, 1935), 8.

CHAPTER XI: REGIONALISM

1. CHW to BM, Oct. 25, 1927, MFP; CHW to LM, "Saturday" [1927], and Jan. 31, 1929, MP; CHW, Shadows and Straws, *JAIA* 15 (1927), 183–84.

2. Chase, "The Future of the Great City," 82–83, and "A Very Private Utopia," 559–62; Chase to BM, Aug. 6, 1930, MFP.

3. Chase, "Slaves of the Machines?" 480–89, "One Dead Level," 137–39, and "The Two Hour War," 325–27.

4. LM, "From a Country Notebook," 313.

5. Announcements in *AR* 63 (1928), 240–44, 68 (1930), 436, and 71 (1932), 155, 328, and 332; *NYT* (Feb. 27, 1927), 16; CS, "The Art Museum of Tomorrow," 5–12, and photographs of the Fieldston School, *AR* 67 (1930), 314–20.

6. HW, "The Place of the Apartment House in the Modern Community," 207–38.

7. BM to Edward T. Hartman, July 11, 1927, MP; LM, "Regionalism and Irregionalism," 137.

8. LM, "Shorter Notices," *Freeman* (Apr. 25, 1923), 167, "The Regional Note," 107–8, and "Downfall or Renewal?" 367–69.

9. LM, *The Golden Day: A Study of American Experience and Culture,* 158, "Devastated Regions," 217–20, and *Findings,* 188–89.

10. LM, *Golden Day,* 273–80, "Regionalism and Irregionalism," 138, and "Frank Lloyd Wright and the New Pioneers," 416; LM to BM, July 25, 1927, MP.

11. LM, "Regionalism," 182–83, and "Regionalism and Irregionalism," 19 (1927), 277–88, and 20 (1928), 18–33, 131–41.

12. BM to HW, Nov. 11, 1928, and to LM, Apr. 4, 1927, MP, "New Exploration," 207–10, to Roger Greeley, Feb. 18, 1930, and to CS, May 19, 1930, MFP.

13. Percy MacKaye, *Kentucky Mountain Fantasies,* xi–xii; review of *Kentucky Mountain Fantasies SG* (Aug. 1926), 520; BM, "New Exploration," 209–10.

14. BM, "Regional Planning," 93–99, and "Our Iron Civilization," 342–43.

15. *A Close-up of the Regional Plan of New York and Its Environs* (1929), copy in EWP; Thomas Adams, *The Building of the City: Regional Plan of New York and Its Environs,* 5, 108, and 122; *NYT* (Oct. 10, 1926), 9. Also see David A. Johnson, "Regional Planning for the Great American Metropolis: New York between the World Wars," 176–93.

16. BM, "New York: A National Peril," 68; BM to CS, July 2, 1930, and R. M. MacIver, Nov. 8, 1930, MFP.

17. LM, "The Plan of New York," 121–26, 146–54; Sussman, ed., *Planning and the Fourth Migration,* 222–59.

18. CS to Aline Stein, Mar. 24, 1932, SP; Thomas Adams, "A Communication in Defense of the Regional Plan," in Sussman, ed., *Planning the Fourth Migration,* 260–67.

19. CS to BM, July 29, Aug. 21, Oct. 3, 1930, MFP; "Program of Regional Planning Conference . . . October 18–19, 1930," typescript, MFP; "A Ten Year Program for a State," *New Republic* 64 (1930), 30–31.

20. LM, "Discussion on the Possibilities of Regional Planning, October 17–19, 1930," typescript, MP.

21. Ibid.; BM to Leifur Magnusson, Oct. 22, 1930, MFP.

22. CS to Aline Stein, Jan. 14, 29, 31, Feb. 19, 1931, SP (excerpts from these letters also in MP); CS to BM, Mar. 5, 1931, MFP; "Tentative List of Those to Be Invited to the Roundtable," MP.

23. LM, *Findings,* 101; Allen Tullos, "The Politics of Regional Development: Lewis Mumford and Howard Odom," 110–20.

24. CS to BM, Mar. 25, 1931, MFP; CS to Aline Stein, Mar. 24, 1931, SP.

25. Edward K. Spann, "Franklin Delano Roosevelt and the Regional Planning Association of America, 1931–36," 185–200; Franklin Delano Roosevelt, "On the Excessive Costs and Taxes in Local Government," 288–302; *NYT* (July 7, 1931), 1, 15; Charles S. Ascher, "Regionalism: Charting the Future," 460.

26. LM, "Regional Planning," 199–208.

27. Chase, "The Concept of Planning," 209–17; *NYT* (July 12, 1931), sec. 1, 5; HW to LM, July 18, 1931, MP.

28. HW to LM, June 26, July 18, 1931: memorandum to Louis Brownlow [1931], MP. Brownlow gives an unreliable account of the conference in his *A Passion for Anonymity,* 268–70. More reliable is Ascher, "Regionalism," 460–61.

29. LM, *Findings,* 198; CS to LM, July 17, 1931, SP.

30. Allen Tate, "Regionalism and Sectionalism," 158–61; John Gould Fletcher, *Life Is My Song,* 360–62.

31. RPAA, "Minutes of the Meeting . . . November 14, 1931," and "Outline for Memo to Governor Roosevelt on State Planning for New Communities," MP.

32. Roosevelt, "Growing Up by Plan," 483, 506–7; CS to BM, July 11, 1932: BM to CS, Nov. 4, 1932, MFP.

CHAPTER XII: WOMEN ON HOUSING

1. *NYT* (Mar. 29, 1928), 25; LM in *Survey* (Mar. 26, 1921), 432. Stein's letters to his wife, an important source of information regarding RPAA activities, are in SP.

2. RPAA, "Minutes of the Meeting . . . October 8–10, 1927," MP; Bing to EEW, Apr. 18, 1928, EWP.

3. M. Bruere, "Spring Planting," 5–13, "Nothing to Lose but the Home," 629–32, "The Black Folks Are Coming On," 432–35, "A Cure for Smoke-Sick Cities," 28, 44, "Putting the Town on Its Feet," 24, 36, "Where Wires Go Wives Don't Strike," 25, 44, and "What Is Giant Power For?" 120–23.

4. Birch, *Wood,* 1–60; *Who's Who* (1922–23), 3371; EEW, "Four Washington Alleys," 250–52.

5. Birch, *Wood,* 62–64; EEW, "What Is a House?" 77–78.

6. Solan Fieldman to EEW, Apr. 20 and 21, 1920; Vance Wood to EEW, Mar. 19, 1920; FLA to EEW, Oct. 21, 1920, EWP.

7. *NYT* (Aug. 2, 1923), 16, ibid. (Feb. 8, 1925), sec. 10, 2, ibid. (Dec. 8, 1925), 20, and ibid. (Jan. 29, 1929), 3; EEW, "How to Get Better Housing," 4–9, 65–71.

8. EEW to Elizabeth Coit, Mar. 18, 1939; CS to EEW, Feb. 11, 1925, Jan. 12, 1933, EWP; Birch, *Wood,* 108–9.

9. Birch, *Wood,* 102–4; *NYT* (Feb. 8, 1925), sec. 10, 2; W. D. Heydecker to EEW, Nov. 17, 23, 1930, EWP.

10. May Schonberg to EEW, Apr. 18, 1928, Mar. 29, 1929, Nov 20, 1930; Bing to EEW, Jan. 28, June 9, 1928; EEW to "Colleagues," July 30, 1929, EWP.

11. EEW to Thomas Adams, May 4, 1927, EWP; Birch, *Wood,* 183 n.

12. EEW, *Recent Trends in American Housing,* 1–4, 45.

13. CS to Aline Stein, Jan. 14, 1931, SP; CS, "Housing and the Depression," 4; RDK to EEW, June 26, 1933, EWP.

14. RPAA, "Minutes of the Meeting . . . May 17, 1933," and "A Housing Policy for the United States," MP.

15. Birch, *Wood,* 173–74. See also Birch, "Woman-Made America: The Case of Early Public Housing Policy," 161–62; Helen Alford to EEW, Mar. 24, [1930]; EEW to Julain E. Berla, Nov. 12, 1932, EWP.

16. RDK to EEW, June 9, July 25, Aug. 7, Sept. 28, 1933; EEW to RDK, June 13, Aug. 26, Oct. 25, Nov. 2, 1933, EWP.

17. Birch, *Wood,* 198 ff.; *NYT* (June 13, 1935), 7, and ibid. (June 23, 1935), sec. 4, 10.

18. EEW, "Letter from Edith Elmer Wood," 196–97, "The Hand of Esau," 556–58, to the editor of *New Republic,* Feb. 27, 1936, and to Loula D. Lasker, June 18, 25, 1936, EWP; Birch, *Wood,* 181.

19. Birch, "Woman-Made America," 153; "Houser Wins Guggenheim Award," *AR* 79 (1936), 341. For the Mumford-Bauer affair see Miller, *Mum-*

ford, 288–325. CS to Aline Stein, Mar. 17, 1931, SP; Catherine Bauer to BM, Aug. 17, 1931, MFP.

20. Bauer, "Who Cares about Architecture?" 326–27, and "The Americanization of Europe," 153–54.

21. Bauer, "Art and Industry," repr. in SP; "Houser Wins Guggenheim," 341; Mumford, *Findings,* 352; *NYT* (May 7, 1932), 19; CS to Aline Stein, Aug. 27, 1932, SP; Bauer to EEW, Mar. 17, 1932, EWP.

22. CS to Aline Stein, Mar. 19, 1931, Feb. 18, Mar. 24, 1933, SP; CS, "Survey of Community Housing Development" (1932–33), SP; CS and Bauer, "Store Buildings and Neighborhood Shopping Centers," 175–87.

23. Bauer to EEW, n.d. [box 90], Mar. 17, Apr. 17, 1932, Apr. 26, Sept. 12, 1934, EWP.

24. Birch, "Woman-Made America," 166–68, and *Wood,* 158, 211; Bauer, "The Swiss Family Borsodi," 490–91; *NYT* (June 29, 1935), 6; Bauer to EEW, Sept. 12, 1934, EWP.

25. Bauer, "Slum Clearance or Housing," 730–31, and "Slums Aren't Necessary," 296–305; *NYT* (Mar. 25, 1934), sec. 4, 5; Albert Mayer, "A Man's House," *New Republic* 82 (1935), 136.

26. EEW quoted in Birch, *Wood,* 212.

CHAPTER XIII: HOUSING—FOR WHOM AND WHERE?

1. RPAA, membership list (Dec. 7, 1931), MP; CS to BM, Jan. 11, 1933, MFP.

2. *AR* 71 (1932), 367–75; RPAA, "Memo to Governor Roosevelt on State Planning for New Communities, January 2, 1932," MP; *NYT* (Apr. 10, 1932), sec. 2, 1.

3. CS to Aline Stein, Mar. 5, 10, 19, 1933. For Hillside Homes, see later in this chapter.

4. CS, "A Housing Policy for the United States" (May 15, 1933); RPAA, "Minutes of the Meeting . . . May 17, 1933," MP; EEW to RDK, June 13, 1933, EWP.

5. RPAA, "A Housing Policy for the United States," *Octagon* (June 1933), repr. in EWP; Birch, *Wood,* 178–79.

6. RDK, "Should Architects Undertake Programs?" 149; *NYT* (May 4, 1930), sec. 14, 1, ibid. (Nov. 23, 1930), 4, ibid. (Apr. 23, 1931), 20, ibid. (Apr. 26, 1931), sec. 11, 2, ibid. (Aug. 17, 1931), 7, and ibid. (Jan. 10, 1932), sec. 13, 3.

7. *NYT* (Apr. 14, 1932), 23, ibid. (Feb. 14, 1932), sec. 11, 2, ibid. (Aug. 31, 1932), 20, ibid. (Jan. 29, 1933), 2, ibid. (Jan.29, 1933), sec. 2, 2, and ibid. (Mar. 19, 1933), sec. 10, 2.

8. CS to Aline Stein, Mar. 20, May 26, June 18, 1933, SP; "Public Works Provided by Industrial Recovery Act," *AR* 74 (1933), 3–8.

9. CS to Aline Stein, July 10, 11, 16, 21, 1933, SP, CS to BM, July 11, 1933, MFP.

10. RDK, "Planning for Changed Needs," 294 ff.; "Housing Director Kohn Tours Country," *AR* 74 (1933), 416–17.

11. Jonathan Mitchell, "Housing by Slow Freight," 236–37; CS to Aline Stein, Nov. 13, 20, and Dec. 10, 1933, SP.

12. "Between the Housers and the Planners: The Recollections of Coleman Woodbury," in Donald A. Krueckeberg, ed., *The American Planner,* 342; CS to Aline Stein, Feb. 3, 6, 12, 26, and Mar. 14, 1934, SP.

13. *NYT* (Mar. 3, 1934), 11; Mitchell, "Housing by Slow Freight," 206; CS to Aline Stein, Mar. 3, June 15, 16, 18, July 2, 7, 1934, SP.

14. Exhange of letters between Harold Ickes and Henry S. Churchill, *New Republic* 80 (1934), 20, 161–62.

15. CS, "Housing and Common Sense," 541–44; *NYT* (June 12, 1932), 12, and ibid. (July 25, 1933), sec. 10, 2; CS, "Rebuild Brooklyn: Address before the Brooklyn League of Women Voters, February 23, 1933," MP.

16. CS to Aline Stein, July 17, Dec. 7, 1933, SP. Stein devotes a chapter to Hillside Homes in his *Toward New Towns,* 83–107.

17. "Hillside Housing Project May Be Financed by R.F.C.," *AR* 72 (1936), 352; CS to BM, Nov. 12, 1932, MFP; CS to Aline Stein, Aug. 30, 1932, Feb. 5, Nov. 24, 30, 1933, SP.

18. CS to Aline Stein, Feb. 10, Aug. 21, 1934, SP; *NYT* (Apr. 12, 1934), ibid. (Dec. 16, 1934), sec. 12, 1–2, ibid. (June 30, 1935), sec. 2, 1, 7, ibid. (Sept. 18, 1935), 42, and ibid. (Apr. 4, 1936), 32; CS, "Speech at Dedication of Hillside Housing Development, June 29, 1935," SP; Louise P. Blackham, "For the Happiness of the Community," 255–56, 276; James Ford, *Slums and Housing,* 708–11; Norbert Brown, "Progress Report on Low-Cost Housing and Slum Clearance," 293–99.

CHAPTER XIV: PLANNING THE TENNESSEE REGION

1. CS to BM, Nov. 12, 1932, MFP.

2. Roosevelt, *Public Papers and Addresses,* 28–29, 116–19, and 139, and *Franklin D. Roosevelt and Conservation, 1911–1945,* Edgar B. Nixon, ed. and

comp. (Hyde Park, N.Y.: Franklin D. Roosevelt Library, 1957), 1:77–89, 133, 144–45, and 151; *NYT* (Apr. 16, 1933), sec. 8, 3. Also see "Quotes from Governor Roosevelt" (n.d.), MP.

3. BM to Chase, July 20, 1936, MP, RPAA, "Memorandum to Governor Roosevelt" (Mar. 23, 1931), MP.

4. RPAA, "Outline of Memo to Governor Roosevelt," 3, 8–9, MP; CS to Aline Stein, Jan. 8–9, 1932, SP.

5. BM, "End or Peak of Civilization?" 441–44; *NYT* (Feb. 4, 1933), 3; "The Tennessee Valley Plan," *New Republic* 74 (1933), 4–6. Also see draft of letter to Roosevelt (Mar. 1, 1933), MP.

6. BM, "An Appalachian Trail," 327–28.

7. "Our Iron Civilization," 342–43; CS to Aline Stein, Mar. 8, 10, 11, 12, 14, 15, 18, 22, 1933, SP.

8. CS to Aline Stein, Mar. 12, 21, 22, 1933, SP.

9. BM, "The Tennessee River Project: First Step in a National Plan," 3.

10. BM, "The Challenge of Muscle Shoals," 445–46, and "Tennessee— Seed of a National Plan," 251–54, 293–94.

11. BM to CS, Apr. 7, May 16, 1933, MFP.

12. BM to CS, Apr. 29, May 16, 30, 1933, July 20, 1935, MFP.

13. BM to CS, Apr. 7, 29, 1933, MFP.

14. BM to CS, May 16, 30, June 9, 20, 1933, MFP; Bryant, *Quality of the Day,* 205.

15. BM to CS, June 20, Sept. 9, Oct. 13, 1933, MFP; BM to Hazel MacKaye, Sept. 21, 1933, and to LM, Oct. 26, 1933, MP; CS to Aline Stein, Nov. 27, Dec. 5, 1933, SP.

16. CS to C. L. Richey, Oct. 7, 1933, MP; F. W. Reeves to R. Bruere, June 24, 1934, MFP; Bryant, *Quality of the Day,* 206.

17. Bryant, *Quality of the Day,* 206–7; BM, "Regional Planning in the Tennessee Valley" (Feb. 5, 1935), ms. in MFP.

18. Bryant, *Quality of the Day,* 207–8; BM to CS, Mar. 28, Apr. 11, Sept. 28, 1934, to R. Bruere, June 24, 1934, and to Chase (copies to LM, CS, and HW), July 20, 1935, MFP.

19. Chase to BM, Apr. 19, 1935; BM to CS, Sept. 28, 1934, and to Chase, July 20, 1935, MFP; Bryant, *Quality of the Day,* 207–10.

20. BM to Chase, July 20, 1935; Bryant, *Quality of the Day,* 208–10.

21. BM to CS, July 31, 1935, MFP.

22. BM, "The Appalachian Trail: A Guide to the Study of Nature," 330; BM to CS, Apr. 29, 1933, and to Chase, July 20, 1935, MFP.

23. Bryant, *Quality of the Day,* 148, 209–10; BM to Robert Sterling Yard, Apr. 1, 1935, and to Chase, July 20, 1935, MFP.

24. BM to LM, Apr. 23, 1936, Dec. 14, 1937, MP; Gordon R. Clapp to BM, June 22, 1936, MFP.

25. BM, "Allocation vs. Allegation in the T.V.A. Inquiry" (1938), MFP.

26. BM, "An Open Letter to the TVA Committee" (July 1938), ms. in MFP.

27. Ibid.

28. Jacob Crane, "Large-Scale Regional Planning: The Unit: Watersheds or States?" 60–66.

CHAPTER XV: NEW DEAL OR NEW ORDER?

1. LM, *Sketches,* 340, "If Engineers Were Kings," 261–62.

2. LM, "Toward A Humanist Synthesis," 583–85.

3. Spiller, ed., *Brooks-Mumford Letters,* 35.

4. LM, "What I Believe," 263–68.

5. Ibid., 266–68, *Sketches,* 472.

6. LM, "In Our Stars: The World Fifty Years from Now," 338–42.

7. LM, "Bellamy's Accurate Utopia," 52; *NYT* (Dec. 30, 1932), 19.

8. LM to BM, Sept. 19, 1933, MP.

9. LM, *NYT* (Feb. 14, 1932), sec. 11, 2, "Breaking the Housing Blockade," 8–11, and "Esthetics and Public Works," 344.

10. Brooks, *Days of the Phoenix,* 142, 153; Spiller, ed., *Brooks-Mumford Letters,* 83, 225.

11. Spiller, ed., *Brooks-Mumford Letters,* 142; LM to BM, July 25, 1940, MP.

12. Spiller, ed., *Brooks-Mumford Letters,* 74, 79; *NYT* (Mar. 14, 1932), 10.

13. LM, *Sketches,* 466, intro. to 1963 ed., *Technics and Civilization,* i–iii, and "The Drama of the Machine," 150–61; CS to Aline Stein, June 25, 1933, SP.

14. Miller, *Mumford,* 325–29; LM, *Technics,* i, 3–6ff., 282–83, and 322–63.

15. LM, *Technics,* 279–96, 382–89.

16. Ibid., 381–89, 400–410, 417–22; LM, *The Conduct of Life,* 235.

17. LM, *The Culture of Cities,* 353–54.

18. Ibid., 3–5, 13–72, 223–99.

19. Ibid., 300–304.

20. Ibid., 306–22.

21. Ibid., 315–401, esp. 331, 347, 362, and 390.

22. Ibid., 329, 348–401. It should be noted regarding the above that nearly all of Mumford's periodical writings from 1934 through 1937 were articles on architecture written for the *New Yorker.* See Elmer S. Newman, *Lewis Mumford: A Bibliography, 1914–1970* (N.Y.: Harcourt Brace Jovanovich, 1971), 30–38.

CHAPTER XVI: THREE WISE MEN

1. BM to LM, Aug. 16, 29, 1936, MP; Chase, *Nemesis of American Business,* 52–54, 72.

2. *NYT* (Nov. 1, 1929), 3; Chase, "The End of an Epoch," 364–65, and *Nemesis,* 166–71.

3. Chase, *Nemesis,* 104–7; *NYT* (Mar. 22, 1931), 8.

4. Chase, "A Ten Year Plan for America," 1–10.

5. Chase, "If I Were Dictator," 536–38.

6. Chase, "A New Deal for America," 169–71, 199–201, 225–26, 282–85.

7. Ibid., 171; *NYT* (Aug. 30, 1932), 15.

8. *NYT* (Dec. 13, 1934), 35, and ibid. (Feb. 26, 1935), 9.

9. Chase, "The Concept of Planning," 213–17, *Rich Land, Poor Land,* 263–64, 277, and "Working with Nature," 624–28.

10. Chase, *Rich Land, Poor Land,* 276, and "Working with Nature," 625–26.

11. Chase, "Cluttered Up with Progress," 634, and *Rich Land, Poor Land,* esp. 55–62; *NYT* (Oct. 28, 1936), 27.

12. Chase, "Old Man River," 177–78; *NYT* (Dec. 13, 1934), 35, and ibid. (Feb. 26, 1935), 9.

13. LM to BM, Oct. 22, 1929, MP.

14. *AR* 61 (1927), 241, ibid. 63 (1928), 240–41, ibid. 68 (1930), 436, and ibid. 71 (1932), 155, 328, and 332; FLA, "How Can We Live in the Sun?" 706; *NYT* (Jan. 17, 1932), sec. 11, 2.

15. CS to Aline Stein, Dec. 14, 1932, Feb. 12, March 1, 11, 1933, SP.

16. CS to Aline Stein, Aug. 18, 1932, SP; FLA, "The Technologist Looks at the Depression, Part I" (July 27, 1932), ms., and "The Facts behind Technology," repr. of *Scholastic* article (1933) made by the Continental Committee on Technology, n.p., SP. Also see FLA, "The Technocrats and the Debt Burden," *New Republic,* 337–38.

17. FLA, "The Facts behind Technology," SP.

18. FLA, "The Technologist Looks at the Depression," ms., SP; CS to Aline Stein, Nov. 25, 1933, SP.

19. CS to Aline Stein, Nov. 25, 1933, SP.

20. FLA to LM (n.d.), MP; CS to Aline Stein, Mar. 5, Feb. 14, 18, Mar. 1, 14, 1934, SP; *NYT* (Apr. 18, 1934), 2, and ibid. (May 30, 1937), sec. 12, 1.

21. CS to Aline Stein, Dec. 14, 1932, SP.

22. CHW, *From Rameses,* xi–xvi, 236–92, and 311–12.

23. Ibid., 323–47.

24. Ibid.

25. Ibid., 338; CHW to LM, July 27, 1933, MP; BM to CS, Apr. 16, 1933, MFP; CS to BM, Oct. 7, 1933, MFP; and CS to Aline Stein, June 22, 1933, SP.

26. CHW, *From Rameses,* 314–15, CHW to LM, Aug. 20, 1936, MP.

27. *NYT* (Nov. 6, 1936), 24.

28. CHW to LM, Aug. 20, 1936, MP.

29. Obituary of CHW, *NYT* (Aug. 13, 1938), 13.

CHAPTER XVII: THE WRIGHT WAY

1. Albert Mayer, "Henry Wright: Creative Planner," 530; CS, "Henry Wright," 25–26; Churchill, "Henry Wright," 293–301, repr. in Kreuckeberg, *American Planner,* 208–24; HW, "The Machine Made House," 76.

2. CS, *Toward New Towns,* 72–77; Charles F. Lewis, "A Moderate Rental Project in Pittsburgh," 217–28; Lubove, *Twentieth Century Pittsburgh,* 70–82.

3. CS and HW, "An Opportunity of Architectural Leadership," 238; HW, "The Six-Cylinder House with Streamline Body," 175.

4. HW, "Exploiting the Land," 305–6; *NYT* (May 13, 1927), 29, ibid. (July 17, 1927), sec. 2, 2, ibid. (Sept. 26, 1927), 6, and ibid. (Feb. 20, 1932), 10; *New Republic* 70 (1932), 57.

5. HW, "Wanted: A Substitute for the Gridiron Street System," 87–89, "To Plan or Not to Plan," 468–69, and "Servicing Apartments for Lower Rentals," 223.

6. HW, "Can Architects Promote More Business?" 288–90, and "Opportunity of Architectural Leadership," 238.

7. HW, "Sinking Slums," 417–19, and "New Homes for a New Deal, Part 2: Abolishing Slums Forever," 41–44.

8. HW, "Servicing Apartments," 223; HW to LM, July 8, Sept. 21, 1933, MP; William Ganson Rose, *Cleveland: The Making of a City,* 919–20.

9. HM to LM, Sept. 21, Nov. 1, 1933, MP.

10. HM to LM, Nov. 1, 1933, Apr. 17, 1934, MP.

11. HM to LM, Nov. 1, 1933, MP.

12. HM, LM, and Mayer, "New Homes for a New Deal, Part 2: Abolishing Slums Forever," 41–44.

13. HW, LM, and Mayer, "New Homes for a New Deal, Part 4: A Concrete Program," 91–94.

14. CS to Aline Stein, Aug. 12, 1932, SP; HW to LM, Aug. 15, 1932, MP.

15. HW, "Hillside Group Housing," 221–22, and *NYT* (Sept. 18, 1932), sec. 10, 1; CS to Aline Stein, Feb. 23, 1934, SP.

16. HW, *Rehousing Urban America,* xi–xii.

17. Ibid., 3–15.

18. *Survey* (Nov. 1935), 345; *American City* (Dec. 1935), 68; *NYT* (Nov. 12, 1935), 17; HW to LM, Nov. 17, 1934, MP.

19. CS, *Toward New Towns,* 182–83; Churchill, *Wright,* repr. in Krueckeberg, *American Planner,* 214–15; "Comparative Architectural Details of Greenbelt Housing," *American Architect and Architecture* (Oct. 1936), 21–36.

20. Obituary of HW, *NYT* (July 10, 1936), 19; CS to LM, (n.d.), SP; Stein, *Wright,* 25–26.

21. Mayer, *Wright,* 530; Henry Saylor, "Diary," *American Architect and Architecture,* 42; CS to BM, Sept. 23, 1937; brochure, "The Henry Wright Library," SP.

CHAPTER XVIII: FADE OUT

1. M. Hughes, ed. *Letters of Lewis Mumford and Frederic J. Osborn: A Transatlantic Dialogue, 1938–1970,* 148–49, 410–11; Stanley Buder, *Visionaries and Planners: The Garden City Movement and the Modern Community,* 178–79.

2. Miller, *Mumford,* 320–45, 365; LM, *Sketches,* 466; LM, speech before the Progressive Education League, reported in *NYT* (Nov. 24, 1934), 17, "On the Road to Collectivism," 361. Also see *NYT* (Dec. 15, 1935), 1, 40.

3. Bryant, *Quality of the Day,* 217–19; BM to LM, Apr. 23, Dec. 14, 1936, MP, "An Open Letter to the TVA Committee" (July 1938), ms., and "Allocation vs. Allegation in the TVA Inquiry," ms., MFP.

4. BM to CS, Dec. 5, 1930, and to Laurence C. Fletcher, Aug. 29, 1937, MFP; Bryant, *Quality of the Day,* 217–22.

5. CS to Aline Stein, Apr. 12, 13, 1931, Feb. 5, 1933, SP; *NYT* (Feb. 21, 1932), sec. 11, 13.

6. Stein, *Toward New Towns,* 115–17.

7. Bauer to EEW, Jan. 12, 1933, and meeting notice, EWP; RPAA, "Minutes of the Meeting . . . May 17, 1933," MP; CS to Aline Stein, Mar. 5, 1933, and to LM, Sept. 5, 1933, SP.

8. LM, "A Modest Man's Contribution," 24; CS to BM, Feb. 12, 1936, MFP; "The Wagner-Steagall Housing Act of 1937," 35–38; and "The Case for New Towns," 39–41.

9. LM to BM, Oct. 25, 1935; BM to LM, Aug. 16, 1936, MP.

10. CS to LM, Nov. 16, 1937, SP; CS to BM, Dec. 21, 1937, MFP; BM to CS, Jan. 11, 29, 1938, MFP.

11. "The New York World's Fair," *American Architect and Architecture* (Nov. 1936), 45–48; *NYT* (Mar. 11, 1937); Saylor, *Diary,* 85–86.

12. Carl F. Feuss to EEW, Dec. 9, 1938, EWP; "The American Institute of Planners Presents 'The City,' " *American City* (June 1939), 129. The film is discussed in William Alexander, *Film on the Left: American Documentary Film from 1931 to 1942,* 247–57; Erik Barnouw, *Documentary: A History of Non-Fiction Film,* 122–23; Harrison Engle, "Thirty Years of Social Inquiry," in Richard M. Barsam, ed., *Non-Fiction Film Theory and Criticism,* 271–95; and "Willard Van Dyke," [interview] in G. Ray Levin, *Documentary Exploration,* 189.

13. CS to BM, May 6, June 15, Aug. 26, 31, 1938, MFP; FLA to LM, May 11, 16, June 21, 1939, May 14, 1941, MP; *American City* (June 1939), 129.

14. BM to CS, May 9, July 25, Sept. 10, 15, 1938; CS to BM, Sept. 13, 16, Oct. 7, 1938, MFP; BM, Christmas card (1939), MP.

15. LM, *Regional Planning in the Pacific Northwest: A Memorandum,* 4–8; LM to BM, July 27, 1938, July 25, 1940, MP.

16. See the reviews of these two books in *SG* (May 1939), 341–42. BM to CS, Apr. 3, 1938, MFP.

17. CS to Bauer, Jan. 10, 1944, Sept. 20, 1950, SP; Hughes, ed., *Mumford-Osborn Letters,* 164–65, 168.

18. Hughes, ed., *Mumford-Osborn Letters,* 193, 335, 355, 371.

BIBLIOGRAPHY

UNPUBLISHED PAPERS

MacKaye Family Papers—Dartmouth College.

Lewis Mumford Papers—University of Pennsylvania.

Clarence Stein Papers—Cornell University.

Charles Whitaker—Louis Sullivan Correspondence—Art Institute of Chicago.

Edith Elmer Wood Papers—Columbia University.

PUBLISHED CORRESPONDENCE

Hughes, M., ed., *Letters of Lewis Mumford and Frederic J. Osborn: A Transatlantic Dialogue, 1938–1970*. New York: Praeger, 1972.

Knapp, Betinna L., ed. *The Lewis Mumford/David Liebovitz Letters, 1923–61*. Troy, N.Y.: Whitston Publishing, 1983.

Pettingill, George E., ed. "The Biography of a Book," *JAIA* 63 (June 1975), 42–45.

———. "A System of Architectural Ornamentation: Further Sullivan-Journal Correspondence," *JAIA* 64 (Sept. 1975), 25–30.

Spiller, Robert E., ed. *The Van Wyck Brooks–Lewis Mumford Letters: The Record of Literary Friendship*. New York: E.P. Dutton, 1970.

BOOKS BY MEMBERS OF THE RPAA

Chase, Stuart. *The Nemesis of American Business*. New York: Macmillan, 1931.

———. *Rich Land, Poor Land*. New York: McGraw Hill, 1936.

———. *The Tragedy of Waste*. New York, 1927.

MacKaye, Benton. *Employment and Natural Resources*. Washington, D.C.: Government Printing Office, 1919.

———. *From Geography to Geotechnics*. Edited by Paul T. Bryant. Urbana: University of Illinois Press, 1968.

———. *The New Exploration: A Philosophy of Regional Planning*. 2nd ed., with an introduction by Lewis Mumford. Urbana: University of Illinois Press, 1962.

Mumford, Lewis. *The Conduct of Life.* New York: Harcourt, Brace, 1951.

―――. *The Culture of Cities.* 2nd ed. New York: Harcourt Brace Jovanovich, 1970.

―――. *Findings and Keepings.* New York: Harcourt Brace Jovanovich, 1975.

―――. *The Golden Day: A Study of American Experience and Culture.* New York: Boni and Liveright, 1926.

―――. *Green Memories.* New York: Harcourt, Brace, 1947.

―――. *My Works and Days.* New York: Harcourt Brace Jovanovich, 1979.

―――. *Regional Planning in the Northwest: A Memorandum.* Portland, Oregon: Northwest Regional Council, 1939.

―――. *Sketches from Life.* New York: Dial Press, 1982.

―――. *Sticks and Stones: A Study of American Architecture.* New York: Boni and Liveright, 1924.

―――. *The Story of Utopias.* 2nd ed. Repr. with new introduction. New York: Viking Press, 1962.

―――. *Technics and Civilization.* 2nd ed. New York: Harcourt, Brace, and World, 1963.

Stein, Clarence. *Toward New Towns for America,* with an introduction by Lewis Mumford. Cambridge, Mass.: MIT, 1966.

Whitaker, Charles Harris. *From Rameses to Rockefeller: The Story of Architecture.* New York: Random House, 1934.

―――, ed. *The Housing Problem in War and in Peace.* Washington, D.C.: Journal of the American Institute of Architects, 1918.

Wood, Edith Elmer. *Recent Trends in American Housing.* New York: Macmillan, 1931.

Wright, Henry. *Rehousing Urban America.* New York: Columbia University Press, 1935.

―――. *Report of the New York State Commission of Housing and Regional Planning.* Repr. in *Planning the Fourth Migration,* ed. by Carl Sussman, 145–94. Cambridge, Mass.: MIT, 1976.

GENERAL BOOKS ABOUT MEMBERS AND RELATED SUBJECTS

Adams, Thomas. *The Building of the City: Regional Plan of New York and Its Environs.* 1931. Repr. New York: Arno, 1974.

Alexander, William. *Film on the Left: American Documentary Film for 1931 to 1942.* Princeton, N.J.: Princeton University Press, 1977.

Barnouw, Erik. *Documentary: A History of Non-Fiction Film.* New York: Oxford University Press, 1977.

Barsam, Richard M., ed. *Non-Fiction Film Theory and Criticism.* Bloomington: Indiana University Press, 1976.

Birch, Eugenie Ladner. *Edith Elmer Wood and the Genesis of Liberal Housing Thought, 1910–1942.* Ph. D. diss. Columbia University, 1976.

Brooks, Van Wyck. *Days of the Phoenix.* New York: E. P. Dutton, 1957.

Brownlow, Louis. *A Passion for Anonymity.* Chicago: University of Chicago Press, 1958.

Bryant, Paul T. *The Quality of the Days: The Achievement of Benton MacKaye.* Ph.D. diss. University of Illinois, 1965.

Buder, Stanley. *Visionaries and Planners: The Garden City Movement and the Modern Community.* New York: Oxford University Press, 1990.

City Housing Corporation. *Eighth Annual Report* (1932).

———. *Radburn: Garden Homes.* N.p., n.d.

Diggins, John P. *The Bard of Savagery: Thorstein Veblen and Modern Social Theory.* New York: Seabury Press, 1978.

Federal Writers Project. *WPA Guide to Washington D.C.* Repr. New York: Pantheon, 1983.

Fletcher, John Gould. *Life Is My Song.* New York: Farrar and Rinehart, 1937.

Ford, James. *Slums and Housing.* Cambridge, Mass.: Harvard University Press, 1936.

Greene, Constance M. *Washington: Capital City, 1879–1950.* Princeton, N.J.: Princeton University Press, 1963.

Hudson, Robert B. *Radburn: A Plan for Living.* New York: American Association for Adult Education, 1934.

Hughes, Thomas P. and Agatha C., eds. *Lewis Mumford: Public Intellectual.* New York: Oxford University Press, 1990.

Krueckeberg, Donald A. *The American Planner: Biographies and Recollections.* New York and London: Methuen, 1983.

Levin, G. Ray. *Documentary Exploration.* Garden City, N.Y.: Doubleday, 1978.

Lewis, Harold M. *Highway Traffic.* Regional Survey volume 3. Repr. New York: Arno, 1974.

Lubove, Roy. *Community Planning in the 1920s: The Contributions of the Regional Planning Association of America.* Pittsburgh: University of Pittsburgh Press, 1963.

———. *Twentieth Century Pittsburgh.* New York: John Wiley: 1969.

MacKaye, Percy. *Kentucky Mountain Fantasies*. New York: Longman, Green, 1926.

―――. *Epoch: The Life of Steele MacKaye*. 2 vols. New York: Boni and Liveright, 1927.

Miller, Donald L. *Lewis Mumford: A Life*. New York: Weidenfeld and Nicolson, 1989.

New York State. *Report of the Commission of Housing and Regional Planning*. Albany: J. B. Lyon, 1925.

―――. *Report of the Commission of Housing and Regional Planning for Permanent Housing Relief*. Albany: J. B. Lyon, 1926.

―――. *Report of the Housing Committee of the Reconstruction Commission*. Albany: J. B. Lyon, 1920.

Rose, William Ganson. *Cleveland: The Making of a City*. Kent, Ohio: Kent State University Press, 1990.

Schaffer, Daniel. *Garden Cities for America: The Radburn Experience*. Philadelphia: Temple University Press, 1982.

Shapiro, Henry D. *Appalachia on Our Mind: The Southern Mountains and Mountaineers in the American Consciousness, 1890–1920*. Chapel Hill, N.C.: University of North Carolina Press, 1978.

Slayden, Ellen Maury. *Washington Wife*. New York: Harper and Row, 1962.

Stalley, Marshall, ed. *Patrick Geddes: Spokesman for Man and the Environment*. New Brunswick, N.J.: Rutgers University Press, 1972.

Sussman, Carl, ed. *Planning the Fourth Migration: The Neglected Vision of the Regional Planning Association of America*. Cambridge, Mass.: MIT, 1976.

Twombly, Robert. *Louis Sullivan*. New York: Viking, 1986.

United States Shipping Board. *Annual Reports*. Washington, D.C.: Government Printing Office, 1918–22.

ARTICLES BY MEMBERS OF THE RPAA

Frederick L. Ackerman

"The Architect's Part in the World's Work." *AR* 37 (1915): 149–58.

"The Battle with Chaos." *JAIA* 3 (1915): 444–47.

"A Brand New Theory of Congestion." *JAIA* 15 (1927): 26.

"Cottage or Tenement?" *New Republic* 14 (1918): 112.

"The Economy of Zoning." *Survey* (Feb. 19, 1921): 732.

"The Hearing," *Survey* 43 (1919–20): 803–4.

"Houses and Ships." *American City* 19 (1918): 85–86.

"How Can We Live in the Sun?" *SG* (March 1930): 706.

"The Influence on Architecture of the Condition of the Worker." *JAIA* 2 (1914): 547–55.

"More Plans for More Chaos." *JAIA* 12 (1924): 133.

"National Planning." *National Municipal Review* 8 (1919): 15–23.

"Our Stake in Congestion." *SG* (May 1925): 141–42.

"Preliminary to City Planning." *JAIA* 8 (1920): 15–18.

"Progress of Building Regulations in New York City." *JAIA* 2 (1914): 350–51.

"The Relation of Art to Education." *JAIA* 4 (1916): 190–93, 234–38, 282–84, and 455–57.

"Shall We Save New York?" *JAIA* 4 (1916): 160–61.

"The Technocrats and the Debt Burden." *New Republic* (May 3, 1933): 337–38.

"War-Time Housing." *American City* 18 (1918): 97–100.

"What Is a House?" In *The Housing Problem in Peace and War,* ed. by Charles M. Whitaker, 22–30.

"Where Goes the City Planning Movement?" *JAIA* 7 (1919): 518–20.

Catherine Bauer

"The Americanization of Europe." *New Republic* 67 (1931): 153–54.

"Slum Clearance or Housing." *Nation* 137 (1933): 730–31.

"Slums Aren't Necessary." *American Mercury* 31 (1934): 296–305.

"Store Buildings and Neighborhood Shopping Centers" [with Clarence Stein]. *AR* 75 (1934): 175–87.

"The Swiss Family Borsodi." *Nation* 137 (1933): 730–31.

"Who Cares about Architecture?" *New Republic* 66 (1931): 326–27.

Alexander M. Bing

"Can We Have Garden Cities In America?" *SG* (May 1925): 172–73, 190.

"New York's First Satellite Town: An Interview with Mr. Alexander Bing." *National Municipal Review* 17 (1928): 142–46.

Martha Brinsley Bruere

"The Black Folks Are Coming." *Survey* (July 15, 1923): 432–35.

"A Cure for Smoke-Sick Cities." *Colliers* (Nov. 1, 1924): 28, 44.

"Following the Hydro." *SG* (Mar. 1924): 591–94.

"Nothing to Lose but the Home." *Survey* (Feb. 15, 1923): 629–32.

"Putting the Town on Its Feet." *Colliers* (Dec. 27, 1924): 24, 36.

"Spring Planting." *SG* (Apr. 1923): 5–13.

"What Has She Done with It?" *SG* (Dec. 1924): 275–76.

"What Is Giant Power For?" *Annals of the American Academy of Political and Social Science* 118 (Mar. 1925): 120–33.

"Where Wires Go Wives Don't Strike." *Colliers* (Jan. 10, 1925): 25, 44.

Robert Bruere

"The Anthracite Paradox." *Survey* (Sept. 15, 1923): 613.

"Antioch." *SG* (June 1927): 259–61, 295–97.

"A Bit of Mellifluous Phraseology," *Survey* (Dec. 15, 1922): 371–72.

"The Coal Disgrace." *Nation* 116 (1923): 261–62.

"Giant Power—Region Builder." *SG* (May 1925): 161–64, 188.

"The Great Obsession." *SG* (Aug. 1925): 473–78.

"The Mind in the Machine." *SG* (Feb. 1927): 581.

"The Non-Partisan Third Party." *Survey* (July 15, 1924): 445–46.

"Our Chained Prometheus." *Harpers* 147 (1923): 610–14.

"Pandora's Box." *SG* (Mar. 1924): 557–60, 646–47.

"Two Governors Prod the Elephant." *Survey* (Apr. 15, 1926): 69–72.

"West Lynn." *SG* (Apr. 1926): 21–27, 49.

Stuart Chase

"Are You Alive?" *Nation* 115 (1922): 68–70.

"Coals to Newcastle." *SG* (May 1925): 143–46.

"Cluttered Up with Progress." *Nation* 127 (1928): 634.

"The Concept of Planning." In *Planning the Fourth Migration,* ed. by Carl Sussman, 209–17.

"The End of an Epoch." *Saturday Review* 7 (1930): 364–65.

"The Future of the Great City." *Harper's Monthly* 160 (1929–30): 82–90.

"Gasless America." *Nation* 123 (1926): 586–87.

"Henry Ford's Utopia." *Nation* 123 (1926): 53–55.

"If I Were Dictator." *Nation* 133 (1931): 536–38.

"My Great-Great Grandfather and I." *Nation* 123 (1926): 190–92.

"A New Deal for America." *New Republic* 71 (1932): 169–71.

"Old Man River." *New Republic* 82 (1935): 177–78.

"On the Threshold." *Forum* 51 (1914): 710–17.

"One Dead Level." *New Republic* 48 (1926): 137–39.

"Portrait of a Radical." *Century Magazine* 86 (1924): 295–304.

"Slaves of the Machines?" *Harper's Monthly* 158 (1928–29): 480–89.

"A Suburban City for the Motor Age." *NYT* (June 24, 1928): sec. 11, 4.

"A Ten Year Plan for America." *Harpers Monthly* 163 (1931): 1–10.

"The Tragedy of Waste." *New Republic* 44 (1925): 37–40.

"The Two Hour War." *New Republic* 58 (1929): 325–27.

"A Very Private Utopia." *Nation* 126 (1928): 559–62.

"A War Budget for the Household." *Independent* 91 (1917): 169–70.

"What Shall We Do to be Saved?" *New Republic* 34 (1923): 13–14.

"Working with Nature." *SG* (Dec. 1937): 624–28.

Robert D. Kohn

"History of the Committee on City Development of the New York Chapter." *JAIA* 1 (1913): 124–26.

"Housing in a Reconstruction Program." *Survey* (May 31, 1919): 341, 392–94.

"Industrial Relations." Parts 1 and 2. *JAIA* 11 (1923): 346–47; 13 (1925): 75.

"Planning for Changed Needs." *AR* 73 (1933): 294 ff.

"Post-War Committee on Architectural Practice." *JAIA* 7 (1918): 118.

"Should Architects Undertake Building Programs?" *AR* 70 (1931): 149.

"The Significance of the Professional Ideal." *Annals of the American Academy of Political and Social Science* 101 (May 1922): 1–5.

Benton MacKaye

"Appalachian Power: Servant or Master?" *SG* (Mar. 1924): 618–19.

"An Appalachian Trail: A Project in Regional Planning." *JAIA* 9 (1921): 325–30.

"The Appalachian Trail: A Guide to the Study of Nature." *Scientific Monthly* 34 (1932): 330–42.

"Cement Railroads." *SG* (November 1932): 541–42, 570.

"The Challenge of Muscle Shoals." *Nation* 136 (1933): 445–46.

"End or Peak of Civilization?" *SG* (Oct. 1932): 441–44.

"The First Soldier Colony." *Public* 22 (1919): 1066–68.

"The Great Appalachian Trail from New Hampshire to the Carolinas." *NYT* (Feb. 18, 1923): sec. 7, 15.

"Industrial Exploration." *Nation* 127 (1927): 70–73, 92–93, and 119–21.

"The Lesson of Alaska." *Public* 22 (1919): 930–32.

"Making New Opportunities for Employment." *Monthly Labor Review* (Apr. 1919): 121–39.

"The New Exploration: Charting the Industrial Wilderness." *SG* (May 1925): 153–57, 192–94.

"The New Northwest Passage." *Nation* 122 (1926): 603–4.

"New York: A National Peril." *Saturday Review* 7 (1930): 68.

"Our Iron Civilization." *Saturday Review* 6 (9129): 342–43.

"A Plan for Cooperation between Farmer and Consumer." *Monthly Labor Review* (Aug. 1920): 1–21.

"Powell as Unsung Lawgiver." *Cosmos Club Bulletin* 22 (Nov. 1969): 2–4.

"Regional Planning." *Sociology Review* 20 (1928): 93–99.

"The Soldier, the Worker, and the Land's Resources." *Monthly Labor Review* (Jan. 1918): 48–56.

"The Tennessee River Project: First Step in a National Plan." *NYT* (Apr. 16, 1933): sec. 8, 3.

"Tennessee—Seed of a National Plan." *SG* (May 1933): 251–54, 293–94.

"The Townless Highway." *New Republic* 62 (1930): 93–95.

"Townless Highway for the Motorist" [with Lewis Mumford]. *Harpers* 163 (1931): 347–56.

"The Town that Took the Wrong Road." *American City* 43 (Dec. 1930): 112–14.

"A Trail through the Appalachians." *Survey* (Nov. 1925): 210.

Lewis Mumford

"The Adolescence of Reform." *Freeman* (Dec. 1, 1920): 272–73.

"American Architecture." *Freeman* (Dec. 19, 1923): 344–46.

"Americanized Europe." *Freeman* (Nov. 22, 1922): 253–54.

"The Art of Love." *Freeman* (Nov. 8, 1922): 213–14.

"Attacking the Housing Problem on Three Fronts." *Nation* 109 (1919): 332–33.

"The Autobiography of an Idea." *New Republic* 39 (1924): 132–33.

"Bellamy's Accurate Utopia." *New Republic* (Aug. 26, 1931): 51–52.

"Breaking the Housing Blockade." *New Republic* 75 (1933): 8–11.

"Community Planning and Housing." *JAIA* 11 (1923): 492–93.

"Devastated Regions." *American Mercury* 3 (1924): 217–20.

"Downfall or Renewal?" *New Republic* 46 (1926): 367–69.

"The Drama of the Machine." *Scribner's Magazine* 88 (1930): 150–61.

"England's American Summer." *Freeman* (June 7, 1922): 296.

"Esthetics and Public Works." *New Republic* 75 (1933): 344.

"The Fate of Garden Cities." *JAIA* 15 (1929): 37–39.

"The Fourth Migration." *SG* (May 1925): 130–33.

"Frank Lloyd Wright and the New Pioneers." *AR* 65 (1929): 414–16.

"From a Country Notebook." *New Republic* 57 (1929): 313–14.

"If Engineers Were Kings." *Freeman* (Nov. 23, 1921): 261–62.

"In Our Stars: The World Fifty Years from Now." *Forum* 88 (1932): 338–42.

"A Modest Man's Contribution to Urban and Regional Planning." *JAIA* 65 (Dec. 1976): 19–28.

"New Homes for a New Deal," part 4, "A Concrete Program" [with Henry Wright and Albert Mayer]. *New Republic* (Mar. 7, 1934): 91–94.

"New Trails for Old." *Freeman* (July 14, 1923): 396–97.

"On the Road to Collectivism." *New Republic* 81 (1935): 361.

"A Philosophy of History." *New Republic* 53 (1929): 140–41.

"The Place of the Community in the School." *Dial* 67 (1919): 245–46.

"The Plan of New York." *New Republic* 71 (1932): 121–26, 146–54.

"Realities vs. Dreams." *JAIA* 13 (1925): 198–99.

"Regionalism." *SG* (Nov. 1926): 182–83.

"Regionalism and Irregionalism." Parts 1–3. *Sociology Review* 19 (1927): 277–88; 20 (1928): 18–33, 131–41.

"The Regional Note." *Freeman* (Oct. 10, 1923): 107–8.

"Regional Planning." In *Planning the Fourth Migration,* ed. by Carl Sussman, 199–208.

"Regions to Live In." *SG* (May 1925): 151–52.

"The State of the State." *Dial* 67 (1919): 59–61.

"Thorstein Veblen." *New Republic* 68 (1931): 314.

"Toward a Humanist Synthesis." *Freeman* (Mar. 2, 1921): 583–85.

"Townless Highway for the Motorist" [with Benton MacKaye]. *Harpers* 163 (1931): 347–56.

"What I Believe." *Forum* 84 (1930): 263–68.

"Who Is Patrick Geddes?" *SG* (Feb. 1925): 523–24.

Clarence Stein

"The Art Museum of Tomorrow." *AR* 67 (1930): 5–12.

"The Case for New Towns." *Planners Journal* (Mar.–June 1939): 39–41.

"Community Planning and Housing." Parts 1 and 2. *JAIA* 9 (1921): 399–400; 10 (1922): 126–27.

"Congestion of Population." *Medical Record* (Feb. 25, 1922): 349.

"Cooperative Homes for Brain Workers." *NYT* (June 7, 1925): sec. 10, 1.

"Co-operative Housing." *Brotherhood of Locomotive Firemen and Engineers Magazine* (Aug. 1925): 168–69.

"Dinosaur Cities." *SG* (May 1925): 134–38.

"The Future of Our Big Cities." *JAIA* 11 (1923): 24–25.

"Henry Wright." *American Architect and Architecture* (Aug. 1936): 25–26.

"Housing and Common Sense." *Nation* 134 (1932): 541–44.

"The Housing Crisis in New York." *Survey* 44 (1920): 659–62.

"Housing New York's Two-Thirds." *Survey* (Feb. 15, 1924): 509–10.

"A Housing Policy for the United States." *Octagon* (June 1933), unpaged reprint, SP.

"Legal Obstacles to City Planning." *JAIA* 10 (1922): 335.

"The New York Puzzle." *JAIA* 12 (1924): 84–85.

"An Opportunity of Architectural Leadership" [with Henry Wright]. *AR* 70 (1931): 238.

"The Regional Planning Association of America." *JAIA* 11 (1923): 292–93.

"Store Buildings and Neighborhood Shopping Centers" [with Catherine Bauer]. *AR* 75 (1934): 175–87.

"The Wagner-Steagall Housing Act of 1937." *American Architect and Architecture* (Nov. 1937): 35–38.

"Wanted: A Place to Play." *Playground* 19 (1925–26): 452, 458.

Charles Harris Whitaker

"Alloy." *Freeman* (May 10, 1922): 198–99.

"Architecture and the Public." *Freeman* (Jan. 19, 1921): 447–48.

"Cities Old and New." Parts 3–4. *JAIA* 14 (1926): 404–7, 510–11.

"A Disease and Its Symptoms." *Freeman* (June 8, 1921): 309–10.

"England's Housing Ventures." *Freeman* (Sept. 8, 1920): 610–12.

"The Federal Building Situation." *JAIA* 11 (1923): 270–72.

"The Fight on the Public Buildings Bill." *NYT* (Dec. 31, 1916): sec. 7, 2.

"Five Architects and One Truth." *JAIA* 12 (1924): 401–5.

"The Forests of Soignes." *JAIA* 2 (1914): 236–45.

"The Housing Issue in the United States." *Public* 22 (1919): 155–57.

"The Impasse in Housing." *Freeman* (Nov. 10, 1920): 202–3.

"The Interrelation of the Professions." *Annals of the American Academy of Political and Social Science* 101 (May 1922): 12–13.

"Land and the Housing Question." *New Republic* 14 (1918): 113–14.

"Locality and Humility." *JAIA* (1923): 417–19.

"New Tale of Two Cities." *Freeman* (Mar. 9, 1921): 610–12.

"On the Relation of Art to Life." *JAIA* 4 (1916): 11–17.

"An Open Letter to the Members of the 64th Congress." *JAIA* 4 (1916): 239–41.

"Our Stupid and Blundering National Policy of Providing Public Buildings." *JAIA* 4 (1916): 44–57, 96–103.

"Post-War Committee on Architectural Practice." *JAIA* 7 (1919): 6–8, 25–28, 390–95.

"The Proposed Disfigurement of Washington." *Outlook* 112 (1916): 489.

"The Smokestack Menace to Washington." *NYT* (Mar. 4, 1916): 10.

"The Vanishing Sanctuary." *Freeman* (Nov. 27, 1920): 251–43.

"Wanted—Ten Million Houses." *Saturday Evening Post* (May 8, 1920): 23, 109–16.

"What Is the Function of Architecture in a Democracy?" *JAIA* 4 (1916): 465–68.

"What Is a House?" *JAIA* 5 (1917): 481–85.

"What Is a House?" In *The Housing Problem in War and in Peace,* ed. by Charles H. Whitaker, 3–8.

"Will the Kitchen Be Outside the House?" *Ladies Home Journal* 36 (Jan. 1919): 66.

Edith Elmer Wood

"Four Washington Alleys." *Survey* 31 (1913–14): 250–52.

"The Hand of Essau." *SG* (Oct. 1936): 556–58.

"How to Get Better Housing." *Journal of Home Economics* 16 (1924): 4–9, 69–70.

"Letter from Edith Elmer Wood." *SG* (Apr. 1936): 196–97.

"What Is a House?" In *The Housing Problem in War and in Peace,* ed. by Charles H. Whitaker, 69–78.

Henry Wright

"Can Architects Promote More Business?" *AR* 68 (1930): 288–90.

"Exploiting the Land." *JAIA* 15 (1927): 305–6.

"Hillside Group Housing." *AR* 72 (1932): 221–22.

"The Machine Made House." *New Republic* 68 (1931): 76.

"New Homes for a New Deal," part 2, "Abolishing Slums Forever." *New Republic* (Feb. 21, 1934): 41–4.

"New Homes for a New Deal," part 4, "A Concrete Program" [with Lewis Mumford and Albert Mayer]. *New Republic* (Mar. 7, 1934): 91–94.

"An Opportunity of Architectural Leadership" [with Clarence Stein]. *AR* 70 (1931): 238.

"The Place of the Apartment House in the Modern Community." *AR* 67 (1930): 207–38.

"Planning a Town for Wholesome Living." *Playground* 22 (1928–29): 682–84.

"The Road to Good Houses." *SG* (May 1925): 165–68, 189.

"Servicing Apartments for Lower Rentals." *AR* 73 (1933): 223–29.

"Shall We Community Plan?" *JAIA* 9 (1921): 320–24.

"Sinking Slums." *SG* (Aug. 1933): 417–19.

"The Six-Cylinder House with Streamline Body." *JAIA* 14 (1926): 175–78.

"To Plan or Not to Plan." *SG* (Oct. 1932): 468–69.

"Utopia a la Mode." *Survey* (May 15, 1925): 251.

"Wanted: A Substitute for the Gridiron Street System." *American City* 42 (1930): 87–89.

GENERAL ARTICLES

Ascher, Charles S. "Regionalism: Charting the Future." *Survey* (Aug. 15, 1931): 460–61.

Baughman, Marjie. "A Prophet Honored Abroad Even More than at Home." *JAIA* 65 (December 1976): 30–33.

Baxter, Sylvester. "The Government's Housing Activities." *AR* 44 (1918): 561–65.

Birch, Eugenie Ladner. "Woman-Made America: The Case of Early Public Housing." In *The American Planner: Biographies and Recollections*, ed. by Donald A. Kruekeberg, 149–75. New York and London: Methuen, 1983.

Blackhan, Louise P. "For the Happiness of the Community." *Recreation* 30 (1936–37): 255–56, 276.

Blair, Karen J. "Pageantry for Women's Rights: The Career of Hazel Mac-Kaye, 1913–1923." *Theatre Survey* 31 (May 1990): 23–46.

Boyd, John Taylor Jr. "Garden Apartments in Cities." *AR* 48 (1920): 69–73.

———. "Industrial Housing Projects." *AR* 47 (1920): 89–92.

Brown, Norbert. "Progress Report on Low-Cost Housing and Slum Clearance." *AR* 70 (1934): 393–94.

Childs, Richard S. "Building a War Town." *Independent* 94 (1918): 469–70.

————. "The Government's Model Villages." *Survey* 41 (1918–19): 484–92.

Churchill, Henry. "Henry Wright, 1878–1936." *JAIA* 26 (1960): 239–99.

Clark, Evan. "Guiding New York State." *NYT* (Apr. 19, 1925): sec. 10, 3, 13.

Covell, Alwyn T. "Co-Operative Group Planning: Henry Wright, Architect and Landscape Architect." *AR* 34 (1913): 467–75.

Crane, Jacob. "Large-Scale Regional Planning: The Unit: Watersheds or States?" *American City* (Jan. 1934): 60–66.

De Wagstaffe, William. "How's Washington Now?" *Forum* 59 (June 1918): 733–40.

Hancock, John. "The New Deal and American Planning." In *Two Centuries of American Planning,* ed. by Daniel Schaffer, 197–230. London: Mansell Publishing, 1988.

Johnson, Alvin. "Land for the Returned Soldier." *New Republic* 14 (1918): 218–20.

Johnson, David A. "Regional Planning for the Great American Metropolis: New York between the World Wars." In *Two Centuries of American Planning,* ed. by Schaffer, 167–96.

Johnson, Hugh B. "In Memory of Benton MacKaye." *JAIA* 65 (Feb. 1976): 68.

Lasker, Loula D. "Sunnyside Up and Down." *SG* (Apr. 1936): 419–23, 439–41.

Lewis, Charles F. "A Moderate Rental Project in Pittsburgh." *AR* 70 (1931): 217–28.

Lubove, Roy. "Homes and 'A Few Well Placed Fruit Trees': An Object Lesson in Federal Housing." *Social Research* 27 (1960): 469–86.

Marcus, Alan I. "Back to the Present: Historians' Treatment of the City as a Social System during the Reign of the Idea of Community." In *American Urbanism,* ed. by Howard Gillette Jr. and Zane L. Miller, 7–25. Westport, Conn.: Greenwood Press, 1987.

Mayer, Alber. "Henry Wright: Creative Planner." *SG* (Sept. 1936): 530.

Mitchell, Jonathan. "Housing by Slow Freight." *New Republic* 80 (1934): 236–37.

Propper, Henry M. "Construction Work Now Under Way." Parts 1 and 2. *American City* 31 (1928): 81–82; 41 (1929): 98–99, 143–44.

————. "When Radburn Opens." *Survey* (Feb. 15, 1929): 645–50.

Rhodes, Harrison. "War-Time Washington." *Harpers* 136 (Mar. 1918): 466–68.

Roosevelt, Franklin Delano. "Growing Up by Plan." *SG* (Feb. 1932): 483, 506–7.

———. "On the Excessive Costs and Taxes in Local Government." *The Public Papers and Addresses of Franklin D. Roosevelt,* vol. 1, *The Genesis of the New Deal, 1928–1932.* New York: Random House, 1938.

Saylor, Henry. "Diary." *American Architect and Architecture* (Aug. 1936): 42, 85–86.

Smith, Alfred E. "Seeing a State Whole." *SG* (May 1925): 158–60.

Smith, Geddes. "Buffalo is Buffalo." *Survey* (Oct. 15, 1926): 92–94.

———. "Problem: Find Four Walls." *Survey* (Dec. 15, 1925): 337–39.

———. "A Town for the Motor Age." *SG* (Mar. 1928): 694–98.

Spann, Edward K. "Franklin Delano Roosevelt and the Regional Planning Association of America, 1931–36." *New York History* 74 (1993): 185–200.

Tate, Allen. "Regionalism and Sectionalism." *New Republic* 65 (1931): 158–61.

Thomas, John L. "Lewis Mumford, Benton MacKaye, and the Regional Vision." In *Lewis Mumford: Public Intellectual,* ed. by Thomas P. and Agatha C. Hughes, 66–99. New York: Oxford University Press, 1990.

Tiller, Theodore. "Washington in War Time." *Review of Reviews* 56 (Dec. 1917): 629–32.

Tullos, Allen. "The Politics of Regional Development: Lewis Mumford and Howard Odom." In *Lewis Mumford: Public Intellectual,* ed. by Hughes and Hughes, 110–20.

Veiller, Lawrence. "Industrial Housing Developments." *AR* 43 (1918): 344–59.

Westbrook, Robert B. "Tribune of the Technostructure: The Popular Economics of Stuart Chase." *American Quarterly* 32 (1980): 387–408.

INDEX

Urban Life and Urban Landscape Series
Zane L. Miller and Henry D. Shapiro, General Editors

The series examines the history of urban life and the development of the urban landscape through works that place social, economic, and political issues in the intellectual and cultural context of their times.

Cincinnati, Queen City of the West: 1819–1838
Daniel Aaron

Proportional Representation and Election Reform in Ohio
Kathleen L. Barber

Fragments of Cities: The New American Downtowns and Neighborhoods
Larry Bennett

*The Lost Dream: Businessmen and City Planning on the Pacific Coast,
1890–1920*
Mansel G. Blackford

*Planning for the Private Interest: Land Use Controls and Residential
Patterns in Columbus, Ohio, 1900–1970*
Patricia Burgess

Cincinnati Observed: Architecture and History
John Clubbe

Suburb in the City: Chestnut Hill, Philadelphia, 1850–1990
David R. Contosta

The Mysteries of the Great City: The Politics of Urban Design, 1877–1937
John D. Fairfield

The Poetics of Cities: Designing Neighborhoods That Work
Mike Greenberg

Building Chicago: Suburban Developers and the Creation of a Divided Metropolis
Ann Durkin Keating

Silent City on a Hill: Landscapes of Memory and Boston's Mount Auburn Cemetery
Blanche Linden-Ward

Plague of Strangers: Social Groups and the Origins of City Services in Cincinnati, 1819–1870
Alan I Marcus

Polish Immigrants and Industrial Chicago: Workers on the South Side, 1880–1922
Dominic A. Pacyga

The New York Approach: Robert Moses, Urban Liberals, and Redevelopment of the Inner City
Joel Schwartz

Hopedale: From Commune to Company Town, 1840–1920
Edward K. Spann

Welcome to Heights High: The Crippling Politics of Restructing America's Public Schools
Diana Tittle

Washing "The Great Unwashed": Public Baths in Urban America, 1840–1920
Marilyn Thornton Williams